WHO OWNS DOMESTIC AB[

The Local Politics of a Social Problem

With the knowledge and sensitivity of a teacher and counsellor, Ruth M. Mann details a community effort to establish a shelter for abused women in a small Ontario municipality. While other literature presents the ostensibly cohesive views of particular interest groups on the issue of domestic violence, Mann exposes the conflicts that actually occur, and the ways these conflicts fuel unintended outcomes. In *Who Owns Domestic Abuse? The Local Politics of a Social Problem*, the author ventures bravely into the politically charged debate over the definition of abuse, and demonstrates that 'owning' a problem does not ensure viable solutions. Rather than promoting a particular response to such problems, Mann uses personal accounts of abuse to make a space for the diverse perspectives of abused women and abusive men. She urges activists and intervenors to argue less and listen more.

RUTH M. MANN is a sociologist at Concordia University, and has worked as a group facilitator in abuse intervention programs for domestically assaultive men, and in a 'challenge of anger' program for women. She is currently conducting research on interventions for violent girls.

Who Owns Domestic Abuse?

The Local Politics
of a Social Problem

Ruth M. Mann

UNIVERSITY OF TORONTO PRESS
Toronto Buffalo London

© University of Toronto Press Incorporated 2000
Toronto Buffalo London
Printed in Canada

ISBN 0-8020-4248-1 (cloth)
ISBN 0-8020-8091-X (paper)

Printed on acid-free paper

Canadian Cataloguing in Publication Data

Mann, Ruth M. (Ruth Marie), 1947–
  Who owns domestic abuse? : the local politics of a social problem

  Includes bibliographical references and index.
  ISBN 0-8020-4248-1 (bound)   ISBN 0-8020-8091-X (pbk.)

  1. Women's shelters – Political aspects – Ontario – Case studies.   2. Women
  – Abuse of – Ontario.   3. Abused women – Housing – Ontario.   I. Title.

  HV1448.C32O58 1999   362.82'9283   C99-931874-8

University of Toronto Press acknowledges the financial assistance to its
publishing program of the Canada Council for the Arts and the Ontario
Arts Council.

University of Toronto Press acknowledges the financial support for its
publishing activities of the Government of Canada through the Book
Publishing Industry Development Program (BPIDP).

Canadä

This book is dedicated to the women and men of the research community who shared their personal, political, and professional struggles and stories – especially to the individuals referred to in the text as Lisa, Bob, Kathryn, Peter, Charles, Susan, Julia, Jim, and Jocelyn. These core respondents were residents of the housing co-operative that befriended and sheltered me, and that introduced me to the larger community of *domestic abuse* activists, abuse intervention professionals, and residents.

Contents

months of shelter operation, based on in-depth interviews. Discussion of similar developments at the established Regional shelter, and at shelters generally.

Preface

Who Owns Domestic Abuse? The Local Politics of a Social Problem is a case study of community activism around domestic violence against women and children in a small-town Southern Ontario municipality, analysed from a sociology of social problems perspective that Joel Best termed contextual constructionism (Best, 1989, 1993). My primary focus is activities associated with attempts to assert, resist, and maintain ownership over the establishment and operation of a shelter for women, and the unintended outcomes of these ownership struggles. I address the lived reality of abuse as a contextual or background feature of this public activity.

The study is relevant to social theory and social policy. On the level of social theory, I address the subjective/objective dualism of definitional processes and experiential realities. My approach is informed by constructionist insights, especially by postmodern concerns with the ways social power and social interests influence knowledge, and the social production of knowledge. Nevertheless, it is grounded in what is essentially a mainstream or 'modernist' approach to research and analysis. As outlined by Herbert Blumer in *Symbolic Interactionism, Perspective and Method* (1969), this approach presupposes both the existence of an empirical social world that stands over and against the observer, and the contingent validity of social scientific knowledge of this world. Consequently, in contradistinction to 'strict' constructionists who regard investigations of conditions as irrelevant to the development of theoretical knowledge of social problems processes, I argue that an analysis of tensions between conditions and the politicized constructions of conditions promoted during social problems mobilizations informs theoretical understandings of the little-explored issue of unintended outcomes. Moreover, I argue that there are important similarities in the dynamics of abuse as political process and in the dynamics of abuse as lived experience, and that an analysis of these similarities advances theoretical understandings both of social problems developments and of the problem of abuse.

On the level of social policy, I address the issue of how to achieve outcomes more consistent with the values and goals of official plans. I argue that actors need to incorporate awareness of the inherently contentious, divisive, and dysfunctional nature of social problems processes into their action plans. This incorporation entails a shift to second-order thinking, to thinking that focuses less on the nature of a specific problem and on arguments for or against proposed solutions, and more on the social problems process itself. This shift is facilitated by awareness that ownership struggles are not only about contending values or interpretations; they are also about emotionally charged and interpersonally constructed 'needs' to monopolize social prestige and social influence. Consequently, 'bad faith' denials of aspects of the problem that involved actors themselves know to be relevant, evasions of responsibility for action, and projections of blame are ubiquitous components of social problems developments.

The continuing high-profile nature of the problem we call abuse, and the prominence of an ongoing feminist backlash, demonstrate the importance of making this analytic shift. This feminist backlash is evidenced in a *National Post* article in November 1998 that sensationalizes ideologically rooted struggles for control over abuse interventions in Canada, and the negative effects of these struggles on abused women (LaFramboise, 1998). The central message is that abused women do not 'like' shelters and related intervention services, and that feminism is to blame for this. My study demonstrates the short-sightedness of this interpretation. Feminists are no more immune to the inherent destructiveness of power struggles than are their opponents, but neither are feminists uniquely responsible. Regardless of which 'side' claims victory in variously situated struggles for 'ownership' over social problems and social practices, when power and control issues dominate, outcomes appear astoundingly similar.

Policy-makers, activists, and social analysts who see a connection between the dynamics of social problems processes and unintended outcomes, and who wish to promote more viable or effective outcomes, may wish to discourage the 'either/or' practices that characteristically drive social problems developments. A proposed shift from an 'either/or' to a 'both/and' approach to social action is facilitated by awareness that action is grounded both in agency and in emotionality, by awareness that various ideological lenses provide sometimes over-lapping but always incomplete and unavoidably distorted views of our interpersonally constructed social worlds, and by awareness that no lens guides us towards a complete or final solution. Demonstrating these provisional 'truths' has been the primary goal of the narrative I name *Who Owns Domestic Abuse?*

Acknowledgments

I wish to acknowledge the contributions and support of several people. First I wish to express appreciation for the support and assistance provided by a number of University of Toronto faculty. Invaluable guidance was provided by the late Norman Bell, who supervised the thesis on which this book is based through early phases of the research process, and by Rosemary Gartner, who took over the position of thesis supervisor in the fall of 1993. Janet Salaff tutored me in the use of field methods. Dennis Magill and Anne Sorenson assisted in the development of the survey. Nancy Howell, Harry Mackler, and Lorna Marsden provided theoretical guidance, and encouragement. Finally, Lorne Tepperman encouraged me to transform the thesis into a book, and Sev Isajiw helped me to frame my response to readers during the peer-review process.

In addition to these faculty members, I wish to acknowledge the special contributions of two friends and colleagues – Dave Tindall, who assisted in the statistical analysis of the survey data, and Luc Theriault, who directed my attention to the radio interview that led me to the research community, and who has provided support and encouragement through to the present.

In addition to these colleagues, I wish to acknowledge the sustained support and encouragement of Virgil Duff, executive editor at University of Toronto Press.

I wish to acknowledge the support of the McLean Foundation.

I also wish to acknowledge the assistance, advice, encouragement, and support of a number of personal friends and family members: David Brandt and Carol MacLennan, Charles and Rhoda Brue, Ted Chamberlin, David Cormack, Larry Dworkin and Julie Levin, Danny and Christine Finkleman, Joseph and Ruth Freed, Murray Glow and Matha Dorian, Kathleen Graham, Peter and Marla Gropper, Zora Gropper, Brian and Cynthia Langille, Daniel Levin and Lillian Bonin, Esther Levin, Jonathan Levin, Elinor Melville, Brenda Moffatt, Peter O'Brien, Gerald and Gladys Rose, Laura and John Sirdevan, Susan and Donald Starr, Daniel and Judith Stoffman, Lydia Vanderstall and Tim Storey, and Elvira and Robin White.

Lastly, I wish to acknowledge the support and encouragement of some very special members of my family – my foster parents, Lucille McDonald and the late James McDonald, my parents-in-law, Myrna Levin and the late Harry Levin, and most especially my husband, Michael Levin, and our children, Marta Morgan, Anna Levin, and Jacob Levin, and Kirk Sutterfield, Allison Mann, and Alexandra Mann.

Acronyms

Children's Aid Society	CAS
Domestic Abuse Committee	DAC
Domestic Violence Committee (housing co-op)	DVC
Probation & Parole	P&P
Regional Sex Abuse Program	RSAP
Regional Woman Abuse Program	RWAP
Regional Women's Shelter	RWS
Township Family Services	TFS
Township Legal Clinic	TLC
Township Regional Police	TRP
Township Resource Centre	TRC
Township Youth Services	TYS
Township Women's Shelter	TWS

WHO OWNS DOMESTIC ABUSE?

1

Theoretical and Political Contexts

Who Owns Domestic Abuse? addresses collective and personal attempts to deal with a problem publicly defined as *domestic abuse* in a Southern Ontario community during an intensive phase of social action centred around the development of a women's shelter. I direct primary attention to the unintended consequences of competition for 'ownership' of the problem and its solution among pro-feminist and non-feminist abuse advocates, professionals, and community leaders. I situate this public activity within the context of 'abuse as a lived experience' as glimpsed through the reported experiences and perceptions of abuse victims, perpetrators, and survivors. This dual examination results in a dialectical portrait of abuse, a portrait that recognizes ongoing reciprocity between experiential realities defined as social problems (Blumer, 1971) and the historically situated struggles of social actors to understand and deal with these realities (Mills, 1959; Best, 1993).

My analysis is guided by the assumption that human subjects participate as agents in the ongoing construction of themselves, their relationships, their institutions, and their societies. Agency operates in multiple contexts, including human emotionality. Human being-in-the-world is historically situated, institutionally structured, ideologically interpreted, interpersonally negotiated, biographically constituted, and existentially (therefore emotionally) experienced. Despite human intentionality and the inescapability of human responsibility, social realities are not as anyone chooses; they are not as anyone 'intends.' Social reality is a contingent ongoing accomplishment, an accomplishment that we participate in and that we undergo. The contradictions inherent to this accomplishment are epitomized in the chaos of love, the anguish of bad faith, the rage of frustrated narcissism, and the soul-wrenching failures of political activism.

These assumptions reflect the influence of postmodern thinking; however, my research orientation is essentially post-positivist (Guba and Lincoln, 1994). With the Herbert Blumer of *Symbolic Interactionism, Perspective and Method* (1969), I seek to develop theoretical knowledge of the empirical social world through investigations of what people actually experience and do in individual and collective spheres of human activity. With Blumer, I regard the empirical social world as 'both the point of departure and the point of return' (Blumer, 1969).[1] I consequently reject the postmodern notion that definitions, and therefore methods, 'are actually constitutive of truth' (Alcoff, 1989).

At the same time, I recognize that social reality is not simply 'out there.' As researchers and analysts, we cannot step outside the 'hermeneutic circle' (Denzin, 1989). Knowledge is inexorably contingent, context-dependent, imperfect, incomplete. Contending definitions of situations, contending facts, contending interests, and contending methodologies reflect the multiplicity of selves, contexts, and interpretive orientations which empirically and experientially interpellate human beings in personal and public spheres of social life. The world exists over and against us, yet we are in this world. We know it only through the various lenses available to us, that is, through the medium, the borrowed language, of consciousness.

These contradictory sets of assumptions reflect the influence of various interpretive sociologies – social interactionism, phenomenology, constructionism, contextualism, existentialism, feminism, Marxism – all of which address the problematic relationship of self to world or society.[2] The research orientation based on these assumptions has much in common with the sociology of social problems perspective that Joel Best (1989, 1993) named 'contextual constructionism.'

Contexts and Issues

Several aspects of the current social context are pertinent to the study. First, abuse is a high profile public issue. During the research period, activists in the research community launched a shelter for women, participated in local and regional efforts to coordinate 'community accountable' abuse interventions, and cooperated in a number of research initiatives. In 1991 and 1992 similar activities were going on in communities across Canada, indeed, across North America. Social

problems sociology identifies this level of intensive public involvement in issues identified as social problems as a later phase in the
career or natural history of a social problem. Second, abuse is a high
profile political issue. At federal, provincial, and local levels feminists
and non-feminists engage in heated competition for 'ownership' of
abuse. Social problems sociology links social problems with social
movements, and identifies competition between those who share the
goals of a movement and those who do not as critical to social problems processes. Third, discourse on abuse is situated within larger
epistemological debates on the nature of social reality, social research,
and social knowledge. Social problems sociology participates in these
debates.

These three contextual issues – the high profile nature of the problem, the highly politicized character of discourse on abuse, and the
contested nature of knowledge and knowledge production – mean that
abuse is an intensely polarized and intensely polarizing field of study.
Social problems sociology provides insights into the dynamics and
consequences of these polarizations.

Social Problems Sociology

Herbert Blumer's 1971 article 'Social Problems as Collective Behavior'
stimulated a sizeable body of research into activities through which
social actors, often in alliance with or in response to recognizable social
movements, create and assert management over social problems. Poverty, juvenile delinquency, mental illness, alcoholism, drunk driving,
child abuse, medicalization, and science are some of the 'constructions'
addressed in social problems sociology during the time that *violence
against women and family violence* entered into discourse as social
problems.[3]

Within the social problems tradition there is a continuing difference of
opinion over whether to retain the subjective/objective dualism in what
Berger and Luckmann call *The Social Construction of Reality* (1966). Constructionists characteristically focus attention on inter-subjective or definitional practices – that is, on how 'putative' conditions, logically prior
to their emergence into public awareness as a problem, acquire recognition, achieve legitimization, undergo mobilization of action, and
become institutionalized or co-opted through the drawing up and
implementation of official, as well as competing, plans of action. Conditions defined as social problems are viewed as one of several histori-

cally, politically, and ideologically constructed realities (Gusfield, 1981, 1984, 1989). Constructionists direct attention towards the deconstruction of claims and the interests behind claims: their own as well as others (Pfohl, 1977, 1985; Schneider, 1993; Troyer, 1993). Through this activity, social problems sociologists have called into question the authoritative knowledge of all 'experts,' self-appointed or professional.

Radical or strict constructionists go further. They argue that knowledge of conditions is irrelevant to the sociology of social problems and that attempts to develop knowledge of conditions impede analysis of social problems processes since knowledge of the 'indisputable character' of a problem is unattainable, beyond the grasp of human subjects (Gusfield, 1984, 1989; Pfohl, 1985; Ibarra and Kitsuse, 1993). Strict constructionists maintain that the 'viability' of a definition or intervention strategy hinges solely on the extent to which it is adopted by the institutions of civil society, and that this has little or nothing to do with the extent to which it corresponds with alleged conditions (Kitsuse and Spector, 1973; Schneider, 1985, 1993). Finally, they argue that investigations of conditions involve researchers in the very definitional processes a sociology of social problems seeks to analyse since investigations of conditions force researchers to 'take sides' in political struggles over the nature of the problem and how to address it.

To avoid falling into this fray, strict constructionists have developed increasingly abstract means of distancing themselves; thus putative conditions have become 'condition categories.' With this shift, the focus of analysis has become social problems theory, which is to say, discourse, not social problems (Ibarra and Kitsuse, 1993; Schneider, 1993; Troyer, 1993). Strict constructionists prefer, indeed insist, that actors be left to face the existential void and political conflict 'unarmed' (Gusfield, 1984).

In contrast, contextual constructionists defend incorporating knowledge of social conditions and what can be known about them into an analysis of social problems processes (Best, 1989, 1993).[4] This more mainstream approach incorporates constructionist or postmodern insights about the historical and political contingency of truth-claims, but does not break entirely with either positivist practices or praxis (Miller, 1993). Indubitable knowledge remains beyond the reach of human subjects. However, 'facts' are treated as something more than 'fictive effects' (Pfohl, 1985). Neither 'discoveries' nor 'inventions,' facts are the products of intelligible human activities. A contextual constructionist uses these products sceptically, cognizant of their status as claims but respectful of their grounding in empirically accessible and morally significant social phenomena (Best, 1989, 1993; Miller, 1993).[5]

As for whether to take sides or stand on the side, most social problems sociologists see this as a false dilemma (Becker, 1967; Best, 1989). In the questions asked, in the theories adopted, and in the methods employed, a side is taken. As for which side to take, the alternatives are to attempt to take the side of 'truth' as this concept is used by Weber (1949, 1958), or to make explicit the political bias that guides inquiry and social criticism (Gusfield, 1981; Miller, 1993). Regardless, most social problems analysts recognize an obligation to respect and to present facts arising from their investigations, even when facts disconfirm the theoretical position guiding inquiry, contradict cherished political goals, or contribute to a non-complimentary portrait of the human subjects whose political action or personal misery is being investigated (Weber, 1949, 1958; Mills, 1959; Becker, 1967; Straus, 1991; Searle, 1993; Jacobson, 1994).

Regardless of whether social problems sociologists adopt a strict or a contextual approach, they recognize that social power impacts on the construction of social phenomena, that power is to some extent constitutive of 'truth.' Moreover, social problems sociologists recognize that they inscribe themselves in these processes (Schneider, 1993). Indeed, it is around the problem of power that objectivism lapses into subjectivism, and subjectivism into objectivism (Hazelrigg, 1985, 1986; Woolgar and Pawluch, 1985; Troyer, 1993). How, as social analysts, are we to disentangle the web of what is from what is claimed to be when truthclaims reverberate back on realities? On the other hand, how can we ignore the power of the lived realities out of which contending truthclaims emerge?

These issues are of particular importance to theorists who recognize that social problems sociology has practical implications regardless of whether analysts regard conditions as 'real' or 'putative' and regardless of whether analysts do or do not 'take sides.' Social problems sociology provides claims-makers with guidelines on how to achieve desired ends (Best, 1989). In professional articles, in the feminist literature, and in the research community, proponents of contending positions use social problems terms like 'mobilization,' 'ownership,' and 'co-optation.' Actors self-consciously use these terms to mobilize support for a preferred perspective. They appear to believe that they can and must assert and maintain ownership over definitions. They appear to believe that they can and must resist co-optation.

The practical importance of these concepts is evidenced in an article by Marcella Schuyler published in *Social Work* in 1976. This article provides pro-feminist social workers with a plan of action for addressing wife or woman abuse based on Blumer's stage analysis of social problems as definitional processes. Regardless of whether social problems theorists intend to, social problems sociology provides actors with 'arms.' As observers, analysts, and commentators, we participate in the dramas of social life.

The Feminist/Non-Feminist Divide

Social actors are confronted with two compelling lenses through which to view the problem of abuse – *violence against women*, grounded in the practices and goals of feminism, and *family violence*, grounded in the practices and goals of sociology and the helping professions (Yllo, 1993). Differences prevail despite widespread recognition that there is no unitary feminist perspective on abuse or any other issue, despite the fact that there is no unitary sociological perspective, and despite the fact that many researchers and commentators work to bridge the divide.[6] Some contend that *violence against women* and *family violence* constructions refer to qualitatively different abuse phenomena, that *violence against women* refers to 'patriarchal terrorism' and *family violence* refers to 'common couple violence' (Loseke, 1992; Johnson, 1995). Regardless, in the public arena, *violence against women* and *family violence* operate as 'either/or' approaches to, and interpretations of, abuse.

Joseph Gusfield (1984) likened social problems processes to a morality play. *Violence against women* is a late-twentieth-century morality play par excellence. This play features male villains and female victims. It is a creation, a discovery, an invention of feminism, an ongoing social movement that emerged in the United States and Canada in the wake of the nineteenth-century anti-slavery movement, the women's temperance movement, and the child protection movement, and that re-emerged in the 1970s in the wake of the civil rights and anti-war movements. Nineteenth-century feminists discovered 'crimes against women,' including rape and incest, but it was not until the 1970s renaissance of feminism that *violence against women* entered into public discourse.[7]

Feminists come in many stripes – liberal, radical, socialist, postmodernist – many are impossible to characterize, and many resist characterization (Flax, 1990; Thompson and Walker, 1995).[8] Feminists in the helping professions commonly describe themselves as 'pro-feminist,' which means that they incorporate feminist concerns and insights into their professional practices. Whether radical, liberal, or simply pro-feminist, most feminists direct attention to structural and ideological factors that cause abuse and that impede efforts to alleviate or end abuse. Some argue that nothing will significantly reduce or stop abuse short of a complete or radical transformation of our entire social, moral, and institutional order:[9]

> A feminist analysis of wife-beating is, at heart, a critique of patriarchy. The central argument is that the brutalization of an individual wife by an individual husband is not an individual or family problem. It is simply one manifestation of a system of male domination of women which has existed historically and cross culturally. (Yllo, 1983: 277–8)

> In a feminist analysis, incest, sexual assault, and wife abuse are understood as intrinsic to a system of male supremacy, the most overt and visible forms of control wielded by men as a class over women, and implicitly sanctioned by the culture. (Avis, 1992: 228)

> When we speak about 'battering' we refer to both the pattern of violent acts *and* their political framework, the pattern of social, institutional, and interpersonal controls that usurp a woman's capacity to determine her destiny and make her vulnerable to a range of secondary consequences. (Stark, 1993: 656)

Feminist research documents the what, how, and why of woman abuse and male-perpetrated child abuse through a variety of research methods. Feminist empiricists measure the extent of male perpetration or female victimization; expose links between patriarchal structures and woman and child abuse; examine links between gender oppression and class, race, and sexual orientation; and refute or qualify claims that direct attention to issues other than gender.[10] In contrast, 'alternative' methodologists assert that *violence against women* is not simply 'out there in the world.'[11] Rather, *violence against women* is 'textual politics,' the self-conscious construction of agents engaged in a Tourainian reconstruction of self, world, and history.[12] For these researchers, a feminist perspective is a 'point of entry,' a lens. This lens, and various 'context specific,' 'institutional ethnographic,' 'collaborative,' and 'layered' methodologies, allow and force researchers to address the context-dependent, subjectively experienced, and institutionally structured reality of violence and abuse.[13] Research demonstrates, or documents, how patriarchy as social context subordinates, silences, and victimizes females. It demonstrates how wife battering or woman abuse functions to maintain male dominance, and it documents the meanings of violence and abuse to the women who experience and resist these practices.

Across methodologies, *violence against women* researchers privilege agency – the knowledgeable, intentional, and therefore morally responsible activities of individuals and groups.[14] In the personal arena, agency is assigned to men who perpetrate and/or collude in abuse, and to women who resist, overcome, and/or rationally attempt to accommodate to abuse (Mahoney, 1994). Feminists support battered women's shelters as a means of supporting and empowering women engaged in these struggles. However, the primary focus of *violence against women* activity is cultural and especially institutional change, a structural outcome dependent on collective, political action. *Violence against women* research is consequently not research 'of' social conditions; it is research 'for' women. It is praxis.[15]

In contrast, *family violence* is a play, a movement, directed by professional practitioners in or proponents of 'the therapeutic society.' Its central theme is damaged selves, male and female, trapped in mutual, often intergenerationally patterned, cycles of abuse and dependency. In *family violence* discourse, the moral is not as clear, the villains and victims are not as easy to identify. Through a broad, apolitical, empirically informed lens, *family violence* intervenors and researchers identify the problem as a social problem, a community responsibility, a social malaise. Key concepts are damaged self-esteem, social support, social reform, healing, and recovery.[16]

Family violence is an emergent of the sociology of the family. As is feminism, sociology is an ongoing social practice rooted in the nineteenth century. It is a close cousin to the social welfare movements that followed and continue to follow in the wake of feminism. *Family violence* sociologists commonly engage in policy-oriented research. However, their principal aim is something other than praxis. Their aim is to develop theoretically coherent and empirically supportable understandings 'of' the social world.

As do feminists, *family violence* researchers employ a variety of methods. They use qualitative methods to explore perceptions and experiences of participants, the salience of contextual issues, and the dynamics of abusive practices – as in Walker's 'cycle of abuse' (1984) and Denzin's (1984) 'phenomenology of domestic family violence.'[17] However, *family violence* research is most commonly associated with survey research and a highly contentious 'act-based' operationalization of abuse designed by Murray Straus (1979), the Conflict Tactics Scale. This widely used self-report instrument allows researchers to measure violence along a continuum ranging from verbal insults to 'minor' acts of violence, such as pushing and shoving, throwing things, and slapping, to 'severe' life-threatening violence, including kicking, choking, beating, and assaults with knives and guns.

Critiques of the Conflict Tactics Scale are largely a consequence of findings – especially findings that women and men express and sustain minor and severe acts of violence at equivalent rates.[18] This apparent gender parity coincides with higher rates of reported violence among lower-income respondents, substance abusers, respondents reporting family-of-origin violence, respondents reporting pro-violent and male-dominant attitudes, respondents reporting conflict over decision-making, and so forth. Domestic *family violence* emerges as a gender-neutral individual or family problem rooted in an overdetermined causal matrix of risky situations, histories, attitudes, and behaviours.

Straus and other *family violence* researchers voice support for feminist efforts to empower women economically and socially through the reform of social institutions. Some, including Straus, identify themselves as feminist or pro-feminist. However, the preferred *family violence* intervention is not social transformation; it is therapy, recommended for all participants in chronically violent and abusive relationships or families – men, women, and children. Ultimately, despite the attention Straus and other *family violence* sociologists direct to violent norms and the need to confront and change these, *family violence* research attributes abuse to practices rooted in the volatile and highly complex psychology of the human species. The primary focus is emotionality, which is to say negative emotionality – the destructive and distorting 'dis-ease' that arises from abusive realities (Denzin, 1984, 1987; Straus, 1991, 1993a, 1993b).

The Postmodern/Modern Divide

Violence against women and *family violence* discourses are situated within a highly esoteric debate on the nature of knowledge, truth, and power.

As researchers and writers, we are compelled to choose between purportedly incommensurable paradigms, postmodernism and modernism. In practice, many straddle or seek to bridge this divide – contextual constructionists, social interactionists, and feminists among them.[19] Nevertheless, postmodern and modern approaches operate as either/or possibilities of how to do theory, research, and writing.

Postmodernists include social problems sociologists who endorse a strict constructionist position and *violence against women* researchers who employ various 'alternative' methodologies. These theorists participate in an epistemologically sophisticated approach to truth grounded in a critique of Western rationality. What distinguishes this approach is the refusal of proponents to recognize or incorporate anything that hints at 'objectivity.' Differences relate to whether analysts adopt a politically detached or a politically engaged position.

Strict constructionists posit an 'Olympian plane' from which to view the dramas of social life (Gusfield, 1981, 1984). Their concern is not with the outcomes of action; it is with processes – specifically, definitional processes associated with the emergence and legitimizations of social problems. From this perspective, social definitions, social knowledge, and social solutions are mere artifacts of a never-ending game of power. Envisioning no 'objective' or 'authentic' reality outside language, strict constructionists see no valid reason for taking 'a side.' On the other hand, as Gusfield points out, there is no logical reason for not adopting a 'Utopian' position and entering the fray (Gusfield, 1981: 198).

Postmodern *violence against women* researchers accept the salience of social definitions and the historic specificity of truth-claims, but utterly reject the idea of disinterested analysis. Instead of an Olympian plane, postmodern feminists posit a social standpoint which locates the actor/analyst, not in 'Utopia,' but in social-historical context. This standpoint demands that attention be directed to outcomes and justifies, indeed necessitates, passionate participation in the contest to win. Social analysis is not simply a language game; analysis is praxis. It entails confrontation, interrogation, subversion. While primary attention is directed to confronting conceptualizations or idealizations, not so-called empirical conditions, it is the existential reality of historically disenfranchised actors that is at stake. A core strategy is to privilege the voices of the marginalized and silenced. This strategy is a tool of empowerment; it is a mechanism for creating knowledge.

Modernists include feminist empiricists, *family violence* sociologists, and contextual constructionists. These theorists continue to participate in a reputedly obsolete but still vital approach to research and analysis grounded in the Western rationalistic tradition (Searle, 1993). Two principal modernist assumptions are that phenomena exist independently of human representations, and that valid, though necessarily provisional, statements can be made about relationships among phenomena (Giddens, 1983, 1992; Best, 1993; Guba and Lincoln, 1994).

Contextual constructionists, feminist empiricists, and *family violence* sociologists are more post-positivist than positivist, even those who rely more or less exclusively on 'empiricist' methods, such as Murray Straus.[20] Modernists differ on whether to adopt a politically detached or a politically engaged position, but all acknowledge the importance of power to outcomes, the salience of meanings to action, and the role of interpretation in analysis. None claim that the world is 'simply out there.' At the same time, the empirically accessible social world, rather than theory or discourse, remains their central or core concern.

Inflammatory Rhetoric

In professional and academic discourse, prominent *violence against women* researchers have labelled *family violence* researchers 'adversaries' of feminism who rely on an 'antiquated epistemology' and 'reductionist,' 'racist,' 'Victorian' constructs (Dobash and Dobash, 1992). Conversely, prominent *family violence* researchers and non-feminist social service professionals have denounced feminists as 'dogmatists,' 'ideologues,' and 'methodological monists' who engage in 'deliberate distortions' (Erickson, 1992; Straus, 1993a). These complementary sets of statements are examples of inflammatory rhetoric, a practice aimed not at resolving issues but at polarizing, de-legitimizing, and discrediting (Meth, 1992).

A debate between Murray Straus and critics of a Conflict Tactics Scale–based analysis of abuse published in *Social Problems* demonstrates the form and consequences of rhetorical practices aimed at discrediting rather than at reconciling positions (Kurz, 1991; Loseke, 1991; Straus, 1991; Dobash et al., 1992). Interlocutors agree that women are the principal victims of domestic violence, and that interventions need to prioritize women's safety.[21] However, they are not able to address the substantive issue of how to interpret contradictions between *family violence* findings that women also perpetrate violence, and *violence against women* evidence, drawn from police and emergency-room records, homicide statistics, and abuse testimonials, that domestic vio-

lence is *violence against women*. Instead, contenders denounce empiricist methodologies, on the one side, and feminist fundamentalism, on
the other.[22]

In *Current Controversies on Family Violence*, Kurz (1993) maintains
that *family violence* and *violence against women* perspectives are irrecon-
cilable, that there is and can be no common ground. Straus (1993a)
maintains that this assertion is based on a deliberate misrepresentation
of both mainstream and feminist perspectives. As in the *Social Problems*
debate, Straus and Kurz talk past, rather than to, each other. Kurz
refuses to recognize gender as one of many factors in an abstracted
overdetermined sociocultural system; Straus refuses to recognize
mainstream sociology as one of several competing ideological practices within the hegemonic meta-narrative feminists call patriarchy.
These refusals are grounded in disparate epistemologies, disparate
paradigms, and disparate politics. Heated arguments about the incom-
patibility of *violence against women* and *family violence* conceptualizations continue. However, as a growing number of researchers across
these two perspectives recognize, alternate language games develop
in contradistinction to each other, not in ignorance of each other
(Giddens, 1976). For those who are willing there is little difficulty
translating across languages, cultures, perspectives, or paradigms. To
accomplish this, however, interlocutors must share a desire to engage
in honest or 'authentic' communication (Habermas, 1987). They must
be willing both to seek and find common ground, and to acknowledge
and respect differences.

In his contribution to *Current Controversies*, Straus (1993a) attempts
to circumvent the necessity either of finding common ground or of
admitting to substantive differences by discrediting Kurz as a feminist.
This attempt entails a flagrant conflation of a liberal pro-feminist orientation, with which Straus is quite comfortable, with feminism. On the
other hand, Kurz speaks as though her radical feminist perspective is
the real, the authentic, the sole voice of feminism. Neither chooses to
recognize her or his opponent's position because both have something
very real to lose. As Loseke and Gelles (1993) note, winning is not just
about rhetoric, theory, or ideology; that is, it is not just about 'conceptualizations.'[23] It is also about research funds, social service jobs, and,
perhaps most importantly, professional prestige.

Polarizations between *violence against women* and *family violence* portraits of abuse prevail despite the fact that there is no unitary 'feminist
perspective' or methodology, despite the fact that *family violence* theo-

rists also differ considerably on how they approach and interpret abuse, and despite the fact that numerous commentators, researchers, and intervenors on both sides seek common ground.[24] These polarizations are a core contextual feature of *violence against women* and *family violence* discourse.

This Study

This investigation of abuse in a geographically distinct Ontario community is grounded in the sociology of social problems approach Joel Best named contextual constructionism; therefore, in the Enlightenment metaphor of discovery. I am a feminist in that I share core feminist understandings, concerns, interests, and goals including, most especially, the goal of equality and equity for women. Nevertheless, I situate my study in mainstream sociological discourse.[25] It is mainstream in the decision to address the subjective/objective dualism of definitional processes and lived experiences. It is mainstream in that I posit neither an Olympian plane nor a privileged standpoint from which to view abuse and other dramas of social life. It is mainstream in that I aim at something other than being on the winning side in struggles over how to define and address abuse. What I do attempt is to 'faithfully' explore the condition of abuse and collective efforts to address this condition, recognizing the complexity of both, recognizing the embeddedness of both in experience and in ideology, and recognizing that as a researcher I cannot but participate in the ideologically constructed and interpersonally experienced realities I analyse.[26]

My explorations are guided by three sets of research questions aimed at the specific goal of furthering understandings 'of' the recurrent and under-theorized problem of unintended outcomes of social problems mobilizations.[27] The first and primary set of questions relate to the character and dynamics of the shelter development process. The second set of questions relate to the ways public or official constructions of abuse 'fit' with variously situated actors' reported experiences and perceptions. The third set of questions relate to the relevance of this case study of abuse as political process and lived experience to the sociology of social problems and to social policy.

My investigation of the character and dynamics of abuse activism focuses on the apparent causes and consequences of an emergent and escalating control orientation that 'took over' in the transition from mobilization of action to the formation of an official plan. This control orientation was fuelled by a number of ideologically 'hot' issues that purportedly divide feminists and non-feminists, namely: (1) whether women are also violent and abusive and the relevance of this to *domestic abuse* intervention; (2) the relationship between *domestic abuse* and alcohol or substance abuse; (3) the relationship between family-of-origin spousal or child abuse and *domestic abuse*; and (4) the relationship between lower-class social status and *domestic abuse*. As I attempt to demonstrate, this control orientation, and the 'bad faith' (Denzin, 1984, 1987) denials, suppressions, and exclusions that accompanied it, produced unintended consequences that contradicted the goals and values of all participants, feminists and non-feminists alike.

My investigations of the 'fit' between public constructions and personal experiences focuses on the relative influence of *violence against women* and *family violence* conceptualizations. As I demonstrate throughout the narrative, activists and professionals rarely expressed unambiguous commitment to a clearly articulated political or ideological position; general residents certainly did not.[28] Consequently, personal accounts tend to draw on and to validate, or perhaps to invalidate, both perspectives. This relates to the 'fact' that neither a *violence against women* nor a *family violence* conceptualization adequately captures either the messy and constantly shifting reality of lived experience, or people's understandings of this reality (McKendy, 1992).

Finally, I address the relevance of this case study to theorizing on the sociology of social problems through an analysis of similarities in the dynamics of abuse as social problems process and the dynamics of abuse as lived experience. My core argument is that both processes are grounded in emotionally charged bids to assert, maintain, and resist control, and in denials of responsibility and projections of blame that mask what Norman Denzin (1984, 1987) calls the 'authentic reality' of the situation.[29]

The epistemologically and politically problematic choices that guide this study are predicated on 'the hope that actors can incorporate into action knowledge of how "objective" causal conditions influence human action so as to transform oppressive and destructive social realities' (Giddens, 1976: 153). With C. Wright Mills and Anthony Giddens, I appreciate and respect the contributions of postmodern theorists on both sides of the feminist / non-feminist divide, but I am not yet ready to renounce modernism, nor am I ready yet to acquiesce to power (Mills, 1959: 193; Giddens, 1983: 22), to force my vision through a singular lens (Yllo, 1993: 59–60), or surrender to demands for epistemological consistency (Best, 1993: 143). My decision to maintain a commitment to empirical evidence and reason, which is to say, science, is ultimately, as Weber states, indefensible. In making such choices, we choose among 'warring gods.' This epistemological fact is, and continues to be, 'the inescapable condition of our historic situation' (Weber, 1958: 152–3).

With these contingencies in mind, I have conducted as 'faithful' and 'truthful' an investigation and interpretation of the activities under study as possible.[30] I have done so accepting, and I ask my readers to accept, that 'others' would interpret my field notes, interview materials, and survey data differently, and that 'others' would draw on different theoretical sources and offer different tellings. A few respondents who played key roles in the 'shelter fray' report finding an early draft of the book 'accurate,' even 'illuminating' (see appendix 8). These endorsements notwithstanding, there is no ethical or methodological resolution to problems associated with my authority, privilege, and responsibility as researcher and author. Whether the story that follows is adequate, credible, compelling, or useful, only my readers can decide.[31]

2

The Study, the Community, and 'The Problem'

I name the research community the Township. In 1991 and 1992 the Township was a collection of smaller towns and villages with intervening rural and recreational lands. It lay on the periphery of one of several Southern Ontario regions composed of similar municipalities.

My research in the Township began with a radio interview on the ways various Ontario communities were responding to domestic violence or wife abuse. This media presentation served as my introduction to three key respondents, Lisa, Bob, and Charles, and to one core agency, the Domestic Violence Committee of a Township housing co-operative. The radio interview was one of several mobilization activities these respondents participated in. Their aim was to awaken public sentiment around the problem of *domestic abuse*, and to promote a community-inclusive and community-empowering response to this problem. The Canadian Broadcasting Corporation was one of several local and extra-local media of communication primed to promote and facilitate this activism.[1]

The radio interview followed a format typical of Domestic Violence Committee presentations. Lisa and Bob 'testified' on their personal struggles to overcome domestic violence. Lisa described her reciprocally violent relationship with Bob, and outlined how the housing co-op had provided a temporary rent subsidy when Bob was 'removed from the home' and placed on a restraining order earlier in the year. She said the co-op's support had made it possible for their family to remain in the community while Bob sought professional help. Next, Bob described the importance of knowing that his family 'would not be put out on the street.' He said this had allowed him to focus on personal problems associated with alcoholism and anger.

He stressed the importance of ongoing emotional support he, Lisa, and their children received from the housing co-op. Both partners emphasized their determination to overcome abuse, and both expressed commitment to a pro-family and pro-community model of abuse intervention.

Charles, who I subsequently learned was a social work professional with career ties to several regional and Township agencies, concluded the interview. He provided a description of the history of the housing co-operative's eight-member Domestic Violence Committee. He stressed the housing co-op's official position that Lisa, Bob, and other couples struggling with domestic violence were the real experts on abuse. He maintained that their 'community' response would not have been possible had Lisa and Bob not agreed to share their knowledge and experiences.

In January 1991 I conducted my first personal interview with Domestic Violence Committee members. I presented myself as a doctoral candidate in the Department of Sociology at the University of Toronto interested in doing a community-based study on domestic violence or woman abuse. By March I had become a regular participant observer in Domestic Violence Committee meetings, which I was allowed to tape-record. These meetings focused on schedules and strategies. I also participated in public presentations. These followed the format of the radio interview described above.

The Domestic Violence Committee included two working-class couples who publicly identified themselves as abuse survivors – Lisa and Bob and Julia and Jim – and two professional couples who worked in abuse intervention or related fields, Charles and Susan and Kathryn and Peter. These eight respondents facilitated expansion of my research into the wider Township community.

First, Domestic Violence Committee members persuaded their co-op board to allow me to occupy a vacant town-house free of charge, where I resided from 1 July to 15 October 1991. As a guest of the co-op, I participated in a seemingly endless stream of cultural events, private parties, and bar-hopping excursions. When a paying tenant took over *my* unit, several co-op families provided me with a key and a couch for sleep-overs, including some who were critical of Domestic Violence Committee activities. Julia and Jim allowed me to set up an office in their laundry room, complete with telephone. It was from this laundry-room office that I administered the survey on violence and abuse to randomly contacted residents in July and August of 1992.

Second, Domestic Violence Committee members introduced me to the Township Resource Centre, a publicly funded agency mandated to identify social needs and develop and coordinate social services.[2] Charles served as the resource centre's executive coordinator in the late 1980s, and again in 1992. He supported the women's action committee that gave birth to the Domestic Abuse Committee, the agency that sponsored the Township Women's Shelter, and he was co-author of the 1990 Township needs study that identified *domestic abuse* as the Township's most pressing social problem. Kathryn was employed as a resource centre community development worker. She was a core Domestic Abuse Committee participant, who served on the emergent Township shelter board. Lisa and Julia were two of several abuse survivors who participated in the series of 'coffee talks' that led to the formation of the Domestic Abuse Committee. Both were awarded jobs as shelter workers when the Township shelter opened in June of 1992. Jim served as a resource centre youth program volunteer, an initiative that served troubled and homeless teens. Susan, Bob, and Peter were unable to fit regular resource centre activities into their work schedules, but participated in Domestic Abuse Committee consciousness-raising and fund-raising events.

Through the summer and fall of 1991, I was a regular participant observer in Domestic Abuse Committee meetings, presentations, and fund-raising events. Through 1992 I interviewed a wide network of activists, professionals, and concerned residents, contacted through the resource centre and the many agencies that coordinated their services through this facility. In personal interviews and at public workshops, I obtained permission to make audio-tapes. At meetings and community events, I took notes during or shortly after proceedings.

In all research contexts, formal and informal, I identified myself as a researcher conducting a community-based study on domestic violence or woman abuse. When interviewing, I relied on 'creative' open-ended interview techniques (Douglas, 1985). I encouraged respondents to take the lead, to describe events and attitudes as part of a conversation on the nature of abuse, its causes, and its solution. I openly shared my personal experiences and my commitments to core feminist goals. At the same time, I made it clear that I had not yet come to closure on a number of contentious abuse-related issues, and that I was interested in the ways women and men across the community experienced and understood 'the problem.' (See Appendices for details of ethics and methods.)

Community Development and Feminism

Abuse activism was grounded in two potentially complementary ideological practices, community development and feminism. As understood by Township activists, both practices aimed at fostering
grass-roots solutions to community-identified problems through the
empowerment of residents. The difference was that feminism aimed at
empowering a specific group in the community, women. It aimed at
empowering women to recognize and resist male-perpetrated abuse
and oppression. In contrast, community development aimed at empowering residents at large. It aimed at empowering residents to join
in the community-wide initiative to combat *domestic abuse*.

In the Township, the ideology of community development preceded
feminism; it arrived with the establishment of the Township Resource
Centre in the early 1980s. According to Charles, community development assumes that residents are 'the experts of their own experience.'
Consequently, it is not the job of resource centre staff to identify, define,
or solve social problems. As Charles emphasized, and as the mission
statement of the Township Resource Centre makes clear, identifying
and solving a social problem is to be a collective, collaborative, community endeavour. Those with 'expert' knowledge are to share, but not
impose, their skills and knowledge. Under no circumstances are residents to be silenced, marginalized, or excluded:

> The Township Resource Centre is a responsive, community directed,
> multi-service, and advocacy centre which delivers a comprehensive range
> of community and social services. A primary goal of the Resource Centre
> is to initiate community development opportunities that empower the
> members of the community to seek appropriate political and collective
> action on their behalf. The Resource Centre endeavors to be forward
> looking, adaptable, universally accessible, and above all – hopeful. (TRC*
> mission statement)

Feminism arrived in the Township in the late 1980s.[3] Its arrival
roughly coincided with the formation of the women's action committee. Early in 1989, during Charles's first tenure as resource centre coordinator, this pro-feminist committee hosted a series of 'coffee talks'
aimed at initiating public education on and awareness of the problem

*See p. xv for a list of acronyms.

of abuse. At the coffee talks, community development workers facilitated dialogue between resource centre–affiliated abuse counsellors and interested residents. These coffee talks resulted in a collaborative decision to define the problem using a broad generic term, *domestic abuse*, and to seek funding for a shelter for women as one component of a comprehensive community-coordinated inter-agency abuse intervention system. At this point, Janet took over Charles's position as resource centre coordinator, and the staff-initiated women's action committee dissolved. The Domestic Abuse Committee emerged as a Township Resource Centre–sponsored, community-based, grass-roots organization.[4]

Through 1991 twelve to twenty individuals regularly attended Thursday-morning Domestic Abuse Committee meetings. Male members included accountant Paul, the only male nominated to the Township shelter board, police inspector Tom, several local business entrepreneurs, members of the Township Resource Centre board, and members of Town Council. Some appeared to regard participation as a professional or civic responsibility. Others participated as a matter of course, as they did in many Township initiatives funded through the resource centre (personal interviews and informal discussions, 1991). Officially, males were as welcome as females. In practice, few men were active, in part because few were free for Thursday-morning meetings.

Women who assumed leadership roles included community development workers Janet, Marlene, Andrea, and Kathryn, social worker Denise, probation and parole officer Mary, attorney Harriet, freelance writer Elaine, and abuse intervention counsellors Fiona, Alice, and Kay. Most of these resource centre–affiliated professionals described themselves as feminist or pro-feminist; that is, most described themselves as service providers who incorporated feminist insights and assumptions into their professional practice. All were pro-women. Their efforts were supported and augmented by resource centre board member Francis, businesswoman Edna, homemaker Leslie, and other 'concerned residents,' including a number of self-identified abuse survivors. Most survivors were current or previous clients of the Regional Women's Shelter, the Regional Woman Abuse Program, the Regional Sex Abuse Program, or Township Family Services. Wendy, who directed the Regional Women's Shelter's outreach program, and Beverly, a counsellor with the Regional Sex Abuse Program, served as Domestic Abuse Committee consultants.

Women at the core of the Domestic Abuse Committee who defined themselves as feminist made a point of distancing themselves from radical feminism. Virtually everyone agreed that males should participate in the Domestic Abuse Committee, and all favoured the inclusion of males on intervention boards, including shelter boards. Several committee members criticized the Regional Women's Shelter for being intentionally radical in rhetoric and practice. Others criticized the insular 'protectionist' or 'separatist' stance encountered in nearby shelters outside the region, whose staff were critical of the Domestic Abuse Committee's vision of a shelter as one component of a community-wide intervention system rather than as the centre or hub of abuse activism.[5] Domestic Abuse Committee members made it clear that they wished to avoid this sort of 'us against them mentality.' They stated that they intended to establish a community-sensitive, inclusive, and pragmatic solution to what all agreed was a multifaceted problem. This solution was to be guided by feminist insights, but it was grounded in the ideology and practices of community development (personal interviews, 1991: Janet, Kathryn, Marlene, Denise, Andrea, Fiona, Julia, Lisa):

> Men who abuse their partners are not monsters ... And if you exclude men you are telling them you think they are all a bunch of monsters. And you can't do that. We wanted to include men because we didn't want to have an us against them sort of thing ... You can't handle hate with hate. (Julia: DVC activist, DAC founding member, abuse survivor, TWS staff; August 1991)

> [E]specially in a small and more rural community, it's important to realize where women are really at. And that they aren't at, you know, men are horrible, and they basically want their relationship ... It's not the same as an urban environment. You have to talk about it as a family issue. It's not just a woman's issue ... And personally, I mean I consider myself a fairly strong feminist but I think it's a matter of pragmatics ... In a small community I think that for a number of reasons you have to, for instance, have men on shelter boards. You know, you have to be accepted by the community. (Janet: DAC founding member, TRC coordinator; July 1991)

Township Resource Centre staff and affiliated professionals made a point of avoiding radical rhetoric. However, Domestic Abuse Committee literature made it clear that *domestic abuse* meant abuse of women, or, in some instances, abuse of women and children. Formally, residents participated both in formulating an official definition of the problem and in developing and implementing an official plan of action. However, resource centre staff and affiliated professionals directed these processes, processes that prioritized educating, or rather re-educating, residents. This agenda was apparently established at the onset:

> In this women's group we started off with an idea that public education and changing values was the place to start and the shelter came along as a sort of necessary service. But throughout we really tried to maintain that commitment to, ah, you know eradicating wife assault has got to come by people changing how they think ... And I think that's quite different from a group coming together specifically to do a shelter, as an end in itself ... The shelter, you could almost call a necessary evil; it's taken such a huge amount of time and energy ... To me the main thing is to get people thinking about the issue and all that stuff, and we've tried to build in from the beginning. (Denise: DAC founder, TWS board; July 1991)

> The Domestic Abuse Committee hasn't done as much of a process, a formal process initially in terms of involvement of the community. It's been very, I'm not being critical it's worked very well ... but there wasn't that kind of a formal, go out to the community and draw people back in for this. It's more been through the press and that kind of thing ... At the coffee talks, ah, well, we had a definition, we had the agenda set out. (Marlene: DAC founder, ex-RWS worker, TRC staff; July 1991)

Domestic Abuse Committee members formally accepted the premise that residents are the experts of their own experience and made a point of incorporating residents' concerns and definitions into their official plan of action, but they were wary of the attitudes associated with residents' experiences. Consequently, the authors of the 1990 needs study reinterpreted residents' contentions that alcohol abuse was the major problem facing the community as resident-identification of domestic violence (Township Needs Study, Report and Summary). Community development worker Marlene justified this redefinition on the grounds that 'residents typically mis-identify domestic violence or wife abuse as alcohol abuse' (personal interview, 1991).

Domestic Abuse Committee activists believed it was important to confront a number of 'false myths' about *domestic abuse*. False myths listed in the Regional Women's Shelter's handbook include the myth that women provoke or initiate abuse; that alcohol causes abuse; that abusive men are mentally ill or sick; and that abuse only occurs in lower-class families or working-class neighbourhoods. At the same time, activists recognized, or believed, that alcohol abuse is associated with more severe and more frequent patterns of domestic violence, that abusers commonly exhibit personality disorders, and that economically deprived populations experience higher rates of domestic or *family violence* (personal interviews, 1991: Janet, Kathryn, Marlene, Denise, Fiona, Alice, Kay, Harriet, Mary). Indeed, activists directed considerable energy to convincing federal and provincial funders that physical wife abuse was more severe and frequent in the Township precisely because of the extent of these and related risks.

Public Images of the Township

A social historical profile of the Township adapted from a regionally sponsored Social Planning Council report, the 1990 Township needs study, Domestic Abuse Committee promotional material, and Township Resource Centre grant applications convey an image of the Township as a problem-ridden community in crisis. These texts were authored by staff moving in and out of positions at the resource centre between 1989 and 1991, and by resource centre–affiliated professionals. They were compiled to convince potential funders that the Township needed and deserved funding for various community development initiatives, including the Township shelter:

> The Township is extremely isolated both economically and socially. Historically a cottage area with a strong farming base it became a centre of relocation for families on relief in the 1940's. During the 1970's and 1980's a housing boom in southern Ontario resulted in a second wave of migration by families in search of affordable housing. Many were forced to accept substandard, dilapidated, unwinterized cottages – in some cases without indoor toilets or electricity. This migration continues.
>
> Within the Region the Township has:
>
> 1) the lowest average family income in the Region, also the highest number of individuals and families with incomes below $10,000;
> 2) the highest illiteracy rate, less than 49% of the Township's adult population has completed grade 9;

3) the highest unemployment rate;

4) the highest rate of lone mothers on social assistance;

5) the highest rate of adult crime and conviction;

6) the highest rate of domestic violence calls: 10 per 1000 compared to 3.2 per 1000 for the Region;

7) the highest rate of women seeking shelter at the Regional Women's Shelter; the Township accounts for 5% of the population of the Region and 12% of Shelter clients;

8) the highest incidence of admissions to Children's Aid Society care;

9) the highest incidence of children with speech, language, behavioral and development problems: 16% are labeled 'exceptional' compared to 10% for the Region as a whole.

Moreover:

10) the Township is one of ten areas in Ontario identified by Royal Canadian Mounted Police as having a serious problem with substance abuse
...

The most widely cited 'fact' supporting images of the Township as problem-ridden was a series of domestic homicides. A media article published in the spring of 1991 identified these as the only domestic homicides to have occurred 'in the entire region' over the eighteen-month period beginning August 1989:

DOMESTIC HOMICIDE #1 – AUGUST, 1989: Mrs. DH-F#1 and her husband are at their home arguing about their marriage breakup when he chokes and then stabs her with a steak knife he leaves lodged in her throat. A few days before Mrs. DH-F#1 had taken their three children to the Regional Women's Shelter, a home for battered women. Her husband is subsequently convicted of second-degree murder and sentenced to life imprisonment with no parole eligibility for 10 years.

DOMESTIC HOMICIDE #2/#3 – NOVEMBER, 1990: Mrs. DH-F#2/3 is stabbed to death by her husband after an argument at their home. Mr. DH-M#2/3 then kills himself with a stab wound to the heart. The couple leave two teen-age children.

DOMESTIC HOMICIDE #4 – MAY, 1990: A mother of two young children is confronted at her home by Mr. DH-M#4 with whom she had recently ended a brief relationship. Armed with a sawed-off shotgun Mr. DH-M#4 shoots the woman in the back before opening fire at the Township Regional Police tactical squad. A police sharp-shooter kills Mr. DH-M#4, the woman survives.

DOMESTIC HOMICIDE #5 – JANUARY, 1991: Mrs. DH-F#5 and her estranged husband encounter each other by chance at the couple's vacant home. The second-degree murder charge against the husband who surrendered to police alleges that after an argument over their divorce, the man stabbed his wife repeatedly and then attacked her with an ax. The couple had two teen-aged children, and one child aged six.

The media article contrasted contending explanations for the 'dangerously high levels of domestic violence' provided by representatives of two emerging camps. The first camp consisted of core Domestic Abuse Committee participants and their supporters. It included attorney Harriet, quoted as saying, 'Violence of one kind or another is part of almost everything that comes through the door of my family law practice'; hospital emergency nurse Susan, who maintained that 'levels of violent abuse far exceed national averages'; and resource centre coordinator Janet, who exclaimed, 'I don't know how we could handle another murder.' This camp attributed the 'crisis level' of domestic violence in the Township to the sexist and otherwise regressive attitudes of residents, characterized as 'behind the times':

There's a different type of lifestyle out here ... It's like going back in time, like to the 50's. People have a different attitude. (Attorney Harriet: DAC, emergent TWS board member)

Attitude is the major problem. And it's there from the municipal politicians on down. I work with teen-agers who have the same attitude as people two generations older. (MPP Linda: DAC supporter, emergent TWS board member)

There's a whole lot of denial, along with a lot of terror. It's like, well, he just slaps me around, it's not like getting shot ... It's a matter of education. (Janet: TRC coordinator, core DAC)

The second camp consisted of local businessmen and male politicians – an emerging Domestic Abuse Committee opposition, though no core members of this 'opposition' participated in the media debate.

This camp attributed the questionably exceptional levels of domestic violence to the high number of female-headed families on social assistance, to high levels of substance abuse, and to a recent influx of residents of lower social economic status:

> Illiteracy and a high number of single mothers and welfare recipients have been long-term issues in this community; just last year the Ontario Provincial Police identified the Township as one of ten with above average substance-abuse problems. (Joe: member of Town Council)

> We've brought in thousands and thousands of people with no roots or ties to the area ... Now they're murdering each other. (Jeff: member of Town Council)

> Those people that moved into the area over the past few years brought a lot of problems with them. (Bill: mayor)

> Any incident gets blown up, it's news. There's no doubt there's domestic violence. Someone says we have more than our fair share and that's true, this area has always had more than its fair share. But some of the percentages being thrown around distort the picture tremendously. (Mark: member of Town Council)

This media debate documents the disparate biases of formally educated professionals, predominantly female, most of whom were 'new' to the community, and lesser-educated established residents, predominantly male. On a second level, it attests to the deep disparities between feminist and non-feminist understandings of abuse. On a third level, it demonstrates the role of 'exaggerated claims and distorted depictions' as contending actors bring their sentiments to bear on the framing of a problem (Blumer, 1971: 303–4).

Official Statistics

A comparative analysis of census data on the Township and neighbouring communities suggests that activists' claims about the social and economic situation in the Township were valid but exaggerated (see tables 1.a, 1.b, and 1.c). For instance, census data confirm that Township incomes were low compared to other communities in the region. However, income levels were consistent with averages in nearby municipalities outside the region. Census data likewise confirm that Township residents were under-educated, under-employed, and somewhat more likely to participate in non-traditional family structures. They were also more likely to rely on the income of one partner; that is, women were less likely to participate in the paid labour force. Again, patterns were generally consistent with those in neighbouring municipalities outside the region. Finally, census data confirm that the Township's population had increased considerably over the previous five to ten years. Similar or markedly higher rates of population increase were evident in many neighbouring communities, inside and outside the region. In other words, census data confirm that the Township was an educationally and economically disadvantaged community stressed by demographic and social changes. They show, however, that it was no more disadvantaged or stressed than other communities on the fringe of Southern Ontario's expansive 'urban belt.'

Most pertinent to the problem of abuse, the Township had a reputation for high rates of violent crime, high rates of domestic violence, and high rates of substance abuse. According to Regional police historical summaries (1989–92) and Canadian Centre for Justice Statistics (1991), rates of violent assault were higher than the regional average but, as with other social characteristics, low or average compared to the province, the nation, or similarly situated urban-peripheral municipalities outside the region (see table 1.d). As for domestic assaults, neither the Township police nor the Regional police compiled statistics on domestic versus non-domestic charges or convictions. However, interviewed Township police reported that rates of violence, domestic and otherwise, were fairly typical. They maintained that the spate of homicides was a 'statistical blip.'[6] Moreover, they maintained that levels of substance abuse were high but no higher than in other communities with similar social demographics.

Residents, Experts, and Activists

Township residents responded to the social problems process in a number of ways. They attended public meetings, public workshops, and fund-raising events. They commented in the local press, participated in the Township needs study, and shared experiences and perspectives in personal interviews. In the summer of 1992, 97 individuals from 150 randomly contacted households, and 32 married or cohabiting partners of these first respondents, participated in the telephone survey on abuse in intimate relationships, administered from my laundry-room office at Julia's and Jim's co-op unit (see appendix 2 for details of sampling procedures and data collection methods).[7]

In a number of contexts, residents resisted Domestic Abuse Committee–promoted constructions of *domestic abuse*. First, many residents resisted constructions of *domestic abuse* as a problem that was primarily or solely male-perpetrated *violence against women*. Many residents volunteered the opinion that 'abuse can be a two-way street,' that 'it takes two to tango,' that 'women can also be abusive.' This opinion was dramatically evidenced in alterations to a Domestic Abuse Committee–designed poster displayed in a doughnut shop in a mall on the outskirts of the Township's most notoriously violent neighbourhood. The poster was altered to attest to the 'fact' that assault of a wife *or husband*, a girlfriend *or boyfriend*, is a crime. Second, residents resisted activists' attempts to downplay alcoholism and related substance problems; most regarded substance abuse as one of several important causes of domestic violence. Third, residents resisted activists' attempts to downplay the consequences of personal histories of child abuse and parental spouse abuse; many maintained that *domestic abuse* refers to both these phenomena, and that both are psychologically damaging, alcohol related, and intergenerational. Lastly, residents resisted activists' attempts to downplay the importance of social economics to *domestic abuse*; many maintained that joblessness was a major contributor to high levels of domestic violence in the Township.

With respect to female culpability, in this study, as in others, Conflict Tactics Scale reports of threats and assaults expressed and sustained over the previous twelve months support a portrait of abuse as either reciprocal or female-perpetrated. These data help explain why the majority of currently partnered respondents resisted the notion that males are primarily or solely responsible for abuse, and it helps explain why so many were willing to excuse defensive violence for women and men alike.[8] (See tables 4 and 5.)

However, accounts of practices that respondents themselves considered abusive support a very different portrait. In qualitative accounts, abuse was overwhelmingly male-perpetrated – over 80 per cent of family-of-origin spousal violence was identified as male-perpetrated, as was 75 per cent of physical child abuse, and 100 per cent of child sexual abuse. Moreover, while several women reported that a current or past boyfriend or husband had subjected them to chronic beatings, assaults while pregnant, stalking, and attacks with knives, guns, and other potentially lethal objects, only one male reported sustaining a comparably serious act of violence.[9] These data help explain respondents' exceptionally strong support for women's shelters, their strong support for the contention that abuse is motivated by a desire for power and control, and their tendency to regard female-perpetrated violence both as more justifiable and as less harmful than male violence.[10] (See tables 4, 5, and 15.)

Contradictions in Conflict Tactics Scale and qualitative accounts of abuse are well documented in the abuse literature. Generally, *violence against women* researchers regard qualitative data as more valid.[11] Most downplay female-perpetration, not because they believe that women are never violent, but because they are cognizant of the serious physical and psychic consequences of male violence on female partners. Moreover, most regard male violence as willed behaviour intricately connected to male dominance, and therefore to human agency.

Family violence researchers who rely mostly on quantitative data privilege a more gender-neutral construction of abuse, not because they are unaware of the serious consequences of violence to women, but because they view wife or woman abuse as a dysfunctional family or relationship process, rooted simultaneously in human emotionality (or psychology) and in social structures.[12]

Members of the Domestic Abuse Committee held varying perspectives on the relevance of gender and other issues. Regardless, the committee directed primary attention to the 'fact' that it was women who were being seriously injured and killed, in society at large and in the Township. Most committee members agreed that female violence was largely defensive or pre-emptive, and that it was irrelevant to the serious problem of female victimization, and the sense of powerlessness women experience as a result of this.

With respect to substance abuse, 90 per cent of survey residents identified substance abuse, specifically alcohol abuse, as a major or important cause of *domestic abuse*, with little variation across gender or social demographic categories, and more than 80 per cent rated substance abuse interventions as important to a community-coordinated effort to alleviate or end *domestic abuse*. Some expressed regret that Township Family Services and Regional Woman Abuse Program counsellors 'refused' to address this aspect of the problem, and dismay that Alcoholics Anonymous was the only substance abuse program available in the community (see tables 4 and 12):

Township Family Services counselling is good but they can't or won't deal with substance abuse ... How can counselling help if you don't deal with alcohol or drug abuse? Maybe it's not all of it, but it's easy 90 per cent ... They say you have to deal with substance problems separately. Well, I was turned down twice by welfare to get money for baby sitting to go to AA. Now the government's paying to send me to Mexico ... I needed counselling to deal with my substance problem a lot earlier. (Female survey respondent, currently single, previous relationship seriously violent)

Respondents' attitudes about substance abuse were consistent with reported experiences. Reports of childhood victimization and family-of-origin wife or spouse abuse were significantly likely to correspond with reports of parental alcohol abuse.[13] Reports of current relationship violence were likewise significantly likely to correspond with reports of current-generation substance abuse, both in the more risk-vulnerable *random* sample and in the more risk-resistant dual partner *couples* sub-sample. These findings help explain why residents resisted Domestic Abuse Committee contentions that alcohol abuse is not a cause of *domestic abuse*. (See tables 4, 7, and 8.)

Across the feminist/non-feminist divide, most 'experts' regard alcohol abuse as a rationalization for abusive or violent behaviour, as a disinhibitor or facilitator, or as a concurrent problem. Few support contentions that alcohol or substance abuse causes domestic violence.[14] Like the majority of experts, the majority of Domestic Abuse Committee activists believed that domestic violence and substance abuse are somehow linked, but that the relationship is not causal. Core activists maintained that abusive males chose to drink knowing that they will abuse their female partners, and that abusers tell their partners that alcohol made them abusive to evade responsibility for their actions. Not all committee members agreed with this position; nevertheless, the Domestic Abuse Committee promoted the idea that attitudes about substance abuse, far more than substance abuse itself, accounted for the 'dangerously high' levels of domestic violence in the Township.

With respect to the relationship between childhood or family-of-origin abuse and violence in adult relationships, 75 per cent of survey respondents identified a history of *family violence* as a major or important cause of domestic violence, with little variation across gender, demographic, or experiential categories. Again, residents' attitudes were consistent with reported experiences. Among partnered respondents generally, correlations between abuse experienced or witnessed as children and violence in adult relationships were statistically significant, as were correlations between childhood or family-of-origin abuse and current relationship distress.[15] These findings help explain why the majority of residents resisted Domestic Abuse Committee contentions that wife or woman abuse is the core problem, and that sexism is the 'root' or most important cause of this problem.[16] (See tables 7, 8, 9, and 14.)

Violence against women researchers characteristically reject the intergenerational hypothesis on the grounds that many survivors manage to avoid replicating abusive family-of-origin patterns.[17] They argue that intergenerational explanations individualize and pathologize abuse, thereby exonerating abusive men and blaming or stigmatizing abused women. They insist that perpetrators and perpetrators alone are responsible for acts of domestic violence, and that sexist attitudes, not feelings, lay behind abusers' decisions to inflict abuse. Consequently, many *violence against women* proponents reject counselling or therapy, either for abusive men or for abused women. Those who favour pro-feminist counselling insist on a gender-specific educational group format that aims at the eradication not only of woman abuse, but also its underlying cause, sexist attitudes.

Family violence researchers recognize that family-of-origin spouse or child abuse does not automatically or inevitably lead to violence in adult relationships; however, many at least partially accept the notion that abuse tends to follow intergenerational patterns.[18] Those who accept this notion direct attention to the mixed, complex, mutating trajectories associated with 'intergenerational vulnerability.' Regardless of whether *family violence* proponents reject or accept the intergenerational hypothesis, and regardless of the importance they assign to sexism, most endorse individual and group counselling or therapy for all family members. Some promote conjoint counselling for violent couples. Regardless, most endorse a cognitive behavioural format aimed at enhancing personal responsibility, individuation, empathy, communication skills, and recognition of feeling states, along with gender issues.[19]

The majority of Domestic Abuse Committee participants recognized or believed that abuse is commonly intergenerational. However, the committee endorsed the pro-feminist position that boys model their behaviour on male role models, in society and in the family, and that these models promote sexist practices. Consequently, the committee focused on sexist attitudes, rather than on the effects of dysfunctional family practices. Helping professionals who held more traditional therapeutic understandings of abuse as trauma-related participated on the committee, but pro-feminist Regional Woman Abuse Program counsellors were more influential.

Finally, with respect to economic stress, 64 per cent of surveyed residents identified economic stress as a major or important cause of *domestic abuse*. Most favoured efforts to economically empower women through job training and employment equity programs. However, many volunteered that more resources needed to be directed to job creation for men and women alike. Some maintained that joblessness was related not only to domestic violence, but also to substance abuse. Most, across genders, social statuses, and experiential histories, regarded economic stress as an important contributor to the allegedly high rates of domestic violence in the Township:

> There's no work here. That has a lot to do with it. The real problems are drink and work. I mean no work. I think no work leads to drinking ... What we need is jobs. (Male survey respondent, 'recovered' alcoholic, long-term marital relationship seriously violent)

Respondents' attitudes were once again largely consistent with reported experiences. Respondents who reported below average household incomes reported higher, though insignificantly higher, rates of violence and abuse, as children and as adults. On the other hand, higher income respondents reported comparable rates of substance abuse and minor violence. These findings generally confirm residents' beliefs that economic stress is an important, but somewhat less important, component of *domestic abuse*. They help explain why residents resisted Domestic Abuse Committee contentions that economic issues are irrelevant to the problem. (See tables 4 and 6.)

Violence against women researchers emphasize findings that abuse occurs across social statuses and experiential histories. Many acknowledge the unholy trio of sexism, classism, and racism, but few are willing to excuse the abusive behaviour of oppressed males. Consequently, *violence against women* proponents direct primary attention to the vulnerable and dependent economic situation of women generally, regardless of the economic resources of their families. Some argue that it is unethical and distorting to 'dredge for differences.'[20]

Family violence researchers agree that violence occurs across social statuses, and they concur that female dependency contributes to wife abuse. Nevertheless, poverty or low social economic status emerges as a consistent 'risk marker' for domestic violence or woman abuse, in both the United States and Canada.[21] This risk 'loads' with others. In study after study, it is unemployed or lower-income substance-abusing males who witnessed or experienced violence as children who are the prime perpetrators of chronic and severe woman abuse, and it is lower-income females who report childhood victimization and who either abuse substances or 'tolerate' substance abusers who are the primary victims.[22] These research concerns and findings target populations and, implicitly, personalities. They reflect a privileging of situational, behavioural, and psychodynamic or emotional 'factors' or processes that implicitly pathologize abuse and the people who experience abuse.

Members of the Domestic Abuse Committee held varying and ambivalent positions on the relationship between social economics and abuse. Regardless, the committee endorsed the *violence against women* position that women across statuses and backgrounds are victims of male violence, that stigmatizing stereotypes are a form of victim-blaming, and that gender oppression and the attitudes that sustain gender oppression are the core or the root 'cause' of abuse.

Myths and Facts

Domestic Abuse Committee activists held conflicting and ambivalent views on all the issues that divide *violence against women* and *family violence* positions. Officially, however, they adopted the stance that the best, and perhaps the only 'real,' way to combat abuse is to change attitudes. Core committee members consequently directed their energies to education around sexism and a presumed widespread tolerance of male abuse of women in the Township, rather than to 'concurrent' issues such as intergenerational child and spouse abuse, substance abuse, economic conditions, and relationship dynamics. This reflects an implicit rejection of *family violence* conceptualizations of abuse as a socially overdetermined interactive process in which at least 'two' participate.

In contrast, the majority of surveyed residents endorsed the view that it 'takes two to tango.' Based on the testimony of those who knew abuse personally, at the level of lived experience, these 'two' are highly likely to be a readily provoked, pro-violent, sexist, substance-abusing male, and a distressed, defensively violent, pro-feminist female, who 'tango' together through a field of coercion and suffering that reaches across extended family networks, and generations (see tables 7, 8, 14, and 15; see also chapter 7).[23]

In their decision to downplay concurrent issues and to treat attitudes as the central or root cause of the problem, Domestic Abuse Committee activists focused attention on something that humans can assumedly elect to do – change how they think. Ironically, the majority of surveyed residents agreed that education aimed at attitudinal change is important to preventing abuse in the future (see table 4). At the same time, most believed that they were simply 'calling a space a spade.' Most regarded substance problems, intergenerational vulnerability, economic stress, and female culpability as obvious aspects of the reality of abuse – aspects that Domestic Abuse Committee activists *refused* to address.[24]

Despite residents' general resistance to Domestic Abuse Committee-sponsored constructions of the problem, support for the shelter and related interventions remained high – evidenced in the survey and in ongoing private and business donations through 1992. However, the Township's 'experts of their own experience' displayed little sympathy for those who purported to advocate on their behalf. Across demographic and experiential categories, the majority preferred that abuse interventions be directed and staffed by abuse professionals and survivors. A sizeable minority welcomed the involvement of concerned residents. However, few supported, and very few preferred, either of the contingents – feminist activists or community leaders – that sought 'ownership' over the shelter and related services during the two years prior to the survey. (See tables 4, 10.a–10.d, and 11.)[25]

Conclusion

This chapter provides a portrait of the Township as an allegedly high-risk but demographically non-exceptional Southern Ontario community whose residents were acutely sensitized to the problem of abuse, highly receptive to research, strongly supportive of intervention initiatives, but openly critical of activist-endorsed conceptualizations of the problem. The following chapter examines how Domestic Abuse Committee activists and their critics used contending perspectives on the nature and causes of abuse and who correctly understands these issues in efforts to assert and maintain 'ownership' over the shelter – a process that polarized activists and community leaders along gender and ideological lines. These polarizations diverted attention from what residents, in formal and informal contexts, continued to assert about the problem and its solution.

3

Mobilization of Action:
Struggles for Control

This chapter examines the ways strategic, contentious, ricocheting practices between or among Domestic Abuse Committee activists and their opponents molded or framed efforts to address the problem of *domestic abuse* in the Township (Schneider, 1985). The general process was one of escalating polarizations. These polarizations emerged from a series of struggles over who specifically should develop and implement the widely agreed upon and broadly supported plan to establish a women's shelter. Major contenders were female Township Resource Centre staff and affiliated professionals at the core of the Domestic Abuse Committee, and a contingent of male volunteers who served on the Township Resource Centre board, men accustomed to taking a lead role in Township activities.

The initial point of contention was over where to locate the new shelter. The central issue, of course, was who would make this decision. Instead of mutual accommodation or compromise, a classic schismogenic process of mutual vilification unfolded, culminating by June 1992 in the virtual divorce of the Township shelter from the Township Resource Centre that sponsored it. This outcome proceeded through developments that mirror the destructive processes that take over families and relationships when struggles to monopolize power dominate interactions (Denzin, 1984; Bateson, 1985; Reiss, 1988).

Behind struggles to achieve or maintain control of the shelter process, backstage as it were, residents contended with the problem itself, with the lived reality of abuse. Residents were invited to come forward to express their concerns and understandings, were in fact admonished 'to take the risk and get involved.' However, activists routinely reinterpreted residents' constructions in ways that reinforced their own definitions and solutions. Residents consequently appear as a sometimes vocal but largely irrelevant audience to what was essentially a struggle between or among contending elites.

Mobilization Activities

Early in 1991 Domestic Abuse Committee activists succeeded in convincing federal and provincial funders that the Township was more needing and deserving of a women's shelter than competing communities. Funding remained contingent, however, on resident support for the shelter – support that could only be demonstrated through significant public and private donations. Consequently, the Domestic Abuse Committee intensified mobilization efforts aimed at educating residents on the nature of abuse, and at fostering consensus that a shelter was needed.

First, the Domestic Abuse Committee sponsored a series of local media articles. These articles focused on incidents or sets of incidents that occurred over an eighteen-month period ending January 1991, and include the domestic homicides described in the previous chapter, the school-yard sexual abuse of a twelve-year-old girl by her male classmates,[1] and the beating of a housing co-op resident by her ex-husband, in which police refused to intervene.[2] These incidents were presented as the tip of an iceberg of abuse. They were intended to prove that the community was in the midst of a crisis and that women and children were the victims of this crisis.

Second, the Domestic Abuse Committee sponsored an Abuse Awareness Workshop, a day-long event held in the spring of 1991, funded by the resource centre and the Women's Directorate.[3] At this point, tensions between the Domestic Abuse Committee and its emerging opposition were nascent, but they had not come to my attention, or generally to the attention of the community. Residents assumedly attended the workshops for one of two reasons – to learn about the problem and to further or initiate their own involvement in implementing a solution. I attended a morning session, described as a Wife Abuse Workshop, and an afternoon session, described as a Community Response Workshop. The workshops are important because they demonstrate the ways feminist and community development approaches were employed to mobilize support for the Domestic Abuse Committee's official plan of action.

The Wife Abuse Workshop

The Wife Abuse Workshop was conducted by pro-feminist staff employed through Township Family Services, the Regional Woman Abuse Program, and the Regional Women's Shelter.[4] The presenters did not identify themselves as members of the Domestic Abuse Committee. However, counsellors Fiona and Alice were regular participants in Thursday-morning Domestic Abuse Committee meetings, and shelter worker Wendy served as a consultant to the committee.

The workshop was very much an expert presentation. The audience, twenty or so women, presumably residents, faced presenters who provided instruction with flip charts and handouts. Just prior to the presentation, I introduced myself as a PhD candidate doing research on community responses to domestic violence through the Domestic Violence Committee of the Township housing co-operative. I requested and received permission to make an audio-tape of the presentation.

At the onset we were told that it is inappropriate to define abuse as *family violence* or domestic violence, that the problem is clearly wife or woman abuse. Having made this clear, Regional Woman Abuse Program presenter Alice and Township Family Services presenter Fiona provided a vivid description of Lenore Walker's (1984) 'cycle of abuse.' As these presenters described the cycle, it consists of four phases: (1) a violent explosion; (2) remorse and forgiveness; (3) closeness – sexual and emotional; and (4) estrangement and tension-building. When tension and mutual isolation peak, the cycle begins again with another violent episode.

According to Fiona and Alice, this cycle is most understandable in terms of a relationship ideal that typifies battering relationships. Fiona reported that, in separate groups, female victims and male perpetrators commonly identify their relationship ideal as entailing total togetherness – a honeymoon that will never end. She represented this relationship ideal as a circle on a circle. Two are one. She said most batterers and victims do not understand the possibility of a relationship in which autonomy and intimacy coexist, diagrammed as two overlapping circles. She said most participants in abusive relationships see the only alternative to total love and togetherness as total separation, diagrammed as two distinct circles. Consequently, even minor disagreements and differences elicit intense anxiety.

Next, Regional Women's Shelter presenter Wendy described the ways gender scripts contribute to the reproduction of this homeostatic pattern: through male scripts to control and female scripts to accommodate. Fiona interjected that abused women commonly admit that they precipitate violence. She said this occurs when the tension becomes unbearable, when violence is imminent, unavoidable. She said that many women find the 'walking on eggs' atmosphere that precedes an explosion less bearable than the explosion itself. Alice stated that women precipitate violence knowing that a temporary phase of calm or closeness will follow the explosion. All three presenters concurred that, regardless of provocation or precipitation, males perpetrate abuse, women endure and resist abuse.

After the presentation, the audience was encouraged to ask questions. Participation was hesitant – a number of questions and answers were too low to pick up on the audio-tape. Presenters tended to address their responses to individuals, rather than to the group. There was no dialogue. Rather, a member of the audience would ask a question, presenters would answer it, and then move on to the next question. One questioner expressed difficulty applying the cycle of violence and the ideal of romantic love to the alcohol-crazed relationship her sister-in-law participated in. Several in the audience nodded assent. Fiona responded that alcohol abuse complicates things, and that concurrent counselling for substance abuse is often needed. She emphasized that alcoholism is a separate problem, and that it must be dealt with separately.

Another woman expressed support for the Township shelter but said she didn't think shelters could do much to stop abuse. She said she knew someone who had gone to a shelter once and claimed she would never go again. Again, there was a murmur of assent. The woman sitting next to her asked what she should tell a friend who believed that shelter workers would make her leave her husband. Wendy assured the women that no one tells an abused woman that she must leave her abuser. She said staff at the Regional shelter actively encourage women to recognize that the decision to end the relationship or to return to their partner is entirely up to them.

At this point, the woman concerned about alcoholism again attempted to get the presenters to address substance abuse. She asked whether there was a way to get someone with a drinking problem to at least think about their situation. Fiona responded that it is important to encourage people to seek help, and that continual support and encouragement often result in help-seeking. She said it was important to support women whatever their problems. She did not respond directly to the alcohol issue.

The Wife Abuse Workshop presenters appeared to have two objectives. First, they tried to educate workshop participants on the relationship between attitudes and behaviours by drawing attention to the ways gender scripts and ideals of romantic love trap women in abusive relationships. Behaviours were presented as a consequence of attitudes, and the dynamics set in motion by these attitudes. Thus, female provocation, one of the false myths listed in the Regional Women's Shelter's handbook, is not really provocation. It is a response to male power, itself a consequence of culturally reinforced expectations both that a male will be in control and that a loving woman will utterly, completely, and constantly meet her man's needs. Second, presenters sought to divert attention from substance issues. This allowed them to avoid discussion that detracted from their main point – that attitudes cause abuse, specifically, attitudes that disempower women. I was left in doubt about the success of the these efforts. As my survey of Township residents demonstrated, and as Best (1990) has noted, residents actively resist constructions of problems that do not seem to fit with their personal experiences.[5]

The Community Response Workshop

The afternoon Community Response Workshop was an exercise in community development. This workshop was co-organized by the housing co-operative's Domestic Violence Committee and the resource centre's Domestic Abuse Committee. Everyone sat in a circle; everyone introduced herself or himself, stating their particular interest in the issue. Participants included four members of the Domestic Violence Committee, several Domestic Abuse Committee members, a few abuse professionals, and a number of general residents. Three of the nine women subsequently nominated to the Township shelter board were present – community development worker Kathryn, freelance journalist Elaine, and concerned resident Leslie.[6] I again introduced myself as a PhD candidate doing research on community responses to abuse with the Township housing co-operative, and again I received permission to make an audio-tape.

Community development worker Marlene and housing co-op resident Charles co-orchestrated or co-facilitated the workshop. Domestic Abuse Committee members played a dominant role, but this was not obvious. I came away feeling that residents had been empowered more than informed. It was later, after I established formal contact with the Domestic Abuse Committee, that I discovered that many of the more vocal residents were already active members:[7]

> Hi everyone, I'm Marlene. I'm a community worker with the Township Resource Centre. As part of the process today we'll go around the circle and introduce ourselves, and if you wouldn't mind, telling us why you're attending the workshop. (Marlene: TRC staff, former RWS worker, core DAC)
>
> I'm Ellie. I live in the Township and I'm here as a concerned resident. I want to know how we can help people who are in trouble, and how we can work with the Domestic Abuse Committee. (Female resident)
>
> I'm Stacey. I live in the community. As a wife and mother I want to make the community a better place for my whole family. (Female resident)
>
> I'm Leslie. I'm a community resident and a member of Domestic Abuse Committee. I want to learn more about how to help the community. (Leslie: DAC, future TWS board)
>
> I'm Martha. I'm with the Anglican Church – I'm the new pastor. I want to find out what's available, and what the contemporary issues are. (Female resident)
>
> I'm Ruth. I'm a researcher with the University of Toronto. I'm doing research with the Domestic Violence Committee on community responses to domestic violence. (Ruth: researcher)
>
> I'm Ed. I'm on the Board of Directors of the Township Resource Centre. I think I'm here today because I'm required to help the community respond to people who have different values, generally. But also I'm quite intrigued at the issues that are related to violence, and how they impact on all of us. (Male resident: TRC board, member of the emerging 'DAC opposition')
>
> I'm Jean. I'm just about to graduate from a community education course, and I'm, ah, learning about this type of thing. (Student: female resident)
>
> I'm Nick. I'm here because I'm interested in these kinds of problems. I'm

here to find out what I can do. I've had so many friends who have been sexually abused, and ah, maybe find out a little more about how it happens. (Male resident)

I'm Lena and she's Pam. We're here, ah, we're staying at the Regional Catholic Home for Young Mothers. We came today, on the bus, ah, at the Home they thought we might learn something. (Two very young and very pregnant young women, who remained silent throughout the discussion)

I'm Lisa, and a member of the Domestic Abuse Committee, also a member of the Domestic Violence Committee of my housing co-op. And my husband had been, and still is, a violent offender who was taken out of the home. The community's response to that was not so much to stop it right away, but at least prevented it from getting worse. (Lisa: DVC, DAC, future TWS worker)

I'm Charles. I'm here today as a member of the Domestic Violence Committee. We were asked to come in and talk a bit about the work we've done, and I hope very quickly we'll be talking back and forth about how it relates to the larger community, and hear stories that other people have of ways of dealing with violence, strategies of coping. (Charles: prior and future coordinator of TRC, child-abuse professional, DVC, DAC supporter, future backer of the DAC opposition)

I'm Kathryn. I'm with the Township Resource Centre, and I'm a Domestic Abuse Committee member and I live in the housing co-op with Lisa and Charles and Susan. And I'm married to a Domestic Violence Committee member. (Kathryn: TRC staff, alternate DVC, DAC, future TWS board)

I'm Susan. I'm here with the Domestic Violence Committee. We think it's important to respond to the problem of domestic violence as a community. (Susan: emergency-room nurse, DVC, DAC supporter)

I'm Elizabeth. I teach child-care courses. I came here hoping I can gather information. (Female resident)

I'm Beverly. I work with the Regional Sex Abuse Program, for survivors of child sex abuse. I'm the clinical coordinator there and the primary reason I'm here today is that I'm representing the Regional Sex Abuse Program.

We find that wife assault and sexual abuse are often occurring in similar situations, or in the same situations. And the primary way we go about our business is that we work in the community as well. (Beverly: RSAP therapist, formerly with the Children's Aid Society, DAC consultant)

I'm Elaine. I'm a reporter with the *Township Weekly*, I'm here to report on the Workshops. I'm also a member of Domestic Abuse Committee. (Elaine: freelance journalist, DAC, future TWS board)

I'm Tina. Well, the first part of the day was a real eye opener to me, 'cause a lot of that stuff that came up took me back to my childhood, the relationship my parents had, and I had never really thought of in that way, in the type of atmosphere that I grew up in. That kind of family thing, that it had gone on for generations and generations. And I thought, I've got two kids. I've got a boy and a girl, and I've got to put a stop. (Female resident who attended the morning Child Abuse Workshop, which ran concurrently with the Wife Abuse Workshop)

After introductions, a general discussion seemed to spontaneously 'take off.' Major themes were the reputation of the Township as a high risk community, the link between violence in families and violence in the community, and the significance of the Domestic Abuse Committee's decision to define abuse generically. As the discussion progressed, a tension between residents who wanted to address the issue of male victimization and activists who wished to side-step this issue emerged. The following are excerpts from a one-hour discussion in which activists and residents appear to achieve consensus over some aspects of abuse, while disagreeing over others:

I think the question Why does it happen here? is, well. I think another way of looking at it is why do we talk about it? ... It's horrible, but you know it's one of those human things. And unless it's being honestly discussed, and honestly addressed, with compassion, there's no end. So it's a public issue here, but it's a shame it's not a public issue, in a bigger way, all across the Province, you know, I mean all across Canada. We're being ridiculed about being public about it, but if we hadn't been talking in our co-operative and in the Township this workshop wouldn't be happening. (Susan: DVC)

You know, I've worked in the Region since maybe 1978, and this community is no different from any other community, in terms of family violence and how much it's happening here. What is deserved is its reputation for being courageous. I mean there's lots of municipalities in the Region, and they tell us these things don't happen there, well we know they do. (Beverly: RSAP)

I was going to suggest that we need to respond as a community because the roles in the community are changing ... for a long long time the Township was a kind of backwoods. I mean when I moved here seven years ago my dad and mum said it was like stepping back into the 1950s. No sewers, hardly a bit of pavement, you remember the good old days? ... But now if you walk into the new supermarket you might see a woman in a sari, I mean this is change. We are a community in transition. And I think we should start with domestic violence, because it starts in the home. (Susan: DVC)

Right, if your families are deteriorating into violence and everything, it's going to affect business. You're going to get increased violence, I mean, this is life. (Lisa: DVC, DAC, future TWS worker)

I think the community has the same moral imperative as a next door neighbour has, I mean the business community, whether it's the grocer or newspaper or whatever. The community has to recognize this is going on, and be supportive, and help get the money for a shelter, and for other services. Because you can't have a healthy community if you don't have healthy families. (Elaine: journalist, DAC, future TWS board).

I think we really need to lay it on thick, with ah education. Get advertisements out, so more people are aware of what's going on. 'Cause some people aren't aware. (Kathryn: TRC staff, DVC, DAC, future TWS board)

Yeah, that's why I'm here, I mean people really need to read about this stuff, and they're not all here today, not all of them. (Elaine: journalist, DAC, future TWS board)

I like your comparison, violence in the family and violence in the community, is there a difference? (Marlene: TRC staff, DAC, former RWS worker)

I mean it's all associated, you can't separate one from the other. (Elaine: journalist, DAC, future TWS board)

Is that why you call it *domestic abuse*? (Ruth: researcher)

Yeah, that's why, I mean we call it *domestic abuse* because abuse starts in the home. It affects women in crisis, but it also affects the children. And like it or not, it affects the men, and unless you find some intervention to stop the abuser it'll never stop. (Lisa: DVC, DAC, future TWS worker)

And not only that, there are women who are abusers as well. (Female resident)

One of the reasons that the Domestic Abuse Committee uses domestic violence or *domestic abuse* is that when we did our poster, instead of putting wife assault on the poster – you know, there might be a girlfriend who wasn't being physically touched but was being kept in a situation, you know, emotionally abused. So we're trying to keep domestic violence clearly generic. (Kathryn: TRC staff, DVC, DAC, future TWS board)

And there are different services, you know some Regional Wife Abuse Program groups are directed at men, and some are directed at women. So certainly *domestic abuse* is a generic term. (Marlene: TRC staff, DAC, former RWS staff)

Well, when it comes down to developing a shelter, maybe then the term will change. (Kathryn: TRC staff, DVC, DAC, future TWS board)

In these excerpts, activists and residents alike try to come to terms with two problematic 'myths' about domestic violence. The first relates to whether abuse is predominantly a low-income or low-class problem. This myth is implicit in claims that levels of abuse were exceptionally high in the Township. In this workshop, activists stated their conviction that the Township was no more violent than other communities; rather, in their view, courageous residents are more willing to talk about violence. This was a position residents seemed to like. In fact, participating activists held conflicting views about this issue. In this workshop and in other public presentations, Charles habitually refuted claims that levels of domestic violence were higher than average, in the Township or in the housing co-op. He maintained that no more than one co-op family in ten had a problem with domestic violence, and that this rate is significantly lower than the national average of one in eight.[8] Others, Susan, Marlene, and Kathryn, in particular, regarded Township domestic violence rates as decidedly higher than average (personal interviews, 1991). Regardless, as noted in the previous chapter, activists tended to regard attitudes rather than social situations as the primary causes of abuse. Consequently, as Kathryn phrased it, they believed that it was necessary 'to lay it on thick' with education.

The second 'myth' relates to the contention that women as well as men perpetrate or provoke violence. Activists temporarily avoided dialogue on this issue by directing the discussion to links between violence in the family and violence in the community. When a resident voiced the opinion that 'there are women who are abusers as well,' Kathryn deftly shifted discussion to the importance of defining abuse in a way that acknowledges the vulnerability of wives, children, and girlfriends, not only to violence but also to emotional abuse. Her statement '... when it comes down to developing a shelter, maybe then the term will change' indicates that she, at least, was uncomfortable with a 'generic' gender-neutral definition of the problem.

Having established the link between violence in the family and violence in the community, Charles took the floor. He provided a short history of the housing co-op's Domestic Violence Committee and then invited Lisa to tell her story. Lisa told her story much as she did in other contexts, with one exception. In radio interviews, media articles, and housing co-op presentations, Lisa reported that she and her husband were both violent and that she often initiated violent incidents. Sometimes she stated that her children regarded her as more violent than their father. She was less explicit in this presentation:

My husband and I separated, last year, after I got a restraining order, when we had a bad incident. Thanks to the co-op I was able to stay in the community with my kids. The co-op got me a subsidy till social services kicked in, so my husband could go for help, to counselling, that kind of thing. We did that, and we were able to work things out, we reconciled ... And we're still working on our relationship. Anyway, we wanted to use ourselves as an example to the community, to other couples or other families that, well, that want to learn how to put an end to abuse. (Lisa)

... Anyway, he had an alcohol problem, an addiction, and now he belongs to the AA fellowship. (Lisa)

... We were, our whole household was, ah, violent. Not only physically, but verbally, or whatnot. You know, everybody abuses everybody every-day, in some form or in some way. But I think it's important that you're aware of the abuse you do, and that you learn how to get a handle on it, and keep control over it. And the community can be a great help, just by giving you support, you know, that you're a worthwhile person. (Lisa)

But how did he, how did your husband feel when you had a reconcilia-tion and he was back and all the neighbours knew? How did other people in the co-op make him feel? (Female resident)

Ah, I think one of the things was that our community offered support, not just for the victim and the children, but for the family. So, ah, to help the perpetrator get the help he needs. Ah, we don't want to break up families. (Lisa)

No, no. (Charles)

They supported our whole family ... Ah, my husband was embarrassed and afraid when he first came back. But I mean people said we believe in you. So, he felt, if they could help me, I could help somebody else, I'm going to say males. (Lisa)

Yes, yes. (Female resident)

If he could help another male before he gets to a violent stage, then it's worth it for him. Ah, he's still going through a lot of problems himself, that he hasn't been able to deal with, but he wants to help another family before it gets to what it did with us. (Lisa)

The biggest impact for me is because we involved abusers, for the first time I had to put to rest reservations, like the abuser's just an animal. Because up until that point I had a very easy time thinking that these men were monsters, or crazy. But I had to recognize, this is a friend of mine. I knew, he's not an animal, he's a human in trouble. I mean, it's really easy to say just support her, and put him away. But you have to stop serial abuse, and you know, the boys in these families are very, very at risk of becoming an abuser. It's like a thousand times greater. (Kathryn)

I think you don't need so much to look at the victim of abuse or at the perpetrator, as at the social – I mean, they're both victims. It's not really one or the other, they're both victims and society has made them both. (Lisa)

I think you have to look at all aspects [almost inaudible, very soft], but you have to ensure the safety, the security, of women and kids, primarily. (Marlene)

But you have to recognize that half of these kids are boys! (Female resident)

Well, you know it's one out of four women have been abused, from physical to sexual to some kind of abuse, and as for the men, we're only beginning to look. (Beverly)

Some might say we also need a shelter for men. (Female resident)

Ah, we do have a shelter for men, my husband went there [referring to the Regional facility for the homeless]. But, ah, I think the problem, we've focused a lot on the victim, but we haven't really taken a look at prevention. Right now women and children are in crisis, that's why we need a women's shelter. But for the future a shelter's not the answer. (Lisa)

We've got to look at changing society. Make people aware that it's wrong. And I mean, like looking at the laws, looking at how we now deal with the perpetrator. He might get a little slap on the wrist and be sent back out to become a serial abuser. He may get a little bit of time, you know. But it is very unlikely that he will get put into therapy, for being an abuser. We need to focus on getting him the kind of help he needs, and having follow-up. So it's not just do something for the victim, you've got to stop the whole thing. (Lisa)

In the above discussion, Lisa addressed three contentious issues – that alcoholism is a core or concurrent abuse problem, that *domestic abuse* victimizes all family members, and that counselling or therapy is necessary to overcome abuse. Interestingly, residents did not choose to focus on the alcohol issue. It was as though acknowledging alcoholism was enough. Instead, residents focused on Lisa's contention that *domestic abuse* victimizes whole families. This contention touches on the intergenerational nature of abuse, and on the troubling 'fact' that residents, Lisa included, tended to subscribe to the 'myth' that women are also abusive.

In contrast to the three Wife Abuse Workshop presenters, Community Response Workshop facilitators did not present an 'expert' position. Instead, they encouraged residents to share their experiences and opinions. Moreover, they refrained from refuting residents' claims that abuse cuts across genders. Instead, Marlene or Kathryn subtly redirected the discussion towards issues that support contentions that *domestic abuse* is gendered. For instance, when Lisa stated, '... they're both victims and society has made them both,' Marlene gently reminded us that 'it is women and children who are in danger, primarily.' Shortly thereafter, Kathryn responded to a resident's observation that 'half of these kids are boys' by sharing the 'fact' that boys who grow up witnessing domestic violence are 'a thousand times' more likely to become abusers than boys who do not.

The 'fact' that males who grow up with domestic violence are 'a thousand times' more likely to abuse or 'beat' their partners is based on an apparent misreading of information provided in the Regional Women's Shelter's handbook in the section refuting 'false myths' about abuse. In this case, the handbook confronted the myth that abuse is 'a private family matter':

> Men who witnessed fathers abusing their mothers are 1000 per cent more likely to batter their partner than men who grew up in non-abusive families; 75 per cent of men who abuse their wives observed violence between their parents. (RWS handbook, 1990)

As is the case for many popular sources, the handbook does not cite the National Family Violence Survey, which produced this finding, nor does it note that women who grow up with domestic violence also express exceptionally high rates of *severe* violence, at rates 600 per cent higher than women who do not (see Straus et al., 1980: 100–1). Straus and colleagues interpret these findings, that adult survivors of parental spousal violence are *ten* times more likely to assault their spouse if male, and *six* times more likely if female, as evidence that domestic violence has similar effects on children of both sexes.[9] *Violence against women* researchers regard this interpretation as untenable since it fails to incorporate evidence that female violence and male violence are qualitatively different.[10]

Domestic Abuse Committee activists Kathryn and Marlene focused on this point, that abuse is gendered, by emphasizing links between woman abuse and other community or societal problems. In contrast, housing co-op activists and participating residents expressed the opinion that abuse is a family problem, emphasizing links between violence in families and violence in communities. Among housing co-op activists, this *family violence* position coincided with recognition or belief that abuse is gendered, that 'the vast majority of abusers, at least 90 per cent, are men' (Charles: DVC presentation, 1991).[11]

The Community Response Workshop concluded with Kathryn's description of the resource centre's efforts to promote grass-roots involvement in community issues through community development. She stated that the Domestic Abuse Committee grew out of 'coffee talks' about women's needs. She made it sound as though this was a more or less spontaneous occurrence. In subsequent interviews, I learned that the coffee talks were outreach initiatives, promoted by posters and flyers, that aimed at raising consciousness about domestic violence, already identified as the most pressing of a number of Township problems in the 1990 needs study. At the Community Response Workshop, residents were told that women participating in the coffee talks had identified child care and housing as pressing problems, and violence against women and children as the most pressing problem of all. Kathryn stated that the Domestic Abuse Committee, and the recently funded Township shelter, grew out of residents' concerns about this most pressing problem.

A female resident asked if men were involved in the Domestic Abuse Committee. Kathryn responded, 'Yes, several men are involved.' She went on to say that the Domestic Abuse Committee was open to everyone in the community, and that new members are always welcome. She ended by telling us that community development workers are always looking for challenges, and that the work to develop a Township shelter had been, and still was, an incredible challenge. She concluded:

> We have a challenge that we want to give to everybody. We've been talking about this element of organizing a community, and taking responsibility as a community. And most of the preceding conversation was about taking things out of hiding, making sure that people don't have to hide. Our challenge is that each of us reaches three people, within a short time, three different people. Tell them something that you've picked up today, and ask them to get involved. Because that's part of community responsibility, taking risks and getting involved. That's our challenge. (Kathryn)

The Community Response Workshop organizers appeared to have

three objectives. The first was to convince residents that *domestic abuse* was a community problem, thus a community responsibility. The second was to convince residents that the Domestic Abuse Committee was the appropriate agency to lead this community response. The third was to educate residents that *domestic abuse* meant, at least primarily, male abuse of women and children. Efforts to educate workshop participants on the gender-specific nature of abuse did not appear particularly successful. On the other hand, residents seemed highly receptive to contentions that abuse is a community responsibility. The camaraderie at the end of the meeting indicated that most were confident that the Domestic Abuse Committee was managing this responsibility well.

We left the Community Response Workshop with a challenge. The challenge was to spread the word, to take risks, to get involved. This non-specific challenge or invitation was offered to all of us, men and women.

From Collaboration to Polarization

Early in 1991, shortly before the Abuse Awareness Workshop, a contingent of male community leaders who occasionally attended Domestic Abuse Committee meetings took the risk of involvement. They secured the offer of a land donation from a developer who had made significant profits from recent land development, and brought the offer of this gift to a Domestic Abuse Committee meeting. The men presented the offer complete with blueprints, cost projections, and preliminary Town Council approval of necessary zoning changes. To the men's consternation, women at the core of the Domestic Abuse Committee told them, on the spot, that their proposed site was inappropriate on several counts, and that the site selection committee would select a more suitable site (personal interviews, 1991).

At this time, a group of women subsequently nominated to the shelter board were in the process of preparing a conditional offer to purchase a large older house that could be renovated to meet standards and budgets stipulated by federal and provincial funders. The house also met criteria identified as important by participants in Domestic Abuse Committee 'outreach' and 'visionizing' events, the second of which was held after this site was selected but prior to its approval by Town Council. It was, core Domestic Abuse Committee participants agreed, a place Township women would want to go to, a place they would want to take their children. The house faced a lake in one of the Township's most picturesque villages; it was beautiful, peaceful. Many Domestic Abuse Committee participants maintained that the site itself would facilitate healing and empowerment. Since the Town Council had approved zoning variances for other group homes in the village, committee members could see no logical reason why the Council would deny their request to have this property rezoned for institutional use.

In contrast, what became known as the alternate site was an undeveloped lot on the outskirts of one of the Township's larger towns. It faced the Township's major retail mall and beer store. More importantly, it lay on the periphery of a notoriously violent neighbourhood, a neighbourhood that housed a number of subsidized rental units and single-parent families.

Domestic Abuse Committee activists voiced their objections to the alternate site when it was initially presented and in subsequent discussions. Activists objected that the area had already been unfairly stigmatized as a hotbed of domestic violence, and that situating the shelter in this neighbourhood reinforced the erroneous belief that abuse is a problem of low-income and welfare-dependent families. They objected that the Township's more rural population needed a quieter site. They objected that abusive men could stalk partners from the beer-store parking lot. Finally, they objected that serious consideration of the site would slow the shelter process since the lot was unzoned and unserviced (personal interviews, 1991; Domestic Abuse Committee meetings, 1991).

The emerging opposition responded to each objection, formally at the Domestic Abuse Committee meeting, and in subsequent lobbying. The men argued that no one had unfairly stigmatized the neighbourhood, which included both a low-rental housing development and the more middle-class subdivision where two of the five domestic homicides in fact occurred. They argued that the proposed site was within walking distance of the multi-service resource centre that housed child-care, counselling, housing, and legal-aid services – all needed by abused women. They argued that restraining orders curtail stalking and that the police, who clearly supported the shelter, would enforce these orders. They argued that several Town Council members had assured them in advance that sewers would be extended and zoning approved. Finally, they argued that federal and provincial funders would be favourably impressed with a donation of this magnitude (personal interviews, 1991).[12]

Soon after the Domestic Abuse Committee's rejection of the alternate site, the men who brought the offer resigned from the Domestic Abuse Committee. Their letter of resignation to the committee, copied to the board of the resource centre and read at an open meeting, concluded: 'Is this how the Township Resource Centre treats a volunteer?' A Domestic Abuse Committee member who served on the site selection committee, and subsequently on the shelter board, commented that the donation seemed somewhat less than 'disinterested.' Rumours of this comment resulted in a demand for a public apology, which the Domestic Abuse Committee refused, and the threat of a slander suit. This threat led committee members to believe that the opposition sought not simply to take over the shelter process, but to undermine the shelter itself. An opposition spokesman retaliated by referring to core Domestic Abuse Committee members as radical feminists at a resource centre board meeting. He maintained that these radicals sought to exclude residents from what was supposed to be a community initiative. Rumours of this comment reinforced Domestic Abuse Committee activists' beliefs that the opposition was bent on subverting both their credibility and the shelter process.

Several Domestic Abuse Committee participants, resource centre employees, and resource centre board members related these events to me. Interpretations varied; however, participants generally agreed that the men who presented the offer had only nominally participated in the Domestic Abuse Committee through 1990. Core members stated that it was unreasonable that 'the old boys' expected to be allowed to play a prominent role this late in the game. On the other hand, a number of Domestic Abuse Committee participants expressed uneasiness about what had happened. Probation and parole officer Mary stated that it would have been polite to at least appear to treat the proposed gift as an option. Concerned resident and resource centre board member Francis said the men who presented the offer were behaving like jerks but that the offer had merit. And resource centre coordinator Janet stated that it might have been a better political strategy to accommodate, or attempt to accommodate, the men who brought the offer (personal interviews, 1991):

I think there are a whole lot of interesting issues here, precisely around this issue of how we should best deal with these people. To some extent we've taken the approach, up until now, partly from our own choice, and partly not from our own choice, of almost having nothing to do with them (the opposition). And one of the issues is whether in fact that's the best strategy, whether that doesn't just play into the hand of 'these inept women.' The interesting issue here is why and how this evolved. (Janet: TRC coordinator, in a discussion on why shelter development initiatives so often spiral out of control, 1991)

Charles urged his friends and colleagues on the Domestic Abuse Committee to adopt a conciliatory stance. He reminded all concerned that the community development mandate demands consideration of all viable suggestions, regardless of possible delays in outcomes, and he reminded all concerned that it is always bad politics to insult volunteers, especially community leaders. Despite this advice from a respected advisor, and despite the reservations of key members, the Domestic Abuse Committee decided to stand firm. This decision was supported by Township Family Services counsellor Fiona, who labelled the opposition's attempt to interfere in the site selection process, their threat to sue, and their claim that the Domestic Abuse Committee had been taken over by radical feminists, bullying tactics. She said the fact that committee members felt abused was itself evidence that they were being abused. She continued to assure us that this was a circumstance in which anger was justifiable, appropriate, and healthy (Domestic Abuse Committee meeting, August 1991).

Through the summer of 1991, residents were largely unaware of these ownership struggles. A local service club raised money for the shelter through the raffle of a recreational vehicle that had been provided at cost by a local merchant. The Saturday before the draw, Kathryn and I sold tickets outside the beer store facing the alternate site. Men, balancing cases of beer on their shoulders, listened while women shared personal stories of survival and resistance. One woman related her struggle to leave a 'rough old man' almost twenty years ago, before there were shelters. She bought tickets for each of her adult daughters. Another woman, whose partner stomped past the booth, commented that she would need the shelter herself soon if things didn't change. Many burly, rough, rustic-looking men expressed disgust that anyone would 'beat on a woman.' A few women and men expressed concern that the Domestic Abuse Committee not forget that men could also be victims.

Service club members boasted that they intended to raise more money than had been pledged by Town Council. In fact, the raffle raised $7000, significantly surpassing the $5000 pledged by the Township. To the dismay of the Domestic Abuse Committee and the service club that sponsored the raffle, however, the *Township Weekly* somehow neglected to cover the event. Only after considerable lobbying by freelance journalist Elaine did the paper publicize the name of the person who won the raffle and the amount of money raised.

Underlying Issues

Three points are important to these initial phases in community polarizations, and to escalations proceeding from them. First, tensions between the Domestic Abuse Committee and its opposition were rooted in gender. The Domestic Abuse Committee was dominated by what might be called 'the new women.' These women were, for the most part, new to the community, young, well educated, assertive, and feminist or pro-feminist. The males who opposed them were established members of the community who took it for granted that they would play a prominent role in community initiatives. They also took it for granted that the community would support anyone who opposed feminism, especially radical feminism. Domestic Abuse Committee activists jokingly referred to these men as 'the old boys.'

The Township's 'new women' recognized that residents were generally unsympathetic to radical feminism. However, they also recognized that residents strongly supported services for abused women, and felt they could depend on residents' support provided they remained focused on this goal. They also recognized that at least some members of both the business and the professional communities supported the ascendant influence of women in public life. As Naomi Wolf (1993) and others have noted, contemporary males experience their power as under siege, and women are only beginning to claim theirs. Wolf termed the consciousness and struggles associated with these developments a genderquake. This genderquake had a discernible impact on emergent and escalating polarizations around the Township shelter. It fuelled the 'whose shelter is this' dynamics implicit in the shelter site controversy.[13]

Second, polarizations were fuelled by tensions between paid and volunteer participants in what was ostensibly a grass-roots initiative (see Kleidman, 1994; Meyer and Whittier, 1994). On formal and practical levels, general residents participated in defining abuse, in promoting public awareness, in fund-raising, and in implementing an official plan of action. But pro-feminist community development workers and the abuse professionals who worked with them orchestrated these processes. These women recognized the need to skilfully incorporate the contributions of volunteers, but they were not prepared to deal with flagrant competition. The complete package that accompanied the proposed site donation set off alarms – even bed linens had been costed. This elicited a 'gut-reaction' that the committee had no choice but to reject the offer or 'the old boys' would assume control over the entire shelter process. This perception coincided with assertions that 'the opposition' regarded abused women as a 'problem population' of welfare-dependent single mothers and their partners, and assertions that it was the committee's duty to resist such stigmatizations.

Conversely, the men who presented the proposed site donation sensed that feminists on the Domestic Abuse Committee were intent on marginalizing them. These men had participated in Township Resource Centre initiatives since its inception. They were experienced in accessing federal and provincial funding, funding that they had helped direct to a broad range of social, cultural, and recreational facilities that they had not, in any practical sense, taken over. As Charles pointed out, to businessmen a fully costed proposal is a demonstration that those making the submission are serious, competent, and committed. When their proposal elicited an on-the-spot rejection, the men felt personally insulted. This initial sense of insult was reinforced by suggestions that the offer was something less than disinterested. The men's letter of resignation – 'Is this how the Township Resource Centre treats a volunteer?' – captures the outrage of men who had no intention of maintaining silence while 'radical feminists' used scarce public funds to promote anti-male attitudes. They had no intention of allowing 'a bunch of radicals' to take over *their* community.

Third, while some community leaders sided with the opposition – for example, the editor of the *Township Weekly* – the majority continued to support the Domestic Abuse Committee. Most members of the Town Council, most participants on the resource centre board, and most members of the business community were confounded by antagonism between the Domestic Abuse Committee and its opposition. This majority seemed uncertain what the conflict was about. Most could not see why the location of the shelter was so important, and therefore why all concerned were making such a big deal of it. To many, participants and observers alike, ongoing developments appeared more like an out-of-control psychodrama than a rational development.

Ensuing Escalations

In the following months, the actions of the Domestic Abuse Committee and its opposition reinforced the worst fears of players on both sides. The first escalation occurred when the Domestic Abuse Committee took steps to incorporate the Township shelter as an autonomous entity, expressly independent from resource centre influence or control. Members of the shelter board included community development worker Kathryn, social worker Denise, probation and parole officer Mary, attorney Harriet, freelance writer Elaine, resource centre board member Francis, businesswoman Edna, homemaker Leslie, assistant MPP Linda, and accountant Paul. This new board hired as a director to oversee renovations, staff hirings, and shelter publicity a 'strong feminist' from a distant community who was experienced in working with 'problem populations,' and whom one of the board members recommended as a feminist and as a professional.

The opposition interpreted the incorporation of the shelter as an autonomous entity, and implicitly the shelter board nominations and hiring decision, as proof that the radicals had taken over the shelter. In an anonymous *Township Weekly* letter to the editor, a 'concerned resident' described the removal of the shelter from the Township Resource Centre's umbrella of services as evidence that shelter activists sought to subvert rather than promote community involvement. Freelance journalist Elaine authored a defence of the shelter board's actions in a competing paper. She maintained that the Domestic Abuse Committee had always assumed that the shelter would achieve autonomy from other community organizations, and that funders expected this.

In the midst of controversies over the integrity and autonomy of the new shelter and its board, the Domestic Abuse Committee sponsored an activity that Charles, the resource centre board, the mayor, and the editor of the *Township Weekly* labelled intentionally provocative. A contingent of Domestic Abuse Committee activists decided to picket the opening of a new animal shelter to raise public awareness of the fact that the protection of animals had received funding prior to *domestic abuse*, historically in North America and again in the Township. The opposition interpreted this protest as further proof that the Domestic Abuse Committee was dominated by radicals opposed to the interests of Township residents. Parenthetically, a few survey respondents volunteered that they considered the protest apt; none suggested that it was inappropriate. Charles had no way of knowing how general residents regarded the protest, but he was acutely aware of the deepening rift between the Domestic Abuse Committee and prominent town leaders. He urged his friends and colleagues on the Domestic Abuse Committee to behave more prudently. Soon after, Janet, Marlene, and Fiona accepted positions with social service agencies outside the Township, and Charles assumed, or resumed, the position of Township Resource Centre coordinator.

The next phase of polarizations came in early 1992. In the midst of struggles to persuade Town Council to approve zoning changes for the lakeside shelter site, the *Township Weekly* published a series of editorials that questioned the competence and good intentions of women nominated to the shelter board. The shelter board convinced a widely respected columnist to denounce the opposition's unrelenting attempts to discredit them in a competing newspaper. Within a week, the owner of a group home near the proposed site decided to capitalize on the controversy. He offered to relocate his facility outside the Township, and to sell his property, already zoned institutional, to the shelter board. Attempts to block this site were futile. The Town Council, and apparently the majority of residents, were fed up with the controversy. The location of the shelter seemed irrelevant, and the opposition's persistent attempts to discredit the Domestic Abuse Committee and shelter board, increasingly irrational.

The final episode in this round of polarizations involved a male member of the resource centre board and a part-time resource centre worker whom he allegedly sexually assaulted. The victim had no connection to the Township shelter, and the assailant was not among the men involved in the shelter site controversy. Nevertheless, the shelter director and several members of the shelter board maintained that they felt personally assaulted by the opposition, among whom they now included Charles. These women reported that a contingent of resource centre employees had recently asked to have the alleged assailant disqualified from board participation because of his racist and sexist attitudes. Charles had insisted that residents could not be excluded because their opinions were less progressive than staff desired. These women maintained that Charles consequently shared responsibility for the assault – notwithstanding the fact Charles had urged the assaulted woman to lay a charge, that he drove her to the police station, and that he insisted that the male in question resign from the resource centre board until the charge was cleared. Charles demanded a formal apology, and when this was refused, threatened to sue (personal interviews, 1992). This was the second threatened lawsuit in less than a year. Neither lawsuit materialized, but these threats of legal action hung over the shelter initiative throughout the research period.

The Shelter Opening and After

Through 1992 the Township Women's Shelter board and newly hired Township shelter staff liaisoned with internationally prominent Battered Women's Movement activists, who they hired to conduct training seminars (personal interviews, 1992). On the day of the shelter opening, several board members described recent developments using, what was for them, a new feminist language. Key concepts were 'resisting co-optation' and 'the male hierarchy.' The women reported that they had decided that it was imperative to resist hierarchical practices. Consequently, they had refrained from issuing special invitations to town dignitaries, including the mayor, the Town Council, and Charles, who continued as the resource centre coordinator. Moreover, no local male was asked to play a role in opening ceremonies. Instead, male performers from outside the Township, native drummers and a 'white ribbon' guitarist, sang, strummed, and drummed for men to join in struggles to end *violence against women*.[14] I found their dramatic contributions artful, even moving. However, they seemed unrelated to the social reality of the Township's overwhelmingly white mainstream community. I noted that men who had 'taken the chance' of active involvement, men like Bob and Jim of the housing co-operative's Domestic Violence Committee, were accorded neither role nor recognition.

Following the ribbon-cutting, freelance journalist Elaine made an impassioned speech that contained an explicit insult to Township males. She told the audience that one male in three is an abuser. 'Look around you,' she repeated, 'one male in three.' Males in the audience included service club supporters, spouses of Township shelter board and staff members, and men who had donated raffle prizes, furniture, plumbing fixtures, and hard cash. It also included resource centre board members, Town Council members, male MPPs, and male representatives of funding organizations. Many had remained loyal to the Domestic Abuse Committee throughout the shelter development process. The mayor, initially 'a strong Domestic Abuse Committee supporter,' left the opening before lunch, reportedly with the $5000 Town Council cheque still in his pocket. Domestic Violence Committee activists Bob and Jim also left early. They later told me they could not help but feel hurt that their efforts had not warranted a thank-you.

Accountant Paul, referred to as the shelter board's 'token male' during the morning ceremonies, had not been accorded a speaking role. Paul asked for the microphone near the end of the evening ceremonies. To the consternation of his female colleagues, he personally thanked the mayor and Town Council for their support in establishing the shelter. Immediately after the opening, Paul resigned. Shortly thereafter, the women passed a formal resolution to restrict future shelter board participation to women.

The resolution to exclude males from the shelter board was the opposite of what residents who participated in the founding of the Domestic Abuse Committee planned. It was the opposite of what residents who participated in the abuse awareness workshops and fund-raising initiatives endorsed. It was the opposite of what community development workers at the core of the Domestic Abuse Committee assumed the community would accept. Finally, it was the opposite of what the Township shelter board espoused in the song *Shelter from a Storm*, composed for the opening. The song was performed at the opening ceremonies and broadcast in a radio interview that same day. The artist prefaced the song with a reminder of our nine months in the womb, and of the life-giving and healing waters of life, symbolized by the lake facing the new shelter:

> We need shelter from a storm, raging in our homes, ah, we need a shelter from a storm. Remembering where we're from, and how our mothers brought us in, wearing white ribbons we begin. Many abusers were abused, this cycle needs reviewed. Like a planter planting seeds, protect this candle from the winds, wearing white ribbons we begin. Everybody surrender, reach out with open hand, everybody remember, loving is God's plan, everybody surrender, every woman, every man. Wearing white ribbons we begin.

> Children need a loving dad, with strong gentle hands and a reassuring voice. Protect your children from within, wearing white ribbons we'll begin. Change your mind, change your life, live in peace with your wife. Your sisters will rejoice. Remembering where we're from, and how our

mothers brought us in. Wearing white ribbons we begin ... (Performed on
opening day and broadcast in a radio interview, June 1992)

By opening day, 'an us against them sort of thing' seemed to have
taken over. Nevertheless, individuals, service clubs, and businesses
continued to donate supplies and money at a rate that astounded
board members and staff. This ongoing support bolstered the shelter
board's perceptions that residents broadly supported the shelter. These
perceptions were confirmed in the survey on violence and abuse, conducted shortly after the shelter opening. Survey respondents supported shelters for women more than any other proposed intervention.
Many expressed unqualified support for the Township shelter. On the
other hand, several volunteered disapproval of the board's decision to
categorically exclude males, a decision announced in the *Township
Weekly* shortly after the opening. (See tables 4, 11, 12, and 13.)

Radicalization and Vilification

Domestic Abuse Committee activists did not regard themselves as radical feminists at the onset of the struggle over where to situate the shelter. They were radicalized through efforts to meet a series of perceived
threats, and through political contacts made in struggles to deal with
these threats. Their radicalization was rooted in rational appraisals of
developments, viewed through an increasingly sharpened feminist
lens, therefore in agency. It was also rooted in emotionally charged
responses to perceived bullying by a small contingent of men who
appeared bent on maintaining power. In a sense, having been named
radical feminists by members of a recognizable male establishment,
Domestic Abuse Committee activists began to act in ways that reinforced this name, and they began to feel good about their new identity.
By the time the shelter opened, freelance journalist Elaine, who
claimed that she had barely thought about feminism before her
involvement with the shelter, publicly identified herself as a radical
feminist. This took place in the same radio presentation that broadcast
Shelter from a Storm. Not all board members were radicalized in the
way Elaine was. Nevertheless, the shelter board assumed a radical
identity. Such is the power of social definitions:

I don't think that before this I would have ever had any occasion to say
that I was a feminist, or ever thought that it was necessary to say it. But

ah, after what we've been through ... Ah, but it's raised the level of awareness with me, and I want to move on, and get really involved in women's
issues much more than I have with the shelter. And ah, if they think that
some of us are radical now, they better look out. (Elaine: freelance journalist, DAC, TWS board, radio interview broadcast the day of the shelter
opening)

Just as the women were radicalized, so was the opposition vilified.
There is no indication that core activists regarded men, in general, or
the 'old boys,' in particular, as enemies prior to the site controversy. It
was the opposition's perceived takeover bid that elicited 'gut reactions'
that prominent men were out to subvert the shelter. By the final act,
one of 'the old boys' made what a jury subsequently dismissed as an
inappropriate pass, and all 'the old boys' were held responsible.[15] The
male held most responsible was Charles, a self-identified pro-feminist
who participated in numerous local and extra-local abuse initiatives,
the male who preached compromise and accommodation. Charles's
response was highly emotional – he was furious at having been identified as 'the enemy,' and began himself to adopt the bullying tactics of
'the male establishment.' He threatened to sue the women who had
insulted him. His response, and accountant Paul's defection, reinforced core activists' beliefs that all the 'old boys' were the same. The
women concluded that they had no choice but to exclude males from
future participation on the shelter board. Again, such is the power of
social definitions.

The struggle between the Domestic Abuse Committee and its opposition evolved into an increasingly destructive contest between
increasingly abstract enemies. There was little of substance in the
issues that vilified and radicalized participants. Nevertheless, few
were able to resist the 'for or against' behaviour exhibited by parties on
both sides. Those who managed to avoid taking sides – for instance,
probation and parole officer Mary – did so by mutely going about their
work, and by going along with democratically arrived at decisions.
Most participants were unable to resist becoming embroiled in the
fray; most were assigned or assumed the role of radical or villain. Thus
community development worker Andrea, one of the few committee
members who defined herself as radical from the onset, became a shelter opponent because she remained loyal to her friend and colleague
Charles.

The radicalized Township shelter board 'won' in that it asserted and maintained control over the Township shelter. However, it paid a price. The extent of that price is examined in the following chapter, which addresses implementation of the Domestic Abuse Committee's plan of action during the first six months of shelter operation.

4

Implementation of a Plan of Action: Struggles with Control

In 'Social Problems as Collective Behavior,' Herbert Blumer (1971) noted that there are typically deep disparities between an official plan and its implementation, that actors tend to bend the plan, substituting their own policies or agendas, and that unforeseen and largely unintended consequences ensue, including the redefinition of the problem and its solution. Blumer concludes: 'I scarcely know of any facet of the general area of social problems research that is more important, less understood, and less studied than that of unforeseen and unintended restructuring ... that arises from the implementation of an official plan' (Blumer, 1971: 305). This chapter examines this 'unforeseen and unintended restructuring.' It describes the ways the Domestic Abuse Committee's vision of what a women's shelter could and should be was bent as differently credentialed staff and board members competed for dominance in the running of the new Township shelter.

The Official Plan

Through 1992 participants on the Domestic Abuse Committee maintained their commitment to a women's shelter as one component of a coordinated community response to abuse. Participants agreed that it was necessary to project a moderate as opposed to a radical feminist profile, one in tune with local sensibilities. Their goal was to provide abused women with a supportive 'healing environment' where they could recover inner resources and break free of abuse. Those nominated to the shelter board endorsed this moderate pro-feminist orientation, as did the shelter director and participating survivors awarded positions as shelter workers. This orientation reflects the influence of community development ideology. It also reflects core actors' interpretations of rumoured problems at the Regional shelter, problems that several Domestic Abuse Committee members erroneously attributed to radical feminism. From the onset, core activists assured each other that they would avoid non-productive wrangles over ideology, wrangles that divide shelter board and staff, and alienate clients and community supporters.

By the time the new shelter opened, several members of the shelter board and staff had adopted a more radical stance. Nevertheless, participants continued to agree that it was important to avoid 'the pitfalls of radicalism.' They continued to agree that the Township shelter should work in cooperation with other abuse intervention agencies, and that it should promote feminist or 'women centred' practices. They continued to agree that the shelter should be a place Township women would want to go, a place they would want to take their children. Finally, they continued to agree that abused women should never be stigmatized, blamed, or shamed. These positive principles and goals were enshrined in the shelter's mission statement:

> The Township Women's Shelter is dedicated to providing all women and their children with safe shelter, support, and information so they can take steps towards ending abuse in their lives. Woman abuse is an unacceptable social injustice. The Township Women's Shelter will achieve its goals, objectives and philosophies in a woman centered way. (Mission statement distributed at the shelter opening, 1992)

Splinterings

Shortly after the opening day, the new shelter staff and board splintered into two contending camps. The first, 'professionalist' camp consisted of the shelter director and those who supported her on the shelter board and in the community. This contingent contended that naïve, romantic, inexperienced, and untrained junior staff and their supporters were refusing to take off 'rose-coloured glasses.' Most, but not all, claimed strong allegiance to feminism. Most also claimed various professional expertise. In opposition stood dissatisfied junior staff and those who supported them on the shelter board and in the community. This second camp endorsed strong identification with abused women regardless of their social situation or the extent of their personal problems. Again, most were strongly feminist, though some were not.

The Township's Abused and Abusive Population

Immediately after opening day, the shelter staff and board found themselves compelled to come to terms with some difficult 'realities' – realities whose difficulty was compounded by what many participants believed were the exceptional characteristics of the Township's abused and abusive 'problem population.' Specifically, the shelter board and staff faced the reality of substance problems; also the realities that not all abused women are nice, that some women lie, and some women are violent. As Denise phrased it, '... we're not dealing with the sort of nice middle-class woman who ends up in this horrible relationship.' Rather, the board and staff were dealing with 'the economic and social reality of the Township,' with a 'population' that needed 'specialized' professional services:

> The economic and social reality of the Township is such that we have had the most incredible number of crises just since the shelter opened just six months ago. We've had sexual abuse by a resident on a child. We've had a number of women with serious substance problems. What we are realizing is that most of the women who come have real substance issues and problems. So we're not dealing with the sort of nice middle-class woman who ends up in this horrible relationship. We are dealing with women who have alcohol problems, women who are not nice to deal with, women who lie and do all different kinds of stuff. For the staff it's been quite the eye opener. Many have had to take off their rose-coloured glasses.
> ...
> In cities specialized shelters are emerging to service this population. But in the Township this *is* the population. We have to serve the community. (Denise: TWS board; December 1992)

Denise's description of the shelter's problem population implicitly supports 'false myths' about the nature and causes of abuse that the Domestic Abuse Committee sought to refute. On the other hand, it is consistent with characterizations of the Township's 'high risk' population in grant applications, the Township needs study, and media reports. Indeed, as 1991 interviews with Janet, Kathryn, Marlene, Denise, Susan, Harriet, Mary, Lisa, Julia, and others demonstrate, everyone 'knew' that poverty and unemployment coincide with high levels of domestic violence in the Township and elsewhere, that substance abuse is typically a concurrent problem, and that some abused women are violent. As Marlene phrased it, Township patterns were consistent with those of abusive populations generally. Yet, Marlene and others on the Domestic Abuse Committee regarded the extent and severity of violence in the Township, and women's acceptance of violence, as exceptional:

> I didn't think it was different in the Township until I came up here, though I had worked with women in the Township for five or six years on a follow-up basis with the Regional shelter and I thought that I knew this area fairly well. A lot of single parents, you know a large number of people on assistance – that kind of stuff. That was consistent. But what was really surprising to me was the extent of violence that women were experiencing here, and the severity, and you know the time over which abuse had been occurring ... You know, being one of a succession of workers at the Regional shelter, perhaps I wasn't getting what I got as an outreach worker because they had already given it [their story] to somebody else. So that could be why I didn't realize, you know, why I was so very surprised.
>
> ...
>
> And, ah, the amount of substance abuse, and ah, the physical violence itself. Physical, you know it wasn't just a push. The use of weapons. The use of anything as a weapon. The planning ... And you know, the women had been in those relationships for a long time, and they were still so young. They'd been in those relationships since their teens and they were hooked in emotionally, really bonded. (Marlene: TWS staff, ex-RWS staff; July 1991)

Knowledge or belief about the exceptional nature of the Township's abused and abusive population influenced the Domestic Abuse Committee to hire a pro-feminist shelter director who had experience working with a 'problem population' rather than abused women.[1] The decision to hire a 'problem population' expert was offset by the decision to award junior staff positions to survivors and homemakers who had participated in the Domestic Abuse Committee. Denise and the new shelter director had previously served on a shelter board, but neither the director, junior staff members, nor any board member had actually worked in a shelter. The director, and most board members, held professional credentials in community development, health, law, enforcement, and social work. Junior staff were uncredentialed. Lisa and Julia had both completed one year of a two-year community college program for shelter workers endorsed by the Ministry of Community and Social

Services, but other junior staff had no qualifications aside from their desire to help abused women achieve survival status.[2] Denise maintained that the board really had no choice in whom it hired:

> We didn't have a choice in terms of who we hired. We had to hire a lot of staff who were very inexperienced, many of whom had never worked outside the home. Some of them were very limited, but being on the board I felt quite good about that, you know, because we were giving them opportunities. (Denise: TWS board; December 1992)

In a time of high unemployment, the Township shelter board had a choice in whom it hired. It chose to hire, indeed to import, a 'problem population' expert as opposed to an 'abused women' expert, and it chose to provide 'opportunities' to local abuse survivors and homemakers rather than employ women from nearby communities who had experience in shelter work. These hiring decisions coincided with the decision to *not* run the Township shelter as a feminist collective, a model promoted in the abuse advocacy course Lisa and Julia participated in, and favoured by Battered Women's Movement spokeswomen, with whom the board consulted.

As Edna confirmed, the decision to institute a hierarchical administrative structure resulted from the director's and board's perception that shelter residents and junior staff were too troubled and too unsophisticated, which is to say, too uneducated, to make responsible or appropriate choices. These perceptions coincided with decisions to empower and support the director to be 'quite directive around certain issues':

> If you come into a shelter thinking that we are all women and this all going to be this wonderful place and suddenly you are confronting a woman possibly sexually abusing a child, the staff could not handle it. Because she has worked with street people, our director had a wonderful ability to be able to be supportive but clear about where the line is drawn. She had to be quite directive around certain issues.
>
> ...
>
> If you have a team where you have people at a pretty sophisticated level of knowledge and understanding and skill level, that is one thing, you can work as a team. Unfortunately what we had was staff doing totally inappropriate things and that is a case of where, of course, the director had to come in. She had to take some very tough stands with some of the

women in residence, which the staff had great difficulty doing. (Edna:
TWS board; December 1992)

Denise and Edna discounted increasingly distressing rumours of client and staff dissatisfaction. They insisted that conflicts within the new
shelter were well within the expected range, and that they had been
blown out of proportion as a result of the inappropriate interference of
'naïvely idealistic' board members and resource centre – affiliated professionals. Denise stated that dissatisfied clients tended to be among the
most 'troubled.' Finally, she likened dissatisfied junior staff to 'teen-
agers having a rebellion phase.' She maintained that it was 'unprofessional' for shelter personnel to publicly air internal problems, that it was
'inappropriate' for staff in affiliated agencies to insinuate themselves
between the director and junior staff, and that it was 'unconscionable'
for all concerned to discuss shelter practices with shelter 'clients':

> It is important to say that among the staff there were only a couple of
> vocal people. The rest of them have very different opinions. Most loved
> her [the director]. They asked her about everything. I think what it was,
> was sort of just like teenagers having a rebellion phase. At first they were
> nervous. Understandably she gave a lot of support. Then they started
> moving into the job, suddenly saying, hey I can do everything now. And
> some were doing some really inappropriate things. I think it is important
> to know it wasn't the whole staff, and I think it's important to recognize
> who it was on staff. Some had really serious problems.
> ...
> What happened is that people who should have refused to become
> involved have been fuelling the fire, at least with the staff [referring to
> Township Resource Centre outreach worker Andrea and Regional
> Woman Abuse Program counsellor Alice]. I am certainly hoping to good-
> ness that they did not talk to clients ... To me crossing the line and dealing
> with the women who live there [the shelter] is an absolute no-no. These
> women are dealing with enough stuff that it is just unconscionable that
> the women who lived there were dragged in. (Denise: TWS board;
> December 1992)

Contentious Practices

Dissenting junior staff saw things very differently. First, those with
personal abuse experience did not regard the women they served as

exceptional. As survivors, they regarded substance abuse, verbal aggression, and female-perpetration as old stories, part and parcel of lifelong struggles to come to terms with repeated victimization. They recognized that they had a responsibility to intervene to protect children. However, they agreed with shelter residents that mandatory participation in group counselling was oppressive. They agreed that curfews, meal-times, bed-times, and program-times were unnecessarily rigid. They agreed that it was insulting to require shelter residents to draw up menus and grocery lists and then routinely override residents' choices for 'nutritional and economic reasons,' as in the director's habitual substitution of block cheese for sliced cheese. And they agreed that it was inappropriate to make an issue of minor damages, unmade beds, and, most notoriously, stained teacups.

Two ex-residents of the new shelter commented on practices they considered both controlling and demeaning. The first described her experience of being denied a private walk with her children because the shelter director had scheduled a group picnic. The second described what became known as the teacup incident. These incidents played a prominent role in escalating disaffection between the more directive professionalists and those who believed it was important to support and empower shelter residents and junior staff:

> I wanted to go with my children for a walk, alone, I wanted to talk to them about what was happening. She [the director] gave me a very cold glare. I have seen that glare from my mother. She gave me the glare and just repeated her statement: I really think a picnic lunch has been packed for all the residents and their children to go out to the beach. I just flew off the handle and said, this is too much, why can't I just go out for a walk with my own children if I want to. In the end we both got half of what we wanted. My two oldest went to the beach with the workers and I had to get lost for an hour with my baby ... I was so livid about it because she denied me my time with my children, which I needed that day. I was really in crisis. I was a new arrival. My whole world was chaotic. I needed time with my kids. It was like being back at home. I was being controlled. It was not what I wanted. I had to be submissive. (Suzanne: ex–Township Women's Shelter resident; October 1992)

> She [the director] came into the kitchen to get a coffee mug out of the cupboard and pulled out one and pulled out another and another and another and they all had tea stains in them. She looked at me as if, how

dare these teacups be in the cupboard this way. I was trying to do my own thing, trying to get my life together. So I put baking soda in the stupid cups and washed them ... All the women that go to that place have had enough of that in their own lives. This is a place they have gone for help, to be treated like that! Whenever she comes through the door, it is for fixing this or for fixing that, she's always right on the workers. (Nicole: ex–Township Women's Shelter resident; October 1992)

Dissenting junior staff reported that they tried to advocate on behalf of women like Suzanne and Nicole, but that all formal avenues for expressing dissatisfaction were closed. First, they reported that they worked in an atmosphere of anxiety that they could lose their job without recourse, at the whim of the director. This feeling originated in their having been compelled to sign a statement acknowledging that they were subject to dismissal without appeal during a one-year probationary period. This statement had been presented subsequent to the opening of the shelter, and subsequent to the junior staff members' assuming their posts as shelter workers. Second, junior staff reported that staff meetings had been turned into information seminars or 'expert' presentations, and that this left them no forum for voicing concerns, airing grievances, and planning responses. Julia reported that staff members complained to each other that Elmer the Safety Elephant was due to be brought in at any time, and that this was about the level of 'education' staff were routinely subjected to. Third, junior staff reported that they had been excluded from participating in a retreat on shelter dynamics, a retreat that had originally been planned for all board and staff. Finally, dissenting junior staff reported that they resented insinuations that their airing of dissatisfactions with colleagues employed through the resource centre, Township Family Services, and the Regional Woman Abuse Program was tantamount to disloyalty. They emphasized the 'fact' that like themselves, these colleagues were active Domestic Abuse Committee participants.

Junior staff and shelter client dissatisfactions coincided with shelter practices that a number of observers labelled unnecessarily insular. Resource centre outreach worker Andrea reported that shelter security was so stringent that she and Regional Woman Abuse Program counsellor Alice were impeded from maintaining contact with clients residing at the shelter. Resource centre coordinator Charles reported that a contingent from the shelter board had lobbied to block a resource centre grant application to expand outreach services for abused women because these services were in competition with those offered through the shelter.[3] Housing co-op activist and health professional Susan reported that shelter practices were so guarded that it was difficult to establish a routine inter-agency relationship:

> I was compiling a directory of services, so I called the Township shelter. Right away I was given over to the director, like no one else could talk. I gave her my name and identified Regional Support Services [for developmentally handicapped adults] and, you know, told her what I was doing. She basically answered my questions but the whole time she kept repeatedly asking what organization I represented, in a very suspicious manner ... I mean when I called the Regional shelter, whoever answered the phone was more than ready to be helpful. (Susan: health professional, DVC activist, DAC supporter; October 1992)

Andrea, Charles, and Susan also commented on an expensive relocation of the entire shelter population to a hotel while workmen performed minor repair work. Board member Kathryn, who expressed ambivalence over the issue, reported that the shelter board had decided abused women should not be exposed to the trauma of having to interact with males in what was supposedly a sanctuary from male violence. Andrea, Charles, and Susan maintained that exposure to males was not inherently traumatic, and that by suggesting it was the shelter was fostering two beliefs the Domestic Abuse Committee had explicitly rejected – the belief that abused women are incompetent, and the belief that men are the enemy.

These purportedly 'insular' practices were compounded by the location of the new shelter. Few shelter clients had a car, and few had the $20 round-trip taxi fare to the Township Resource Centre and the many abuse-related services offered through this facility. Consequently, the shelter had to arrange for 'approved volunteers' to chauffeur groups of shelter residents to the resource centre and back.

Professional Co-optation

Early in 1993 the professionalist camp replaced a number of untrained or dissatisfied junior staff with workers who had expertise in nursing, child care, and social work, replicating patterns observed in shelters for well over a decade (Ferraro, 1983). Coincidently with these replacements, five members of the shelter board resigned: parole officer Mary, freelance journalist Elaine, community development worker Kathryn, long-term resident and resource centre board member Francis, and concerned resident Leslie – all officially for personal reasons. This left social worker Denise, attorney Harriet, businesswoman Edna, and assistant MPP Linda to recruit new female board members. Board vacancies were filled by mainstream professionals employed in education and general health, not by abuse professionals or abuse survivors.

Shortly before the spate of resignations and replacements, a group of ex-residents sent a letter of protest to the shelter board, which they copied to provincial funders. The professionalist contingent persuaded the majority of board members and funders that it was essential to back the director. Those who could not tolerate what was beginning to look like an endless struggle, or who could not support what they believed were increasingly authoritarian, non-feminist practices, withdrew from the fray. The professionalist contingent, all 'fairly strong' feminists, were left in power.

Resistance

On the two-year anniversary of the shelter opening, a small group of ex-residents picketed the shelter. These women contended that the shelter continued to engage in practices that systematically undermined the autonomy and competence of the women it served. That same week, the *Township Weekly* ran an editorial on shelter residents' dissatisfactions, dissatisfactions that reportedly persisted through 1996, despite a succession of shelter directors.

Township Resource Centre women's outreach worker Andrea expressed the sentiment of the dissenters when staff and client dissatisfactions were first emerging. She maintained that the Township shelter had effectively taken on the role of the abuser. She reminded me of the Domestic Abuse Committee's early concerns that the Township shelter be more supportive and less controlling than several ex–Regional shelter residents reported finding that facility. She asserted that it was not only the right, it was the duty, of responsible Domestic Abuse Committee participants to criticize and monitor the shelter they had worked to establish:

> It is no different than power dynamics going on in an abusive relationship – it is just a different label put on it. Justifying it, saying, you know, we just really want to work within the shelter to fix this problem, and what

you're doing is just feeding the opposition, that's abusive. It's no different from what I hear an abusive man saying to his wife and family – we don't need help, we don't need a counsellor, this is a family problem and we'll keep it in the family. Is it any different?

...

Most of us who worked in the Domestic Abuse Committee feel that we put the work into this community, that we educated the community, that we fought our heads off with the community to make this shelter work, and we deserve to be able to criticize it and to monitor it. (Andrea: TRC women's outreach worker; October 1992)

The Regional Women's Shelter

Early developments at the twelve-year-old Regional shelter were reportedly very similar to developments at the new Township shelter. At both shelters, staff conflicts and client dissatisfaction were grounded in the problematic of control, and in the difficulties of dealing with the troubling behaviours and attitudes of some abused and abusive women. Regional shelter outreach worker Wendy, a co-presenter at the 1991 Abuse Awareness Workshop, shelter worker Eloise, and shelter worker Pat participated in an informal group discussion and individual taped interviews during the summer of 1991. Ex–Regional shelter worker Marlene also discussed problems and practices at the Regional shelter in a 1991 interview. Marlene, Wendy, and Pat were all involved with the Regional shelter when it opened in the late 1970s.

Wendy and Marlene both reported that this shelter had been developed by a group of service providers responding to emergency needs of women and children that were not being met through traditional child welfare or social assistance channels. They reported that abuse emerged as a prominent issue as a result of the testimony of the women seeking shelter, as had 'grass-roots feminism.' In 1991 the shelter continued to provide refuge to both homeless and abused women, though, as in the case of most Ontario shelters, it did not accept violent women, women with active substance problems, or women with serious mental health problems. The Regional shelter was directed by a community board that included female and male professionals from the Family Services Association, the Regional Woman Abuse Program, the Regional police, and other community agencies. Formally, the shelter operated as a hierarchy, headed by a director who reported to the board. Practically, however, decision-making was, and always had been, 'pretty consensual' (Wendy, 1991).

Wendy, Marlene, and Pat reported that, from the onset, most staff were strongly feminist and that many were abuse survivors. The majority now had professional credentials. Several had earned these while working at the shelter. Many, Wendy among them, defined themselves as 'pretty radical.' However, staff had learned the importance of avoiding 'radicalism.' According to Wendy, radicalism consists of an unwillingness to consider alternatives. At the Regional shelter, this had coincided with propensities to over-control fellow staff and clients. Wendy maintained that openness and a relinquishment of control better reflect feminist principles:

> We're an interesting blend of staff. We have some who are quite radical, and others who are not, though I don't think we have anyone who is a 'Real woman' or anything like that. I don't know if we could stand that, so as a staff we're feminist. And some are pretty extreme. But that's OK, we accept our own individual differences in staff. And I think that carries through to the clients too. In my estimation, radical is somebody who doesn't listen. And we really don't have anybody like that. I think that we're all probably pretty opinionated but we also respect the fact that other people have a right to theirs too. And you know, there are some pretty fierce battles, sometimes, that go on. But we all do basically respect each other's competence, and I think that is why it works. There's never any question of whether anybody else is competent. You might not agree with them but that doesn't mean they're not competent. (Wendy: RWS staff; July 1991)

Wendy reported that there had been a major change in shelter dynamics when the staff collectively decided to 'lighten up' on control, a few years previously:

> It was more or less a mutual decision among all staff that we felt that things were far too controlled. It just didn't make any sense. There were too many programs, too much pressure ... And as soon as we changed the focus of the program, everything changed. No problems with vandalism or any of that sort of stuff, things that were major problems in the past. (Wendy: RWS staff; July 1991)

Pat similarly reported that tensions in the shelter dissipated as staff came to accept less than ideal hygiene standards, routine damage to property, children acting out, client resistance to curfews (largely imposed by funders), and client resistance to feminist interpretations of abuse. All interviewed staff reported that it was a known 'fact' shelters run more smoothly when the competence of co-workers and residents is acknowledged, when autonomy is maximized.

Wendy emphasized her conviction that it is imperative that staff resist temptations to be over-directive. She reported that shelter residents needed to be encouraged to make their own decisions even when these decisions seem self-defeating. She reported that staff had learned that it was counter-productive to attempt to influence the women's decisions 'in any way':

> Often times women do ask to be told what to do, because they're scared. And we try very hard not to do any of that, because we don't want to control. We want them to take control of their own life. And so, no matter what her decision is about her life, whether it's to reconcile or not, or whatever, we support her in that decision ... And we certainly don't want her to feel like we're trying to influence her in any way. That's one of the reasons why we don't prominently display things [political/educational material]. (Wendy: RWS staff; July 1991)

In a way that was consistent with these principles of supportive empowerment, the shelter made no attempt to control or monitor with whom staff or residents interacted, whether partners or researchers. Marlene, Eloise, and Wendy all reported that the shelter makes a concerted attempt to promote openness. They also stated that they self-consciously avoided disseminating alienating images of 'men as the enemy.' This was evidenced in the apparent lack of concern of staff and residents with workmen who repaired kitchen cabinets during the interviews. Generally, security was not emphasized. Children wandered in and out of the foyer that served as the shelter's sole barrier to a busy commercial street. Wendy reported that 'surprisingly enough' the highly visible Regional shelter was not troubled by harassment:

> They [husbands/partners] do come to the door occasionally. Ah, not a lot, they usually don't feel too comfortable coming here. But we don't restrict the women from talking to them or seeing them in any way. I think you've got to be real careful when you're a shelter that you don't start taking on the role of the abusive partner – in the name of saving the woman. (Wendy: RWS staff; July 1991)

Regional shelter staff identified power and control as the major component and driving force of abuse, and they regarded abuses of power by supervisors, service providers, and parents as comparable to male-perpetrated woman abuse. Nevertheless, Regional shelter staff vehemently rejected the notion that domestic violence is gender-neutral. Marlene, Wendy, Eloise, and Pat fully agreed that sexist attitudes and patriarchal structures cause abuse:

> I think that most of the men who are abusing their partners see them as property and as being somehow less important than they are ... As for why women stay, again it's socialization. You look at what women are told about relationships, that you're supposed to hang in there no matter what and give him another chance. A lot of women are hearing this and not only from their parents but from their contemporaries as well. Ah. And a lot of it is economic. They're frightened that they can't make it on their own. (Wendy: RWS staff; July 1991)

Regional Women's Shelter staff refuted a number of 'false myths' about abuse that implicitly justified 'directive' rather than 'supportive' practices at the new Township shelter. First, Wendy and other Regional shelter staff rejected the 'false myth' that women provoke abuse, through the use of violence or otherwise. However, Wendy and Marlene both regarded female-perpetrated violence against children as a real problem. According to Marlene, many shelter clients direct at their children aggression they are afraid to direct at their abusive partners.[4] Marlene argued that this projective abuse is legitimized by beliefs that control of children is equivalent to good parenting:

> In their relationships, I think the majority [of women] were taking the passive role, most aren't violent. However, their kind of control would come through when they were around their kids. But, well, I guess you'd have to, you'd have to define abuse of kids. You know, really, from my definition, yes I think they are abusive with their kids. You know, my definition is pretty strict. You know physical discipline, harsh discipline. From my personal perspective, that would be abuse. Especially thinking about the relationship between physical discipline and power and control. I mean that's the issue. A slap is a way to get what you want. But it's a tough one because physical discipline is acceptable in many many circles ... Many women really have a problem with it. They really want to

control that kid. Ah, and they believed that was how you do it. They didn't know any other way. (Marlene: ex-RWS worker; July 1991)

To discourage abusive or punitive parenting, the Regional Women's Shelter enforced a 'no hitting rule.' Marlene reported that many shelter residents subverted this rule by disciplining children in the privacy of a bedroom. Marlene and Wendy both indicated that they have a clear responsibility to intervene when a child is being abused, but many situations are ambiguous:

> Certainly, the women don't like the no-hitting rule. It wasn't unusual for a woman to take a child up to a bedroom for a spanking when no one was looking ... Sometimes staff intervene, sometimes, not often. It was really tough. It's a really fine line, because, you know, people didn't want to interfere, and yet, again, you get back to some of the social norms. You know, do we interfere, or don't you? Do you let abuse occur, or don't you? And I really truly believe that that's the core of it. I think that people do have to interfere, they do have to take a chance. (Marlene: ex-RWS worker; July 1991)

Second, Regional shelter staff rejected the 'myth' that alcohol abuse causes domestic violence. At the same time, they acknowledged that many abusers have substance problems. Marlene lamented the tendency of both Regional shelter clients and Township women to regard this concurrent problem as a cause:

> They [shelter residents] really connected alcohol with violence, very very clearly. The level of violence, and the connection to alcohol was really a big one ... They were saying alcohol was the cause. It was a little bit worrisome because it's not a matter of simply saying go to AA and stop drinking and things will be fine ... Abused women really don't seem to have the level of understanding of, you know, socialization behind abuse, roles, that sort of thing. (Marlene: ex-RWS worker; July 1991)

Third, Regional shelter staff rejected the 'myth' that childhood traumas make people abusive. However, staff freely acknowledged that histories of child abuse and parental spouse abuse are common among victims and perpetrators alike, and they recognized that some women need professional help to deal with these issues. Wendy maintained that child sexual abuse was a major issue among abused women. She reported that a large majority of shelter clients are child sexual abuse survivors:

> A lot of women come from situations where they saw their parents abuse each other. But, ah, probably a higher percentage of women have been sexually abused, themselves. I think if we ever sat down and started asking that question, that we would find it was 70 per cent or 80 per cent have been sexually abused as children. It just keeps coming up over and over and over again ... Most report that their husbands were beaten as kids, or that they saw their mothers beaten. (Wendy: RWS staff; July 1991)

Fourth, Regional shelter staff rejected the 'false myth' that abuse is predominantly a low-income or low-class phenomenon. Wendy reported that more educated, more affluent women have more options, so that they tend to be under-represented in shelters. Wendy interpreted the documented 'fact' that Township women were disproportionately represented at the Regional facility, not as evidence that Township women experienced more abuse, but as evidence that they had fewer alternatives. In contrast to Marlene, Wendy saw no difference in the type or severity of abuse reported by women from the Township. She reported that the Regional shelter provided refuge to some very well off and decidedly well educated women, and that regardless of their social situation abused women tell very similar stories. Moreover, regardless of their social situation, abused women display astounding coping skills, and most are highly competent.

While residing at the Regional shelter, women are encouraged to participate in group counselling aimed at education and empowerment. Participation is encouraged, not required. Education focuses on gender issues, relationship dynamics, and parenting practices. Empowerment focuses on helping women to recognize victimization processes and personal choices. Shelter residents are encouraged to serve as advisors to each other, to engage in peer counselling. They are not encouraged to seek psychotherapy. Women who 'have issues of their own that they want to work on' are referred to appropriate services outside the shelter:

> The purpose of the group on Monday is to get women to talk about their common experiences and to give them information about abuse ... [What] we try to do is respond to each woman's individual needs, and give her

the information that she asks for so she can make her own choices ... We want them to take control of their own life. And so no matter what her decision is about her life, whether it's to reconcile or not, or whatever, we support her in that decision. (Wendy: RWS staff; July 1991)

I used to be amazed sometimes when I would think what is it we could do to help some of these women. And I would go out in the living room, and they were doing it among themselves. You know, bonding, and finding solutions with each other. We're only here just to support them, and to offer alternatives, so they can see their options. (Pat: TWS staff; July 1991)

I have a real problem with the idea of providing therapy. These women have no place else to go, most of them, and I think to ask the woman to go into therapy as a condition of having a roof over her head is really criminal. I really don't believe that that's appropriate. I work with them in terms of just here-and-now counselling kinds of things ... Ah, if they believe that they have issues that they want to work on, aside from those issues, then I'll refer them outside of the shelter. (Wendy: RWS staff; July 1991)

Wendy reported that most abused women returned to abusive partners several times before effecting a permanent break, and that many never achieve this. She reported that most who return choose to sever all contact with the shelter. Pat and Eloise agreed with Wendy that the only appropriate response was for shelter workers to accept and respect abused women's choices:

I think that by maintaining contact with the shelter that they [ex-residents] feel that they're somehow being disloyal ... We had a woman who was living in our second-stage housing who was with us for two years. Her husband used to stick cigarettes in her eyes and do all kinds of stuff to her. Really bad abuse. And he was in a treatment program and she decided to reconcile. Her major reason was, I think, because she was really frightened to do it on her own, with her kids. And she was also pregnant at the time. And she went back, making the agreement that she would continue to maintain contact with me for the follow-up. But she changed her mind, she didn't want to. She didn't want anything more to do with us. You have to respect that it's her choice. (Wendy: RWS staff; July 1991)

Shelters in Context

Since the 1970s women's shelters have spread rapidly across North America and the United Kingdom. Nearly simultaneously, three shelter models emerged. The first is a feminist or liberationist model, characterized by strong, even radical, feminist ideology and non-hierarchical decision-making practices. The second is a non-feminist or professional protectionist model, grounded in mainstream social service or therapeutic ideologies and traditional organizational practices. The third is a pro-feminist model, a model that combines feminist and professional approaches.[5]

Liberationist shelters aim at promoting female empowerment and individual autonomy; however, their primary goal is to raise the consciousness of women, not just individually but as a class (Beaudry, 1985). A feminist shelter is more than a service for abused women; it is a site from which to work towards the transformation of society. Proponents insist that abused women's problems are social, not psychological. Solutions entail political activism, not therapy. Shelter workers serve as social advocates, not service providers. Shelter recipients are referred to as 'residents,' not 'clients.' These practices and principles coincide with non-hierarchical decision-making and peer counselling (Dobash and Dobash, 1992).

In contrast, protectionist and pro-feminist shelters function as resource centres for women and children in crisis. Their aim is to meet short-term personal and social needs of abused women and children. These include the need and/or desire for education, and, in some shelters, psychotherapy. While orientations can be either strongly professionalist or strongly feminist, most such shelters offer a combination of feminist and professional orientations. The blending is a result of ideological overlap between social service and feminist ideologies, and organizational transitions to accommodate funders. Staff typically assume the dual role of counsellors to, and advocates for, 'clients.' Hierarchical organizational practices prevail, practices that purportedly maximize efficiency and accountability.

Several researchers attribute undesirable or dysfunctional shelter practices to the professional co-optation of shelters (Ferraro, 1983; Dobash and Dobash, 1992; Gagne, 1996). On the other hand, researchers report the same kinds of problems across ideological and organizational boundaries. Covert hierarchies tend to emerge where formal hierarchies do not; as do stringent limits on shelter residents' freedoms, and 'expert' analysis of abuse conveyed through 'consciousness-raising' or 'education' on gender, parenting, cycle-of-violence relationship dynamics, and so forth. This rule-bound, highly didactic environment tends to reproduce the controlling practices imposed by abusers. It tends to convey messages that battered women are inept wives, abusive parents, and social dupes. Irrespective of a shelter's ideological orientation or organizational structure, abused women tend to resent and resist these shelter practices. This resentment and resistance fuel staff dissatisfactions and staff burn-out.[6]

Researchers attribute problems in shelters to three related processes, all three of which are in evidence in accounts of problems at both the Regional and the Township shelters. First, staff and board members tend to become embroiled in power and control struggles. In some shelters, these struggles centre on differences between more radical and less radical feminists, or between feminists and professionalists. In others, class issues seem more salient, as when differently credentialed staff compete for the power to influence, determine, or interpret policy. Second, there is a tendency for shelter workers to experience burn-out. Burn-out results from exhaustion associated with wrangles over shelter policy and practice, and disappointments at perceived failures to save or change abused women. Third, shelters serve, or disproportionately serve, a poor and, in many cases, an under-educated, chronically unemployed, and almost inevitably disenchanted 'surplus population,' a population whom agents of social control have been trying to contain since the seventeenth century (Pizzey and Shapiro, 1982; MacLeod, 1987; Davis, 1988; Gordon, 1988).[7]

Across ideological and organizational boundaries, despite and against the best intentions of feminists, pro-feminists, and professionalists alike, shelters emerge as a new version of the 'total institution' (Davis, 1988; McDonald and Peressini, 1991). As Goffman made explicit in his classic work *Asylums* (1961), the primary function of total institutions is re-socialization of inadequately or inappropriately socialized members of society. A secondary function is institutional efficiency. When women's shelters allow either or both of these functions to dominate, abused women experience re-victimization, not support and empowerment.

Township Residents and Shelters

Township residents expressed strong support for the new shelter. This support was evidenced in public meetings, in fund-raising events, in the survey on violence and abuse, and in an ongoing flow of private donations that continued well past the shelter opening.

Several female survey respondents who reported abuse intervention experience also reported staying at a women's shelter, usually the Regional shelter. The majority of these women expressed strong support for shelters. Nevertheless, female abuse intervention clients were five times more likely than women with no client experience to rate shelters not helpful or only somewhat helpful. The tendency for a markedly higher percentage of intervention clients to be wary of formal interventions relates to the well-documented propensity for intervenors to unwittingly re-victimize people who come to them for assistance.[8] No one knows this better than intervention clients. (See table 11.)[9]

Domestic Abuse Committee activists entertained hopes that, unlike other shelters, and unlike the Regional shelter, the Township shelter would be more than a place abused women would use, that it would be a place where abused women would want to go. They forgot that shelters are not a vacation resort, but rather a dreaded last resort. They forgot that most shelter clients contend with a number of concurrent problems, problems that impede attempts to respond positively to the 'education' and 'support' shelters and related abuse interventions provide. They forgot that abused women need opportunities and encouragement to express their angers and dissatisfactions. Most importantly, they forgot that the voices of abused women are now legitimized. Activists forgot that people would inevitably hear both about client dissatisfactions, and about their own futile attempts to discredit and silence the women they purported to serve.

Unintended Outcomes

At the new Township shelter, a 'moderate' pro-feminist professionalist contingent instituted practices aimed at containing and silencing dissent, discrediting interference, and intensifying control. These practices were rooted in key actors' interpretation of realities behind a number of 'myths' about abuse, realities that reinforced or fostered beliefs that abused women, and uneducated women, are ill-equipped emotionally and cognitively to make appropriate choices. They were rooted in erroneous perceptions that undesirable shelter practices were the result of radical feminism and naïve idealism, and they were rooted in fears that 'the male hierarchy' lay in wait to discredit the Township shelter, and shelters generally. These perceptions and fears led to practices, justified under a banner of professionalism, that undermined the goals and principles of virtually all participants. They produced a shelter environment that no involved actor intended.

Rumours of dissatisfactions at the neighbouring Regional shelter were confirmed by several staff, who reported that this facility had also been burdened with a dysfunctional control orientation during its first decade of operation. At the Regional shelter, controlling practices coincided with the privileging of radicalism rather than professionalism. As previous researchers have also noted, neither of these 'isms' prevents a shelter from falling into the dreaded trap described by Wendy – the trap of 'taking on the role of the abuser in the name of saving the woman.'

Wendy and other Regional shelter staff reported that they had collectively adopted a strategy aimed at averting this outcome, and that this strategy works. It consists of openly acknowledging criticism, accepting differences, accommodating mistakes, and, most importantly, relinquishing control. It is a strategy that recognizes the possibility that all women are agents, that all women knowledgeably and competently participate in the ongoing flow of events in their world, regardless of their social situation, educational accomplishments, professional credentials, ideological commitments, or personal troubles (see Giddens, 1979; Loseke and Cahill, 1984; Hoff, 1991; Bowker, 1993; Mahoney, 1994). This strategy is consistent with feminist principles, and it is consistent with community development principles. As I will demonstrate in the next chapter, it is also consistent with therapeutic principles.

5

Counselling and
Therapeutic Intervenors

Therapists and counsellors employed through the Regional Woman Abuse Program and the Regional Sex Abuse Program participated in Domestic Abuse Committee activities, as core participants, workshop presenters, and consultants. With colleagues in private practice, they implemented court-mandated and voluntary counselling programs promoted through the police, the courts, the Regional welfare office, the Children's Aid Society, and the Township Resource Centre.[1] This chapter focuses on how their services and orientations fit with the Domestic Abuse Committee's vision of a community-coordinated inter-agency response to *domestic abuse*.

My analysis focuses on practices and perceptions relevant to the four issues that fuelled polarizations during mobilization of action and shelter operation: the relevance of gender; substance abuse; intergenerational processes; and the alleged exceptional nature of the Township's under-educated and under-employed 'problem population.' As noted in chapters 1 and 2, some *violence against women* proponents identify a *family violence* perspective on these issues as hegemonic (see, for instance, Dobash and Dobash, 1992; Smith, 1997). In this chapter, I treat *violence against women* and *family violence* perspectives more as contending hegemonies. Both make empirically supportable claims about the social world, and both exert a powerful influence on people's understandings.

Pro-feminist and Mainstream Therapeutic Counselling

Through head-on confrontations with attitudes and practices that foster male violence against wives and girlfriends, pro-feminist psycho-educational programs for abusers and victims make a point of resisting tendencies to 'individualize' abuse. The core assumption is that individuals make choices based on socially structured beliefs, and that social structures, and the belief systems that support them, are both gendered and willed. Consequently, educational counselling focuses on the repudiation of all forms of male power and control over women, not on feelings or needs. This orientation reflects not simply a theoretical privileging of agency, which is to say, knowledgeability and intentionality, but also a denial or suppression of emotionality (McKendy, 1992; Smith, 1997). Holmes and Lundy (1990) describe the assumptions and goals of such a program operating in Ottawa, Ontario. They label competing 'insight' and 'cognitive behavioural' approaches that address feelings, fears, anger problems, and communication deficits as 'single faceted and narrow':[2]

> Men abuse women because of what they believe, not what they feel, so our approach [is] to attempt to systematically uncover the beliefs and intents of abusers, and the effects of their violence. (Holmes and Lundy, 1990: 14)

> [A] profeminist approach situates male violence, and what is needed to eliminate it, within a socio-political context. This approach recognizes that gender relations are relations of power and dominance, and that women experience gender inequality and oppression within a variety of social structures in society. Male authority inside the family is supported by social relations and structures outside the family. In this context, *violence against women* is an important means by which their subordination to men is maintained. (Holmes and Lundy, 1990: 13)

A more traditional therapeutic approach works on the assumption that human behaviour is the product of complex interactions among emotions, cognitions, and ego ideals. Programs for abusers typically focus on gender issues, but not exclusively; they also address anger problems, enmeshment, communication and empathy deficits, and intimacy needs. Wallace and Nosko (1991) describe one such program operating in Toronto, Ontario (see also Nosko and Wallace, 1988). This program focuses on the relevance of enmeshment or a lack of individuation to violence. A core assumption is that enmeshment results from attachment anxieties associated with childhood trauma, especially for males, who use dominance to ward off terror of abandonment and shame associated with this terror. Counsellors rely on supportive group processes to guide men from shame to guilt, from narcissism to empathy, from denial to responsibility. This orientation reflects a theoretical privileging of emotionality. It assumes both a need for, and a possibility of, individual healing and recovery.[3]

Whether pro-feminist or more traditionally therapeutic, court-mandated programs for male abusers operate as an adjunct to a court system mandated to punish, incapacitate, and reform individuals convicted of spouse or partner assault.[4] Similarly, support groups for abused women operate as an adjunct to women's shelters and related services mandated to protect women, and to enhance their social and economic power.

Pro-feminist Counselling in the Township

In the Township, pro-feminist group counselling for male perpetrators and female victims of domestic violence was provided through the Regional Woman Abuse Program. This program had been working in conjunction with the courts for the better part of a decade. The majority of male clients were court-mandated. All female clients were voluntary.

Interviewed counsellors included Fiona, Alice, Kay, and John. Fiona, Alice, and Kay combined Regional Woman Abuse Program counselling with individual, couple, and family therapy offered through Township Family Services. John combined Regional Woman Abuse Program counselling with community mental health work at the Regional hospital. All three women were active members of the Domestic Abuse Committee; Fiona was the most influential of the three. Fiona and Alice served as co-presenters with Regional shelter worker Wendy at the 1991 Wife Abuse Workshop. All counsellors were interviewed in the summer of 1991.

Fiona, Alice, Kay, and John identified themselves, and their program, as 'strongly' pro-feminist. All four insisted that sexist beliefs, and the social institutions that foster these beliefs, explain both why men are abusive and why women tolerate abuse. John was particularly explicit. He made it clear that sexist attitudes are the cause of abuse, and that the Regional Woman Abuse Program's major intervention focus was getting clients to discard these beliefs:

> My philosophy comes from the pro-feminist approach of working with
> men. We are looking at gender equalities, economic equalities, social,

political – we look at society. For example, we look at the people who control society. We look at the businesses and politics and on and on, and
these are all men-controlled ... Men are socialized differently. We are
taught not to express our feelings, not to show any emotion, not to be
weak, to be strong and positive and be leaders. We've grown up with taking a leadership role and it is instilled in us very early. We take that into
society. We are made to feel we have to be in control. Sexist beliefs are the
cause of abuse. The major focus is to discard sexist beliefs. (John: RWAP;
summer 1991)

[T]he main focus is taking responsibility, cutting through the denial, making the men really take stock of what they have done, and then doing
some skills-training around anger management and attitudinal change.
We are trying to get men to do lots more than just curb their anger. We
want them to really look at the whole power and control issue and that
goes on beyond their relationship. We want them to look at society, and
what society has done. (Fiona: RWAP; summer 1991)

Male perpetrators and female victims receive counselling in separate
groups. Men's groups focus on getting the men to recognize that abuse
is a choice, and that they and they alone are responsible for making
this choice. Counselling focuses on helping men to identify the full
range of violent behaviours and attitudes, on teaching men how to
manage their anger, on teaching men how to empathize with their
partners, and, most importantly, on getting men to accept that they
must renounce or relinquish power and control. Regional Woman
Abuse Program counsellors reported that most abusers believe that it
is their partner who has all the power, and that it is their partner who
causes the abuse:[5]

There are a lot of men who feel very strongly that they are not responsible. They blame their partners for their abuse. They insist that it's their
partner who's the real abuser. Being an unwilling client is a big issue for
us. So irrespective of what has happened out there, we slowly focus on
the men – meaning that they have to take responsibility for their behaviours. They have to recognize what they have done, recognize that they
have a choice. (John: RWAP; summer 1991)

Women's groups focus on the mirror opposite of men's groups.
Women's groups focus on getting women to stop taking responsibility

for violence or abuse. Consequently, women are not provided with counselling on how to manage anger. Rather, women are encouraged to recognize and express anger as part of 'assertiveness training.' Nor are women encouraged to develop or practise empathy. Rather, women are encouraged to stop trying to understand their partner's behaviour. Finally, women are not encouraged to consider how their own abusive or controlling behaviours feed or provoke abuse. Instead, women are educated on the inappropriateness of allowing partners to set rules or allocate responsibilities. Regional Woman Abuse Program counsellors agreed that these strategies are necessary to counter gender socialization, and something Fiona termed 'the victimization process':

> We don't want women to be more empathetic. Women are generally overly empathetic already. I mean, they don't want to leave their partner because they feel he can't make it on his own. They worry about him.
> ...
> The effect of the victimization is that women lose, that and they begin to believe what they are told. They begin to believe that they are worthless, and if it wasn't for this wonderful man who just gets aggravated by their stupidity, and therefore beats them up for their own benefit – well, eventually women really do believe it. It is hard for us who haven't been there to grasp the enormity of that effect. (Fiona: RWAP; summer 1991)

John declined to comment on the existence or extent of female-perpetrated violence. Fiona admitted that some women are violent, but described female violence as mostly minor. In contrast, Kay stated that serious forms of female violence commonly come up in women's groups, and that one of the last myths is the myth that women are nonviolent. Regardless, all four counsellors maintained that it is important to retain a focus on male violence. All insisted that women's use of violence, and women's use of power and control, are qualitatively different from men's. Most importantly, Regional Woman Abuse Program counsellors maintained that, for women, anger is a healthy and appropriate response to male power and control tactics:

> *Female violence* has been coming up in my groups, and we are beginning to address it. I think the next thing is looking at all those myths around – women are not violent, it is always the man. I wonder, is this the next thing, looking at how women act aggressively even if it is verbal aggres-

sion? But what we see is even if she is verbally abusive, whatever, he ends up with more power. So, regardless, she ends up more the loser ... Even if she is fighting back. He has more physical power and he has more financial power. (Kay: RWAP; summer 1991)

We don't look at ways women can be over-controlling or abusive for the simple reason that for the women who have gone through a lengthy victimization process they first need to feel good about themselves, they first need to feel empowered, and they first need to feel their own strength. Now their own strength initially is anger and being assertive and refusing to get caught up in his stuff. (Fiona: RWAP; summer 1991)

Regional Woman Abuse Program counsellors saw men and women as occupying complementary roles scripted by patriarchal social norms, including norms of romantic love. They identified these norms as contributing to the predisposition of abusers and abused to become enmeshed. Counsellors reported that enmeshment issues were compounded by the tendency for most abusive men and many abused women to find the intensity of abuse preferable to the boredom of a normal relationship. Fiona reported that many abusive men admit that they 'get off' on violence. On the other hand, as she also suggested in the 1991 Wife Abuse Workshop, many abused women admit that they feel rewarded by the emotional and sexual intimacy that follows violent episodes:

For violent relationships it is really a big vacuum, you know, if he can put a stop to the abuse. Men have said that too. They've said: 'What do I do? I got a rush, when I hit her. I got a real rush, it's a higher high than anything else that I've ever experienced. Beats sex, you know. So what do I do? My life's going to be like this? Flat!' So you ask, then what else they enjoy doing, what is almost as good? They say: 'Well, gliding, you know, or driving a motorcycle too fast, or race car driving.' (Fiona: RWAP; summer 1991)

We've got this diagram where you've got two healthy individuals that are pretty solid, but in violent relationships they are really shaky the two of them. They try to complete the circle by tying together as one. There is a lot of stuff about we are one. (Kay: RWAP; summer 1991)

Counsellors described abusers as Jekyll and Hyde types, who have a tender, generous, romantic side, but also a side that is distrustful, obsessed with control, rigidly sexist, socially isolated, selfish, highly dependent, and needy. These contradictory characteristics coincide with intense jealousy, insecurity, unpredictability, and anger – characteristics that contribute to the 'walking on eggs' atmosphere reported by many female partners. In contrast, counsellors described abused women as non-assertive, too willing to forgive and forget, unable to express anger, overly dependent on their relationship, and too 'other absorbed':

> Jealousy is a very intense element, especially for men who have come from backgrounds where they have been through a lot of losses and rejections in relationships. With jealousy comes an intense need to control.
> ...
> There is a lack of tolerance for differences. These are people who are very needy and dependent and socially isolated. All the emotional and social needs are being met through that relationship, the men even more than the women. (John: RWAP; summer 1991)

> There is a very warm wonderful component, or quality, to some of these men. Not all of them, but you find it much of the time. And, and it's that Dr Jekyll and Mr Hyde thing. The positive is so positive. You know, if the guy throws the chili against the wall and then goes out and buys a diamond ring, you may not remember the chili very long but the diamond ring lasts a while. You know, the problem is the women fantasize that you can get rid of all the bad and keep all the good, but the good is too good to be realistic. They both need to move more towards the middle.
> ...
> The man is too involved with himself and the woman is too other absorbed. That's how these couples work. (Fiona: RWAP; summer 1991)

Counsellors reported that many male clients have current or past problems with alcohol and other substances, but all four stressed their belief that alcohol does not cause men to abuse their partners; rather, alcohol is a factor that contributes to the frequency and severity of violent practices. All were in agreement that this concurrent issue should not be a focus of woman abuse counselling. No interviewed Regional Woman Abuse Program counsellor addressed the issue of substance abuse among victims:

> I think the alcohol allows it to become more predominant and perhaps

escalates the violence. I absolutely refuse to believe that alcohol causes it. I refuse to believe that alcoholics are any more abusive than normal men. In my mind the men who are abusive and have an alcohol problem use the alcohol as a means of allowing themselves to escalate the violence. They would have been abusive anyway – maybe not to that extent and maybe less frequently. (Fiona: RWAP; summer 1991)

Alcohol is a factor. It doesn't cause abuse but it contributes to abuse and I want to make that clear. (John: RWAP; summer 1991)

I think a person can have an alcoholic personality. A lot of the time alcohol is involved, whether you're talking about physical abuse or incest. But alcoholism and abuse are two different problems. The man comes to us, but he has two problems. He has to work on them separately. (Alice: RWAP; summer 1991)

Fiona, Alice, and Kay reported that more than half of all female clients report child sexual abuse, and that almost all perpetrators report physical, sexual, or emotional child abuse or family-of-origin wife abuse. John tended to dismiss these childhood issues. He reported that abusive men are all too willing to seize on personal histories to rationalize or excuse their behaviours. Counsellors agreed that family-of-origin abuse should not be a primary focus of woman abuse counselling, that, like substance abuse, childhood trauma was a concurrent issue, not a cause:

With the women, more than half are incest survivors ... Lately, I have seen more men saying they have been sexually abused. Men are starting to talk about it. It's a new issue. A lot of men experienced severe physical child abuse. (Alice: RWAP; summer 1991)

I don't see violent backgrounds so much in the women. I see women who have been sexually abused who then seem to seek out, ah. But definitely in the men there is the factor of having been traumatized either by physical violence or sexual abuse and then becoming abusive, and not necessarily sexually abusive but becoming physically abusive in their relationship. They have seen their father being abusive to their mother, they have been physically abused themselves and there has been a great deal of deprivation in their childhood. I don't think there has been a man in the group who has not had one of those in their background. (Fiona: RWAP; summer 1991)

About 75 per cent of the men witnessed or experienced severe abuse, in some form. But a lot of them will want to say that – to try to justify their behaviour. We try to take that away from them, so we don't make an issue of what happened to them as children. We tell them there are a lot of people who also came from abusive families who are not abusive themselves. (John: RWAP; summer 1991)

In deference to *violence against women* critics who condemn therapy for perpetrators and victims of domestic violence, Regional Woman Abuse Program counsellors made it clear that their program was 'not about treatment,' especially that women's groups were not about treatment. Nevertheless, counsellors Fiona, Kay, and Alice expressed concern about the relationship between child sexual abuse and adult relationship violence, especially the apparent tendency for child sex abuse survivors to fall prey to physical woman abuse. Counsellors acknowledged that many clients need concurrent therapy to deal with personal issues. It was the policy of the Regional Woman Abuse Program to refer clients with concurrent problems to other agencies, including the Regional Sex Abuse Program.[6] As Fiona noted, and as confirmed in the survey, Township and Regional programs for woman abuse, child abuse, and substance abuse tend to serve 'the same,' or at least a significantly overlapping, 'problem population':

Basically, we're talking with the same population, you know. That's why I'm so opposed to working in this field with problem populations, you know – alcoholics, wife beaters, child abusers, child molesters – because it doesn't make sense ... You end up with a lot of overlap. It's very difficult to sort these issues out. (Fiona: RWAP; summer 1991)

Mainstream or Traditional Counselling in the Township

Compared to the Regional Woman Abuse Program, the Regional Sex Abuse Program was more traditionally therapeutic. The Regional Sex Abuse Program had also provided court-mandated counselling for the better part of a decade. In addition to male perpetrators of incest and child sex abuse, the program ran groups for child and adolescent victims, non-offending parents, and adult survivors. Counsellors Beverly and Ralph participated in individual interviews in September of 1992. Beverly served as a consultant to the Domestic Abuse Committee but did not attend weekly meetings. I first encountered her at the 1991 Community Response Workshop.

Private therapist Nancy also relied on a more traditional therapeutic approach. Her clients were referred through the Children's Aid Society, the Regional hospital, and private physicians. Nancy was not affiliated with the Regional Sex Abuse Program, but many of her clients previously, concurrently, or subsequently participated in Regional Sex Abuse Program groups. I was introduced to Nancy through her daughter, a *random* participant in the 1992 survey on violence and abuse. Nancy participated in a single interview in the fall of 1992.

Child sex abuse counsellors saw their client population somewhat differently than Regional Woman Abuse counsellors. First, child sex abuse counsellors saw victim and perpetrator roles as fluid. They reported that most child sex abuse offenders were themselves victims, and that most victims, whether female or male, also offended:

> We are finding more and more that male offenders were themselves victims ... Five of seven offenders in one group have experienced child sexual abuse [checking file], yes, the adult male offender was himself a victim in five out of seven in this group. Three of these were victimized by fathers, one by someone in the extended family, one by someone outside the family ... At present males are over-represented in our victim and survivor groups. (Beverly: RSAP; summer 1992)

> More and more women are acknowledging that they too have offended to the extent where we have changed our intake form. Now we ask if you yourself sexually abused? And they are very grateful to be asked. It is something that gnaws on them. (Ralph: RSAP; summer 1992)

> They [child and adolescent victims] also report re-enactments of the abuse with other siblings, or cousins, as an example. Boys report having oral sex with one another, and girls tell about initiating sex with brothers, or sexually touching younger children in a variety of contexts. We are hearing about it a lot from young women and girls in their teens just by asking the questions. We see the other too [sexual abuse of own child by female survivor/victims] but not with a well-fixed frequency. (Beverly: RSAP; summer 1992)

Beverly, Ralph, and Nancy reported that offenders, victims, and survivors tend to share the same set of characteristics, across ages and genders. Though most researchers do not make this claim, the three counsellors' descriptions of victims, offenders, and survivors generally mirror those in the child sex abuse literature.[7]

First, the three counsellors described male offenders as emotionally and sexually estranged from wives, as highly puritanical, and as generally lacking in social support. They reported that many have impotence problems:

> Offenders are very isolated ... It is sad. They are so closed. They desperately need nurturing, and they need to know they can get it and how to get it appropriately.
>
> ...
>
> These men are incredibly isolated ... They cannot relate to their own sexuality. They see sex as dirty. Their sexual lives are flat, not fulfilling. And the abuses [incest] usually occur when the wife is out of the house ... It happens when the wife is not available to them emotionally or physically. (Ralph: RSAP; summer 1992)

The counsellors described female survivors and non-offending parents as somewhat less isolated, but as equally likely as offenders to be emotionally distant, from partners and from children, and to be puritanical and frequently frigid. Counsellors stated that non-offending mothers were often themselves child victims.

Finally, counsellors described child victims as emotionally alienated from parents and siblings, ashamed, intensely angry, highly aggressive, and often suicidal. They reported that child victims commonly experience emotional abuse both through the seductive manipulative behaviour of the offending parent and through the rejecting condemning behaviour of the non-offending parent. As children, and as adults, many place primary blame on mothers – both because mothers failed to stop the abuse and because mothers rejected and blamed them for the shameful, unmentionable, and secret behaviour they were coerced or compelled to participate in:

> My people [clients] all hate their mothers because mothers are there to protect and nurture and keep you safe and secure. Obviously they weren't kept safe or secure when they were being abused in the family. Some people feel it is hard to get a handle on what emotional abuse is.

Withholding love and affection is emotional abuse. (Nancy: private therapist; summer 1992)

There is a lot of anger against mothers. The more experience I am getting the more convinced I become that virtually every child discloses, not necessarily verbally, but discloses in some other non-verbal way. But you have to be an observant, astute, or perceptive adult to pick up on the attitudinal changes. The mothers don't for any number of reasons. They go into denial. They don't want to believe in their minds. (Ralph: RSAP; summer 1992)

They are daddy's pretty little girl but to mother they're a little slut ... It is emotional abuse that makes it more difficult for the victim to heal and recover because they are so desperately needing of that person's [the offender's] love and affection. They have been so put down and humiliated. The only time they are getting love and affection is during the abuse so they desperately look forward to it and might even initiate it. That really compounds the problem. It makes it a lot more difficult for them. (Nancy: private therapist; summer 1992)

The mother and father are unequipped to identify the child's needs and are more concerned with their own. Those children grow up with a minimal amount of self-esteem for themselves and experience disrespect and abuse from others and really find it the norm to be abused as opposed to feeling something is the matter. For a mother to recognize that her child is being [sexually] abused is a very complicated process. The defence mechanisms are built up so much that to see what's behind the acting out behaviours that were her own as a child, right in front of her, it's just too difficult to face. (Beverly: RSAP; summer 1992)

Counsellors reported that child victims of both sexes commonly initiate sexual activity with younger children and peers, and that victims of either sex both 'unknowingly' invite and promiscuously seek out sexual activity with adults. Counsellors described this pattern as especially noticeable among females because of societal norms that condemn girls and women who engage in indiscriminate sex. Counsellors reported that, regardless of gender, boundary problems, apparent in inappropriate and self-demeaning sexual practices, continue into adulthood, as does vulnerability to sexual exploitation:

Incest victims are vulnerable to sexual victimization because they unknowingly send out sexual cues, they unknowingly say I'm sexual. And they don't know how to refuse, they feel they can't say no, they don't know boundaries.

...

Often there's that adolescent stage where they [females] are very promiscuous, and when they come out of that they withdraw from sex. Again what happens here goes back to that desperately needing child. During adolescence they'll do anything to feel loved. But then you go into negative emotional chaos again ... I am worthless, I am shamed, I am filthy and dirty. (Nancy: private therapist; summer 1992)

In one group, 50 per cent of the offenders were being sexually assaulted at work and didn't know it. Their bosses were coming up and groping them. These are male bosses. Such things as taking hoses and stuffing them up their pant legs into their crotch. They did not construe it as abuse. They thought that it was just boys being boys. They didn't like it, they felt put down, humiliated, but they didn't know how to object. My colleague and I were just astounded. These are men that had offended and they acknowledged that what they were doing in their family was wrong, and yet they didn't construe what was happening to them as being assaulted. (Ralph: RSAP; summer 1992)

Counsellors reported that male and female clients alike tend to subscribe to rigid sex roles. However, they regarded the rigid sexist attitudes, and the dysfunctional power and control orientations that accompany these, more as a consequence than as a cause of child sexual abuse:

People who feel out of control have to control other people. As for sexism, there's a lot of sexism, a lot of rigidity. But I think that sexism no matter which way you are looking at it, whether it is from a man's or woman's perspective, is a need to gain power. It is a role and identity for people who don't have a real strong sense of self. Sexism is not as important as abuse itself. Again, I think abuse causes abuse. (Beverly: RSAP; summer 1992)

In sexual abuse they have lost control. They have lost that level of control and power and it is important that you give it back to them – at least some of it. (Ralph: RSAP; summer 1992)

The three counsellors similarly regarded substance problems as more of a consequence than a cause of interpersonal abuse:

> The addictions problem is interesting because we have specialists who work in alcoholism or drug addiction and not a high percentage of our offender population are into drugs and alcohol – 50 per cent at the most. It defies the myth. I would say that addiction to alcohol or drugs is more an outcome, a way victims cope, or try to cope. (Beverly: RSAP; summer 1992)

> I am not sure that alcoholism is a cause or the outcome. There is a high correlation between drug and alcohol abuse and sexual abuse. But we don't find it a major theme among offenders. We find it more among victims. (Ralph: RSAP; summer 1992)

Therapist Nancy routinely disclosed her personal abuse history to clients – to bridge interpersonal distance and to provide assurance that it is possible to overcome abuse. Nancy reported that she grew up witnessing severe wife abuse inflicted by an alcoholic father, and physical child abuse inflicted by a mother who was herself a victim of physical and sexual child abuse. While still in her teens, Nancy married into 'a lying alcoholic family' dominated by a 'pathologically violent' wife/mother subsequently diagnosed with multiple personality disorder. According to Nancy, it was as predictable that her husband batter her as it was that she struggled for years to tolerate his abuse. After finally leaving, she entered therapy, completed a four-year social work program, established a successful counselling practice, and raised two non-violent children. Nancy maintained that were it not for therapy, she would have passed on the emotional chaos of perpetration and victimization to her children:

> It goes from generation to generation ... Just because their mothers or fathers were abusive doesn't mean they are going to become abusers, but there is a very high risk. Abused children don't have a high sense of self, so they will go into abusive relationships or become self-abusive through alcohol. They develop various addictions – alcohol, drugs, sex, work. One way or another people will continue the abuse. They will become abusers or will seek out abusive relationships. Their need for that emotional chaos is very powerful ... They love the abuser, and they seek the same abuse. (Nancy: private therapist; summer 1992)

Beverly and Ralph did not disclose personal information, to me or assumedly to clients. However, they agreed with Nancy that many family dysfunctions, including wife abuse, are causally related to child abuse, in general, and child sexual abuse, in particular. All three child sex abuse counsellors were in agreement that 'abuse causes abuse':

I am a strong proponent of it [the intergenerational explanation]. When I start treatment, the first questions I ask, in the first two or three sessions, are family-of-origin questions. To me, once I have done that, all the pieces seem to come together ... Virtually all the offenders either came from abusive backgrounds or backgrounds where there was profound deprivation, which certainly explains but does not justify why they have done what they have done ... Our data suggests it [child sexual abuse] is the causal factor for a lot of other dysfunctions. In the battered woman syndrome, a woman permits herself to be battered and comes back for more, progressively losing more and more of her self-esteem. We ask, why is this woman's self-esteem so low? And what we find is a history of child sexual abuse. (Ralph: RSAP; summer 1992)

I think abuse causes abuse. It occurs because these vulnerable adults [who were themselves abused] turn to inappropriate ways for having their needs met. (Beverly: RSAP; summer 1992)

The counsellors described two intergenerational patterns. In the first pattern, abuse 'mutates' from one generation to another: for example, when female victims or survivors of child sexual abuse fall prey to woman abuse, and/or emotionally or physically abuse their children or spouses; or, when physically or emotionally abused males perpetrate child sexual abuse or woman abuse. In the second pattern, evident in about a third of Regional Sex Abuse Program cases, incest manifests as an entrenched intergenerational phenomenon. Nancy related case-history material on both patterns:

One of my men who suffered physical and emotional child abuse, who was always put down as a child and as an adult, ended up by sexually abusing his children. Both his parents were extremely aggressive. Even at age seventeen he was made to get on his knees and beg to his father. This man was so demeaned, and never got any positive messages. He never felt any power. He was treated worse than an animal. He could never relate to women at all. When he married, he married a very dominant

very aggressive woman, and she picked up where his parents left off. She didn't abuse him physically, but she would put him down in front of people, she would lock him out and make him beg to come back in again, and get him crying and sobbing. Sexually, she ridiculed him – he couldn't perform, do this, do that, he couldn't get it up. So the only time he could get aroused was with children. He abused children in his family of both sexes – fondling them, caressing them, having them touch his genitals, that kind of thing. He abused one of his daughter's friends as well.
...

There are cases like one of my women clients now, where incest is just a part of life. 'I am going to teach you sex because I don't want you out there looking foolish. My mother and father taught me, so now I'm going to teach you.' These fathers are very protective and jealous of their daughters, that kind of thing. They teach their daughters that it's normal so their daughters think, dad is teaching us. (Nancy: private therapist; summer 1992)

Regardless of whether they were working with offenders or victims, all three counsellors focused on developing empathy and a sense of connectedness, through 'authentic' supportive interactions, or through group processes. Nancy's work relied more on confrontations with both experiences and abusers. Beverly and Ralph preferred to focus on the emotional effects of experiences. Regardless, child sex abuse counsellors saw positive self-esteem as the key to self-responsibility, and the key to preventing re-offence or re-victimization. Their primary aim was not to change attitudes, but to change selves:

Mostly we legitimize and validate any person's experience and get them connected to their feelings. Sometimes they will feel very conflicted, very awful or guilty ... Our approach is very much process-oriented, using what is going on in the group. I've certainly learned that disclosing the actual full details of the abuse is a lot less necessary than I once thought it was. It is secondary ... The more important thing is to be inquiring about the meaning of their experiences rather than the details. How it made them feel. (Beverly: RSAP; summer 1992)

It's important to share experiences ... You want offenders to come to accept responsibility, but it is not laid on. There is not a strong didactic, educational thrust to it. There might be educational components periodically, but we start off just generally talking about what their families were like. You take them back as far as they can go and bring them up to the present time, in terms of who they are as a person. (Ralph: RSAP; summer 1992)

In the fall of 1992, the Regional Sex Abuse Program was in the process of extending an experiment with 'gender-blended' treatment groups to adolescent and adult victims and survivors. This experiment resulted from increased demand for victim services for males, from a growing suspicion that victimization and perpetration are experientially unitary, and from 'discoveries' that gender-blending – used for some time in pre-adolescent treatment groups and in adult post-treatment support groups – challenges sexist stereotypes, promotes empathy, and facilitates recovery, for males and females alike. Regional Sex Abuse Program counsellors regarded these cognitive and emotional restructurings as necessary if clients were to succeed in breaking intergenerational cycles:

> Since learning that offenders are victims and victims offend, we are not quite sure what to treat first – the victim piece or the offending piece, to treat them concurrently or treat them in a mixed configuration or an extended configuration. (Ralph: RSAP; summer 1992)

> With the children we've found it is very good for them to see that not all boys are offenders and not all girls are victims. They will be stronger kids as a result of that as opposed to aligning themselves with the victim or the offender stance – boys are to abuse and girls are to be hurt ... We're thinking mixed groups might be quite a good opportunity for women to learn to relate with men in a better way, and vice versa. This would help to break the intergenerational cycle. (Beverly: RSAP; summer 1992)

Beverly reported that recent acknowledgment that males experience victimization and that females commonly offend is a consequence of the evolving ability of professionals to hear what clients are telling them. She noted that colleagues in affiliated agencies resisted the idea of gender-blended treatment groups, especially colleagues in the Regional Woman Abuse Program. These colleagues insisted that victimization affects men and women differently, and that men and women engage in very different forms of perpetration. Beverly's work with child abuse victims and offenders had convinced her that differences rooted in gender were minimal. She expressed confidence that professionals in other agencies would also eventually shed 'myths' that lead them to disregard evidence that abuse issues transcend gender:

> Resistance to mixing the genders is more from the professional community than from the clients. A myth we sustain in this profession is that men can't talk to women and women can't talk to men and that we shouldn't put them together because it will be too hard. You know, women will be intimidated, men won't listen, men will overpower ... I think dealing with both men and women is something all agencies are going to have to face sooner or later. (Beverly: RSAP; summer 1992)

Coordinating Services

Counsellors working through the Regional Woman Abuse Program and the Regional Sex Abuse Program saw abusive and abused individuals and families somewhat differently, but they were in agreement that they were serving 'the same' multi-problem population. These perceptions are supported by reports of strong overlap between battering and child sexual abuse as reported by clients of the Regional Woman Abuse Program, the Regional Sex Abuse Program, and the Regional shelter. Perceptions of population overlap are also supported by statistically significant correlations between physical and sexual child abuse and serious dating and marital violence in the 1992 survey on violence and abuse (see tables 7 and 8). Finally, they are supported by an extensive body of empirical research on male 'batterers,'[8] 'battered women,'[9] and 'battering relationships'[10] – research that consistently identifies child abuse in general, and child sexual abuse, in particular, as a potent risk marker for violence in adult relationships.[11]

Regional woman abuse counsellors and Regional sex abuse counsellors respected the need to cooperate with and support each other, despite having to compete for funding. This cooperation and support was facilitated by mutual agreement to maintain treatment boundaries, and by the flexible ways Regional Woman Abuse Program counsellors practised pro-feminist counselling. Formally, the program places primary emphasis on processes and practices associated with a feminist perspective. Practically, counsellors struggled with the complex, emotionally confusing reality of abuse, and they combined feminist and therapeutic principles. As therapists, they recognized, or believed, that 'violence is a man's unwept tears' (Kay: RWAP; summer

1991). As therapists, they recognized, or believed, that for women and men alike, violence, anger, and the need to control originate in the personal pain of other-inflicted and self-inflicted abuse:

> I just don't believe that men are bad inherently and that women inherently are better. I have always believed in feminist principles but there is this jarring thing that something isn't right. I just recently realized ... you can't mix political beliefs and therapeutic beliefs, and political theories and therapeutic theories ... The main programs need to have a therapeutic base and they need to be guided by therapeutic principles, and the women's movement and the shelter movement needs to be guided by political principles, so the two don't mix. While the political has an impact, it should not be dominant. (Fiona: RWAP; summer 1991)

The Exceptional Nature of Abuse in the Township

A major issue in the press and at public meetings was whether abuse was or was not more severe or more frequent in the Township than in other Canadian communities.

Regional Woman Abuse Program counsellors were reluctant to stereotype the Township as an exceptionally abusive community. All considered more 'middle-class' forms of emotional abuse just as serious as physical abuse. Nevertheless, all four associated the obvious physical nature of abuse and residents' apparent willingness of accept abuse with high levels of alcohol consumption, low social economic status, and low educational achievement, and all four associated these patterns with sexism. None could be accused of wearing 'rose-coloured glasses.' On the other hand, all suggested that the Township's abused and abusive population was somehow exceptional:

> In the Township, it is more out there, more visible. The downside is that it is almost accepted as part of the community, but the upside is that people talk about it. (Kay: RWAP; summer 1991)

> I think something social is happening there because – I have to be careful because I don't want to label or stereotype the Township – but for me it is more of a socio-economic, education type of issue. Some of the men say the Township is very violent, and sexist. More men from the Township seem to have alcohol problems. They tend to be more physically violent. (John: RWAP; summer 1991)

I don't think there's more abuse in the Township than in other parts of the Region. I believe it is expressed more, and perhaps it is more physical. When I talk about *family violence* itself, the more insidious is the emotional and mental abuse. I would say perhaps that the outright physical abuse is, well, maybe more obvious. This seems to be a class issue, to some extent. A cultural issue, but it's all abuse. (Fiona: RWAP; summer 1991)

In contrast, the more traditionally therapeutic child sex abuse counsellors rejected the idea that abuse was any different in the Township than in other, more affluent communities, inside or outside the Region. All three reported that they found the same patterns among advantaged and disadvantaged families. None identified the Township as more substance-dependent than most other Canadian communities. None identified clients from the Township as more troubled, more sexist, or more prone to physical violence than abused and abusive individuals generally. None was willing to identify either abused and abusive people in the Township, or abused and abusive people generally, as 'a problem population':

We get clients from all across the Region. It's not more pronounced or different in any one community. Abuse goes across the spectrum. (Ralph: RSAP; summer 1992)

Township Residents and Abuse Counselling

The majority of survey respondents rated all proposed counselling services as important abuse interventions. Respondents who reported childhood or adult abuse supported woman abuse and child sexual abuse interventions at even higher rates than respondents not reporting these experiences. On the other hand, currently violent and relationship-distressed respondents displayed less support for substance abuse interventions. This is noteworthy since it was individuals reporting violence and relationship distress who were most likely to report that they or their partner struggled with this 'concurrent' problem. Contrary to the expectations of activists and resource centre–affiliated professionals, members of the Township's abused and abusive 'problem population' appeared more likely to recognize that violence issues and substance issues are somehow separate. (See tables 4 and 12.)

Also contrary to the expectations of Township activists, and in contrast to the attitudes of the majority of surveyed residents, respondents reporting adult relationship violence were highly likely to rate sexism as important to the problem, whether female or male. This finding coincides with the strong tendency for female respondents reporting violence to rate feminists as at least acceptable abuse intervenors – though, like the majority of surveyed residents, most preferred abuse professionals and abuse survivors.[12] (See tables 4, 10.a–10.d, and 14.)

These findings suggest that the Township's abused and abusive population 'knew' considerably more about the nature and causes of abuse than Domestic Abuse Committee activists assumed.[13] More importantly, they demonstrate that the people most in need of abuse interventions are most receptive to the services aimed at the two most troubling abuse patterns of all – wife battery and the sexual abuse of children. Finally, they suggest that intervention services have the best chance of overcoming client resistance or 'disenchantment' when they are directed and implemented by trained professionals, whether pro-feminist or non-feminist, who either have personal abuse experience, or who make a point of working with and listening to people who do.[14]

Relevance of Abuse Counselling to the Shelter Process

In the summer of 1991, before the escalation of polarizations over who would direct the shelter development process, Regional Woman Abuse Program counsellor Fiona voiced an opinion with which colleagues who remained in the Township appeared to agree.[15] Accountability must be to abused women, not to a political movement or to a professional agency:

> I think the accountability to the woman has to be number one. That is where I see the difference. I am not sure if the shelter movement is the most benign. It can't be ... As a shelter movement, you cannot consider other areas of interest or put other needs first. But I think accountability to the women has to come first, always. (Fiona: RWAP; summer 1991)

During the first six months of shelter operation, the Township shelter board drew on professionalist ideologies to resist the attempts of Regional Woman Abuse Program counsellor Alice to mediate between junior staff who attempted to advocate on behalf of shelter residents, and the shelter director and *her* board. Instead, the shelter director and board went on a weekend retreat, where they were advised by a hired outside expert on how to handle shelter dynamics, that is, on how to handle problematic staff and clients.

A number of respondents active in the Domestic Abuse Committee, including some who participated in the widely criticized 'executive' retreat, interpreted the shelter board's refusal to accept Regional Woman Abuse Program counsellor Alice's offer to mediate, and the formal exclusion of junior staff from decision-making, as indications of the shelter board's increasingly controlling and insular stance – a stance that resulted in the systematic silencing both of survivors who worked in the shelter, and of the women who relied on their services.

These insular and silencing practices coincided with the attempts of an emergent professionalist contingent of Domestic Abuse Committee activists to wear and/or use dual lenses – feminist and professional – and to strategically adjust these lenses to justify progressive monopolizations of power. These power bids were not rooted in a desire to be abusive or controlling; rather, they were rooted in the good intentions of women who wanted to solve the problem of abuse, who wanted, that is, to do something about the Township's 'problem population.' Good intentions notwithstanding, when the shelter board denied abused women a legitimate voice, it violated a central feminist principle. At the same time, it violated a central therapeutic principle.

It is impossible to determine how things might have developed had counsellor Fiona remained in the Township to advise board members during the early months of shelter operation. It is also impossible to determine how things might have developed had the Domestic Abuse Committee allowed or granted traditionally therapeutic counsellors more of a voice. It seems reasonable to suggest, however, that in either instance core activists might have heard that obsessive control needs are derivatives of victimization processes, that examination of how one feels provides insight into how we all feel, that learning to respect and understand our self coincides with learning to respect and understand others, and that learning to resist abuse coincides with learning to resist perpetrating abuse.

Had the Domestic Abuse Committee incorporated these basic therapeutic perspectives into their plan of action, they might have been better able to avoid the spiral of mutual denigration, polarization, and paranoia manifested in the increasingly zero-sum struggle for ownership over the shelter. Had an 'us against them sort of thing' not taken over the Township shelter board, the director and junior staff might all have entered into the implementation phase more ready to air and to receive criticisms, more experienced in the difficult business of collaborative decision-making, and less defensive. Finally, had the Domestic Abuse Committee been more willing to listen to the counsel of all participants, the shelter board might have been less inclined to define the Township's abused and abusive population as something 'exceptional,' as something outside themselves.

This possibility becomes even clearer in the context of the next chapter, which examines the perspectives and practices of law-enforcement, legal, and medical professionals who served on the Domestic Abuse Committee and shelter board.

6

Law Enforcement, Legal, and Medical Intervenors

This chapter examines the abuse-related practices and perspectives of law enforcement, legal, and medical professionals involved with or publicly supportive of the shelter process. As in the previous chapter, my analysis focuses on tensions between pro-feminist and more mainstream therapeutic understandings of abuse, and the effects of these on efforts of Domestic Abuse Committee activists to establish a women's shelter as part of a coordinated community response to *domestic abuse*. Again, I organize the discussion around the four issues that fuelled polarizations: the relevance of gender to abuse; the relevance of alcohol problems to abuse; the relevance of intergenerational family processes to abuse; and the nature of the Township's allegedly exceptional 'problem population.' Again, I treat *violence against women* and *family violence* conceptualizations as contending hegemonies.

The law enforcement, legal, and medical professionals who were interviewed include police inspector Tom, probation and parole officers Mary and Tim, attorney Harriet, law student Brenda, nurse Susan, and physician Kate. With the exception of physician Kate, who displayed Domestic Abuse Committee promotional material on her family clinic bulletin board, all enforcement, legal, and medical professionals who were interviewed were members of the Domestic Abuse Committee, or participated in Domestic Abuse Committee initiatives through the housing co-operative Domestic Violence Committee. Attorney Harriet and probation officer Mary served on the Township Women's Shelter board.

The Police

In August of 1991 I dropped by the Township police precinct with the

aim of arranging a formal interview with inspector Tom and one or
more junior officers. Subsequent to an informal discussion with the
desk sergeant and another junior officer, I obtained an interview with
the inspector. Inspector Tom reported that he had worked in a number
of Canadian communities prior to assuming his post in the Township
in 1954. Though he was not able to attend Domestic Abuse Committee
meetings on a regular basis, Inspector Tom considered himself an
active member of the committee.

Inspector Tom and the two junior officers reported a disjunction
between official police responsibilities and police practice towards
domestic abuse, and they reported disparity between police and official
Domestic Abuse Committee perspectives on the problem. As the
inspector reported, police responsibilities are clear. The police are
responsible for stopping or preventing domestic assaults, for laying
charges against assailants, and for offering assistance to victims.[1]
Junior officers reported that the Township police routinely provided
women with Domestic Abuse Committee information cards.[2] They
also routinely chauffeured abused women to the Regional Women's
Shelter, located approximately forty-five kilometres south of the Township. All three interviewed officers expressed relief that the Domestic
Abuse Committee had obtained funding for what all agreed was a
badly needed Township shelter for women.

I asked the inspector to confirm a number of 'facts' cited in the
Regional Women's Shelter's handbook and the Domestic Abuse Committee's promotional materials – that Township police receive significantly more calls per capita than the Regional average, 10 per one
thousand population compared to 3.2 per thousand; that wife battering is the leading cause of homicide in Canada; and that aside from
traffic violations the most common request for police service is for
domestic violence.[3]

The inspector said he could neither confirm nor disconfirm Township
and Regional disparities in the incidence of domestic violence rates
since separate statistics were not kept on domestic and extra-domestic
assaults at Township or Regional levels. As for homicides, he said that
most were probably domestic related but it would not be correct to say
that most homicides result from wife battering. Domestic homicide victims include current and ex-spouses, siblings, children, parents, live-in
lovers, and the lovers of spouses and live-in partners. As for requests for
police services, according to the inspector these overwhelmingly relate
to property crime, not assault. The inspector backed up this assertion

with data. Out of 235 incidents included in the July 'incident summary' on his desk, 19 were for assault, including 2 for sexual assault, 'with maybe half domestics.' In comparison, 75 were for theft under $1000, 43 were for break and enter, 21 were for theft over $1000, 11 were for fraud, and 18 were for wilful damage.[4] A similar pattern was evident in incident reports for May and June. These reports indicate that assaults account for 10 per cent to 15 per cent of police activity.

The inspector also disputed claims that domestic violence is the most common problem requiring police intervention, but he confirmed claims that the police 'don't like' domestics. According to the inspector, this dislike is a consequence of the dangerous and ambiguous nature of domestic violence:

> I don't know where they are coming up with their numbers. I will say this. It is the number one call you don't want to go on. The others are a breeze compared to that one. If the domestic flares up, then you could be in trouble. As a general rule two police officers respond to a domestic call. That is a policy that has been instituted by the department, because we have had a lot of officers hurt in domestic situations that are cut or assaulted or hit with a baseball bat. That happens a lot. You know, not so many have guns, but a lot of people have baseball bats. (Inspector Tom: TRP; summer 1991)

Inspector Tom said it could be problematic deciding whom to charge when violence is mutual. According to the inspector, the general practice is to charge the male, to assume that the male is the aggressor. He said that this is usually in fact the case, and that, regardless, it is usually the woman who sustains greater injury. He reported that most often, however, there is no visible evidence of assault:

> When you go to a domestic situation, if she says she has been assaulted and you have reasonable probable grounds to believe it, that she in fact has been assaulted, you feel confident about laying a charge. But often, it's her word against his. It always helps to have a bruise, it helps to have evidence. If you don't have a bruise, then you've got to take her word for it. (Inspector Tom: TRP; summer 1991)

The inspector reported that taking a woman's word that she's been assaulted is problematic because so many women change their mind. He reported that a common pattern is for a woman to cooperate in laying a charge, a necessary step in getting a peace bond or restraining order, but then to invite her partner back before the case comes to court. More troublesome than reconciliations are cases in which abused women refuse to cooperate on the witness stand:

> If they don't abide by it, she takes him back, even though it's in violation of the order, it's difficult to say to him, 'Hey, you're under arrest, uh, because you violated the bail restrictions,' when in actual fact she says, 'But I invited him back.' Of course, if he assaults her again, you arrest him for violating bail, and you lay another assault charge.
>
> ...
>
> When a woman takes the stand and says we've reconciled, he's quit drinking, we're doing better – I don't mind that. At least they're facing it, they're trying. But when the woman comes in and swears on the Bible that the assault never happened, that she fell – you can't help but feel a fool. You're standing there as the officer who took this man's freedom away, and you say to yourself, I'm not going to fall for that trap again. An officer who has four or five or half a dozen of them like that becomes cautious. (Inspector Tom: TRP; summer 1991)

The inspector reported that police are most cautious in dealing with repeat calls. He described three kinds of repeat calls – repeat calls to the same couple, repeat calls in which a known male assailant is with a new partner, and repeat calls in which a known female victim is with a new partner. He reported that in some cases officers recognize both partners from previous relationships.

The inspector said that it never fails to amaze rookies that so many families are non-supportive of abused daughters:

> I've had situations where the wife's parents said, 'You made your bed, you lie in it, you're not coming home with me.' I would have thought that having a police officer there, the police officer takes the wife to her mother's or her father's or both, it doesn't matter, that they would take a little bit better attitude – that they would at least say all right, you can stay here for tonight but you've got to sort out your problems tomorrow. I've had situations where there is this police officer standing there and the parents say, 'You're not staying here.' It's hard to comprehend, but I would say this happens in 10 to 25 per cent of the cases. Before women's shelters you saw it more. Then abused women really had no place to go. (Inspector Tom: TRP; summer 1991)

The inspector did not associate these 'exceptional' patterns with social class. He said people on social assistance are no more likely to have trouble with domestic violence than those who are not, and he pointed out that none of the highly publicized domestic homicides occurred among families on social assistance:

> We have just as many calls in other areas of the town as we do in the sub-sidized housing developments. Domestics are not necessarily for the poor or the people on welfare. It takes in a whole gambit of people. Sometimes they surprise you. You stand there, your eyes are rolling, and you say to yourself, I'll never be able to afford a place like this one. Jeez. You start muttering to yourself you know, and figure, what do they have to worry about? (Inspector Tom: TRP; summer 1991)

The inspector also rejected the idea that the incidence of domestic violence was exceptionally high in the Township. He reported that rates of abuse seemed higher in the Township than in some neighbour-ing communities because 'there's a lot of drinking.' He said that in communities across Canada when you find high levels of alcohol con-sumption, you also find high levels of domestic violence. He said many alcoholics are non-abusive. Nevertheless, alcoholism is invari-ably a factor in chronically violent relationships, that is, in 'repeat domestics.' He volunteered that many core Domestic Abuse Commit-tee activists sought to downplay the alcohol and violence link, and he attributed this to their tendency to look at wife or woman abuse in iso-lation. Inspector Tom said that unless one looks at the larger picture, it is easy to get an exaggerated notion of the extent and nature of abuse.

Inspector Tom and junior colleagues were ambivalent about the impact of traditional or sexist attitudes towards male and female roles on abuse. The inspector said that most women in traditional relation-ships, including his wife, cannot comprehend why a woman would put up with physical violence.[5] However, he agreed with core Domes-tic Abuse Committee activists that male dominant beliefs contribute to the abuse of women. He said that abusive males tend to be extremely domineering, and that women who 'tolerate abuse' act as though they believe abuse is their lot. He said that women's toleration of abuse is probably the single most important factor in patterns of recurrent abuse, more important than substance abuse. However, he regarded toleration of abuse more as a personal attribute, related to family his-tory, than as a consequence of traditional gender roles. Inspector Tom maintained that most people in traditional marriages neither justify nor tolerate abuse.

Inspector Tom and junior officers agreed that domestic violence is a problem that cannot be eradicated, or even seriously reduced, through enforcement alone.[6] The inspector lauded the Domestic Abuse Committee for taking a lead in educating women and children to resist abuse. He also lauded the Domestic Abuse Committee's efforts to obtain funding for a shelter. As for counselling services, the inspector said court-mandated programs like the Regional Woman Abuse Program probably help deter recurrence, but that the best counselling available anywhere was provided through Township Family Services, which he described as 'an excellent agency, the best in the Region.'

Inspector Tom and the two junior officers voiced support for the idea of an inter-agency abuse intervention system promoted by the Domestic Abuse Committee. However, inspector Tom reported finding core Domestic Abuse Committee members 'somewhat narrow-minded.' According to inspector Tom, a successful inter-agency response system requires a 'broad perspective,' one which incorporates the knowledge and experience of all agency participants.

Probation and Parole

Two experienced probation and parole officers served the Township, a female and a male. Both worked out of the Township Resource Centre. Officer Mary was active in the development of the Township shelter and served on the Township shelter board through 1992. Both were established residents of the community, and both participated on the Domestic Abuse Committee, though officer Tim did not take an active role in discussions.

The two officers participated in a joint interview in November of 1991. Initially officer Tim cited 'expert opinions' expressed at a recent Regional professional development workshop on domestic violence sponsored by a provincial police and parole association. Officer Mary quickly moved from these official, pro-feminist interpretations to practice. Tim followed her lead. Both officers had worked in parole for over twenty years.[7]

Officers Mary and Tim agreed that probation and parole clients commonly grow up in 'dysfunctional families,' and that they tend to sustain or perpetrate abuse in adult relationships. They further agreed that family patterns related to alcohol and other addictions, not sexism, were the principal causes not only of domestic violence but of criminal activity generally.

The officers reported that their short-term focus was on assisting clients in meeting court-mandated requirements. Over the long term, they encourage lifestyle changes deemed necessary to avoid recidivism.[8] The officers reported that over 80 per cent of their clients are male. Whether male or female, most are on probation for extra-domestic offences, with property crimes the most common. Regardless, most report violence or abuse in a current or past dating or spousal relationship. Reports of mutual violence are most common. The majority also report childhood or family-of-origin abuse. Finally, most struggle with a host of addictions.

Officers Mary and Tim agreed that the most common, and perhaps the root, addiction is addiction to alcohol. Both subscribed to the view that alcoholism is more than a propensity to drink too much, that alcoholism is a disease, a sickness, that is both genetically and socially determined. As officer Tim expressed it, alcoholism plays a causal role in other problems because it distorts the personality. Thus it is not significant whether an alcoholic is drinking at the time of a violent or criminal incident. Officer Tim maintained that many alcoholics are most abusive, most nasty, when they are not drinking. He said that behaviours rooted in alcoholism take on a life of their own, especially in the mid and late stages of this progressive disease. However, officer Tim emphasized that the alcohol-violence link is 'tricky':

> Alcohol is a tricky connection. The people in the field [abuse therapists, etc.] wouldn't acknowledge it as a cause in any way, shape, or form. It is a factor, but its position in a constellation of factors is a little bit confused ... It is a progressive disease that goes through changes of personality. It is characteristic for an alcoholic to become violent, but violence wouldn't characterize every alcoholic. This is more in the late middle stage. (Officer Tim: P&P; summer 1991)

> In the last ten years they kept putting alcohol abuse on the back burner, but all the while it couldn't be completely dismissed. It has come on strong with greater, sophisticated research techniques. Even when someone's parents weren't alcoholics, it's likely that their grandparents were. (Officer Mary: P&P; summer 1991)

According to officers Mary and Tim, substance and family-of-origin

issues are as central to understanding and combating domestic violence as they are to understanding and combating crime. Both maintained that issues of alcoholism and intergenerational *family violence*
drive the dysfunctional power-and-control dynamics characteristic of
abusive relationships:

> There is this power struggle going on, 'sexual jealousy' quote unquote.
> The woman tends to have been isolated. There is always such scrutiny.
> This kind of man has an ego, he wants power, he wants control, control is
> a big issue. You have to look at the control/dysfunctional family theory.
> (Officer Tim: P&P; summer 1991)

> Control is a big part of it. The control comes from being hurt as children.
> Therefore they don't want anyone to hurt them so they get stronger in
> their control. Both men and women, it's not just men who have trouble
> with control. (Officer Mary: P&P; summer 1991)

Both officers maintained that, regardless of gender, violent and
abusive individuals want to overcome abusive patterns and build pro-
ductive lives. Both stressed that alcoholism and other addictions are
treatable through twelve-step programs such as Alcoholics Anonymous, through detox programs, and through individual and group
counselling. As did the child sex abuse counsellors who were interviewed, officer Mary said that the key to positive change is building
self-esteem.

Officer Mary described wife abuse prevention programs as useful,
but short-sighted. She expressed concern that the Regional Woman
Abuse Program ignored or downplayed substance abuse. She stated
that in a two-year follow-up of court-mandated clients of this program,
two of every three men had reverted to violence, and substance problems clearly contributed to this. Officer Mary identified 'refusals' to
address substance issues as a major flaw in the Domestic Abuse Committee's response to the problem of abuse.

Officer Mary also expressed concern that violence and other forms of
abuse by women are overlooked or denied in the Regional Woman
Abuse Program. She said that female-perpetrated violence is not as
common, but that violent women exhibit very similar characteristics to
violent men. She said the 'fact' that a significant minority of women are
violent needs to be incorporated into discussions of *domestic abuse,* and

stated that more resources need to be directed towards programs for men:

> I went shopping with this religious group and I suggested that many domestic situations are alcohol related and one of the women just lambasted me that we are not going to minimize this because of alcohol. She insisted that men must take total responsibility for what they are doing. But I have some on my caseload where women totally victimize men. These are women on for assault (extra-domestic). I have one guy who, from all the people I've talked to, is the victim. It is the woman who has continued to beat him up, to do different things to him. When he had had enough he held her back, but when the police arrived he was the one they charged.
>
> ...
>
> The big problem now is that the men don't have the services. They are already in the court system before they go to the Regional Woman Abuse Program, they're already in trouble. If men have been abused as a child, or if their wife is abusive, who do they go to? Who's ready to believe them? (Officer Mary: P&P; summer 1991)

As for sexism, both officers acknowledged that sexist attitudes are rampant in the probation and parole population. However, neither believed that sexism was the principal cause of abuse. Officer Mary said that it is true that abusers are domineering, but that it is erroneous to equate traditional values with the denigration of women. Both officers maintained that traditional values dictate respect between a man and a woman. As did both the child sex abuse counsellors and inspector Tom, officers Mary and Tim regarded rigid attitudes more as a consequence of negative self-esteem rooted in childhood abuse, than as a cause of abusive behaviour.

Neither officer Mary nor officer Tim seemed to be wearing 'rose-coloured glasses.' Rather, both sought to combat something they regarded as a multifaceted problem through participation in a community-coordinated inter-agency response. Both maintained that an effective abuse intervention system would entail four essential components – women's crisis services, substance abuse services, therapeutic services, and police and probation services. Officer Mary pointed out that efforts were being made to develop this sort of system at both Township and Regional levels. She stated that she and several other core Domestic Abuse Committee activists participated in both initiatives. However, she said that through 1991, talk of a comprehensive inter-agency response system was just that, talk.

Legal Professionals

In the summer of 1991, I interviewed two female legal professionals: attorney Harriet, who practised family law in the Township; and Brenda, a law student who staffed a summer drop-in service for victims of wife abuse at the Township Legal Clinic. Both participated on the Domestic Abuse Committee. Attorney Harriet served on the Township shelter board through 1993.

Attorney Harriet had approximately four years experience practising family law in Ontario, two in the Township, and two in a more urban municipality to the south. Over the previous two years, she had represented approximately one hundred Township residents, men and women. She dealt with divorce, property, support, custody, and paternity cases, often through Legal Aid. She said male clients typically seek rights to joint custody or enforcement of child visitation orders, and that female clients typically seek to obtain or enforce rights to property and support.

Contrary to her statement in the press that 'violence of one kind or another is part of almost everything that comes through the door of my family law practice' (see chapter 2), attorney Harriet reported that physical violence has been an issue in no more than four of her one hundred Township cases. She was convinced that more clients experienced abuse, but said few disclosed spousal violence since there are no financial benefits associated with victimization. On the other hand, she reported that largely non-supportable allegations of child abuse were commonplace. Attorney Harriet stated that, regardless of gender, family law clients engage in a host of evasions, lies, manipulations, and power ploys aimed at the singular goal of making their ex-partner 'pay.'

Attorney Harriet said that the women who do disclose spouse abuse display emotional over-involvement and dependency at levels difficult to comprehend. She said many Township women need counselling on how to handle finances, parenting, and post-divorce relationships, and that women who report abuse desperately need such counselling. She said abused women are especially in need of counselling on how to handle relationships:

These women are very emotionally involved. When they come in, all you see is hate and anger. They tell stories about what they've been through. But they tell me they're still in love. I think, god, you couldn't possibly love this person. They initiate a suit, but then they call like a month, two months later. They tell me, 'Oh well, we're reconciled' ... One client is a twenty-two-year-old girl. She was married to one man, left, got pregnant. She thinks it's her lover's baby, but she's not sure. She starts living with her lover. Later she got pregnant by her lover again. Then she left him because he got into cocaine, and was getting violent. She went back to living with her husband, who had also been abusive. Her husband is suing for custody of the first child, claiming it's his. The lover is suing for custody of the second child, that she's currently carrying ... The lover was just charged with assault. He came after her and trapped her in the car and slammed the car door on her four-and-a-half-month pregnant stomach, saying, 'If I can't be the father to it, no one will.' He's from a bizarre family of troublemakers. In this town there are some family names which pop up all the time. (Attorney Harriet: summer 1991)

Attorney Harriet identified the Township's 'small-town mentality' as a major contributor to what she maintained were exceptionally high levels of abuse. She associated this mentality with the 'rampant sexism' espoused by male clients and accepted by female clients, and also with 'irresponsible' sexual practices. Attorney Harriet maintained that the Township's major recreational activity was adultery, and that levels of promiscuity among youth were 'astounding.' She recounted a number of what she termed 'bizarre' cases involving clients who had sex with multiple partners without birth control. She said in Ontario a woman has to sue her child's father for support in order to qualify for social assistance, and that several clients have had to launch paternity suits against a series of partners before locating their child's father. She said implicated males were astounded to learn that they are responsible for biological offspring regardless of the sexual behaviour of a woman. She stated that, in the Township, neither women or men were assuming responsibility for birth control and that neither men nor women approached parenting responsibly. She attributed this to the generally low educational and income levels of Township residents.

Attorney Harriet was one of the shelter board's strongest opponents of the 'alternate' shelter site. Her objections to the site were mainly that the proposed 'gift' was a takeover bid. She seemed less concerned that the site was 'inherently stigmatizing.' Indeed, attorney Harriet made it clear from the onset that she regarded the Township as a 'problem population.' If anyone on the shelter board was wearing 'rose-coloured glasses,' it was certainly not her.

Law student Brenda grew up in the Township. In the previous year, she had worked at an urban clinic affiliated with her law school in another province, where she counselled numerous abused women, and where she participated in the defence of three men charged with wife assault. In the spring of 1991, Brenda applied for and obtained the grant that funded the Township Legal Clinic's 1991 domestic violence drop-in initiative, a resource centre – affiliated service. She had single-handedly promoted the drop-in initiative through wife abuse posters, flyers, and media ads, and by mid-July she had counselled about twenty-five women.[9]

In contrast to attorney Harriet, Brenda very much liked small-town living. However, she said that this was not what the Township currently provided. As did many other long-term residents, Brenda attributed a high incidence of social problems less to the attitudes or characteristics of residents than to processes of social change. Brenda maintained that the tax base simply didn't allow for such amenities as a transportation system or an indoor sports arena, and that this helped account for high levels of abuse. Brenda said small towns were dependent on the personal initiative of residents, and that newer residents didn't understand this. She said these problems were compounded by the 'fact' that so many residents, both established residents and newcomers, were stressed by long commutes to work in the more urbanized south. She said they were even more stressed by high debt loads:

> I've had clients from both the high-end and the low-end subdivisions, and they both have outrageous debt problems. It doesn't start the violence pattern, but it certainly makes it more frequent. And probably more severe. (Brenda: TLC; summer 1991)

Brenda regarded economic factors as salient, but she rejected the idea that the economic characteristics of Township residents were a major factor in the incidence of serious violence. Rather, Brenda saw abuse as rooted in family experience. Both she and attorney Harriet recounted experiences with women who wanted help but who resisted laying charges. Both reported working with women who obtained a restraining order or peace bond who then invited their estranged partner to violate the order. Both reported high levels of emotional dependency, and negative self-esteem. The difference was that attorney Harriet saw these as exceptional patterns, related to the special characteristics of Township residents, and Brenda regarded them as typical of abused women generally.

Brenda said that at the urban clinic and in the Township she could spot an abused woman from the minute she walked through the door – not because of visible bruising, which you almost never saw, but because of the haunted uncertain look in the abused woman's eyes. She said women at the urban clinic told the same horrendous stories as women in the Township. In both contexts, women typically claimed to be *only* victims of emotional abuse, control, or obsessive jealousy until you won their confidence. Then most admitted to having been hit once or maybe twice, or actually from time to time over a number of years.

As did attorney Harriet, Brenda believed that abused women needed counselling, but she stressed neither life skills nor relationship dynamics. Brenda didn't have 'answers,' but she believed it was important to address the intergenerational nature of abuse. She regarded court-mandated counselling for men and supportive counselling for women and children as essential to breaking intergenerational cycles. Brenda stressed her conviction that intervenors cannot ignore children, since children who grow up in abusive families are the abused and abusive women and men of the next generation:

> Large numbers of these men come from violent homes where they've seen their mother's get beaten up by their father, or mentally abused, or a combination. And they think that this is acceptable behaviour. So they've got this violent tendency. Women, too, they're usually from violent families. By and large right now what we see is women who have grown up in violent homes, and have worked their asses off, seeing their moms abused, to be the perfect little girl for dad. They think, if mom can't do it right maybe I can. And I think that gets them into a relationship in which they think it's OK to be beaten, physically or emotionally, or both. And even though they may get out of one violent relationship, they go right back into another one.
>
> ...
>
> And I think that's why it's really important that the kids who are in violent situations, and who get out, get counselling ... But I don't think it's always a cycle. I guess that's what makes it harder, because when it's not a cycle, how do you explain it? Obviously it has to start somewhere. And

where does it start? I don't have those answers. But as much as possible, let's stop it at this generation. (Brenda: TLC; summer 1991)

Medical Practitioners

Two medical practitioners participated in the study. The first was Kate, a physician who participated in a single interview in the summer of 1991. Physician Kate actively promoted the Domestic Abuse Committee – affiliated abuse intervention services at her family practice clinic in one of the Township's smaller towns. She had been practising medicine in the Township for approximately seven years. The second was nurse Susan, a housing co-operative Domestic Violence Committee activist and a core respondent throughout the research process. Nurse Susan had worked for several years in emergency at the Regional hospital. At the time of the interviews, she worked with developmentally and emotionally handicapped adults through a Regional agency.

Physician Kate operated her family practice clinic in a small town on the northern periphery of the Township. She reported that she had grown up in a typical small-town Ontario community, a town considerably different from the 'backwoods' community that housed her family medical clinic. Physician Kate said that if the Township was the poor cousin of the Region, as people commonly asserted, then this town was the black sheep of the Township.

Physician Kate said she believed that abuse levels in the Township were higher than average, and attributed this to two factors: high levels of alcohol consumption and sexism.[10] She said her knowledge of abuse was based on accounts of victims, and on reports provided by victims' neighbours and relatives. In agreement with police inspector Tom, she said rates of abuse were no different among the more affluent newer residents than among established residents. However, she noted some class patterns. She said male abusers seem almost inevitably to come from abusive families, regardless of socio-economic status, but that women who reported intergenerational abuse were overwhelmingly working-class. She said physical abuse in middle-class families is equally pervasive, but that it tends to be less severe and more hidden:

> I definitely see a fairly strong family history in the people I see. It is very rare for me to find someone who is an abuser and he has not come from a family where he has witnessed physical abuse. As for the women, some yes and some no. I would find that, one shouldn't use these terms, but the

women from the lower socio-economic groups in my practice – often it went on in their homes. The women from the higher socio economic groups, and they are often employed and this and that, it often did not happen in their home and has slowly and insidiously crept into their relationship. And no one is more shocked than they are about where they find themselves.

...

As for severity, I would say it is less obviously physical in the middle classes. The women with the bruised necks and black eyes or where the neighbours have told me she doesn't come out for a whole week, usually they are from lower socio-economic groups although you do see it at a higher one as well. Middle-class women don't share it with you, they will hide it like crazy. (Physician Kate: summer 1991)

Physician Kate reported that working-class abusers avoid interaction with herself and other professionals, but that abusers in middle-class families are over-involved in issues like their wives' birth control or their children's inoculations – responsibilities most men entrust to their wives. As did Regional Woman Abuse Program counsellor Fiona, she described abusive men as too charming, too nice, implicitly as Jekyll and Hyde types:

In the lower socio-economic groups, men would never come in. I would never even see them. But the middle and upper class that beat their wives and kids, they are always in here. They are really into what is happening with their woman or their kid, too much so. It is an over-involvement. It is not appropriate, it really sticks out as being inappropriate.

...

You know, he's too wonderful and it is not real. Prince Charming. They are just too self-confident. They are asking about things that they have no business asking. Any man I have ever had come in with his wife or girlfriend or fiancée to discuss birth control is beating her. It is really bizarre. I am batting 100 per cent. He wants to come in to impress me with how wonderful and supportive and charming he is. (Physician Kate: summer 1991)

Physician Kate reported that, regardless of class, physical abuse was almost always alcohol related. As did officer Tim, physician Kate expressed ambivalence about how to interpret the alcohol abuse and substance abuse link. She noted that at least half of all people with substance problems are not violent, and, as did many Domestic Abuse Committee members, she lamented the tendency for abused women to focus blame on alcohol. Nevertheless, physician Kate prominently displayed substance abuse programs on her 'abuse services' bulletin board:

> The role of alcohol is huge, huge, huge. I know they will say that alcohol will not cause abuse and you can treat the alcoholism and the abuse continues or you can stop the abuse and the alcoholism continues, but in my experience it is present far more than 90 per cent of the time.
>
> ...
>
> It can be in both partners but most often it's the male. It never happens when he is not drinking. It only happens when he is drinking and therefore, of course, it focuses all her attention of blame on the alcohol. (Physician Kate: summer 1991)

Along with the pro-feminist activists at the core of the Domestic Abuse Committee, physician Kate saw sexism as a primary issue. Moreover, as did attorney Harriet, she regarded sexual promiscuity as somehow related to sexism. She reported that she heard stories of girlfriends being slapped in the halls of the high school and at parties, and that more than once she had witnessed boys slap girls on the street outside the convenience store that served as the town's major teen hangout. She said that across social statuses in the Township, regardless of whether the families involved had been long-term residents or were newly arrived, teens seemed to accept the idea that boyfriends would hit their girlfriends if they 'got out of line.' She said nearly all her adolescent patients were sexually active and that the girls told her they could neither refuse to participate in sex nor insist that their boyfriends wear condoms – that if they did, they wouldn't have a boyfriend. Physician Kate said most adolescent girls in the Township considered this unimaginable.

Physician Kate believed that higher than average rates of *domestic abuse* coincided with what attorney Harriet called the 'mentality' of Township residents. However, physician Kate emphasized her conviction that abuse and the sexist attitudes associated with abuse were equally common among newcomers and established residents. She maintained that the major focus had to be education, most especially education of children and youth. As did law student Brenda, physician Kate wanted to see services for children and youth as a central feature of the Township's community-coordinated response to abuse. Along with police inspector Tom and law student Brenda, she emphasized the pervasiveness of these problems across social statuses.

Nurse Susan, who saw herself 'more as a humanist ... than a feminist,' recounted her emergency-room experience in an informal discussion, recorded in field notes in September of 1992. As did physician Kate, she noted the tendency for chronic abusive patterns to be intergenerational and for chronic domestic violence to coincide with alcohol abuse. As was the case with both physician Kate and attorney Harriet, nurse Susan was also troubled by abused women's acceptance of violence, and by their willingness to engage in what was considered inappropriate sexual behaviour.

Nurse Susan reported that she had dealt with women who sought emergency care again and again with serious injuries, who, instead of expressing fury at having been abused, expressed concern about the welfare of their abusers. She recounted a story of walking into an examining room to find a battered woman engaged in sexual intercourse with the male who hours ago had broken her collarbone, bloodied her face, and knocked out her teeth. She recounted another story of a chronically battered women who engaged in sex in the recovery room hours after giving birth. As did Regional Sex Abuse Program counsellors, nurse Susan associated these phenomena with 'boundary problems.' However, she stressed that 'battered' women seeking emergency hospital care are exceptional, outside the norm. She believed that most abused women are closer to normal on a continuum of abuse; and that, on one level or another, abuse affects most women and most people:

> I don't think these women are typical of abused women in society, they're extreme cases. I don't go along with victim blaming, but, you know, a lot of the nurses lost sympathy. It's hard to respect someone who doesn't seem to respect herself. But these women have probably been abused since childhood. It's unbelievable how much child physical and sexual abuse occurs in problem populations, like the special needs clients I currently work with. (Nurse Susan: DVC; summer 1992)

Nurse Susan acknowledged that women could also be abusive, even violent, and she vehemently rejected the idea that all men, or even all abusive men, were villains. However, along with core Domestic Abuse Committee activists, nurse Susan believed that males are the primary abusers. Moreover, as did physician Kate and the majority of core

Domestic Abuse Committee activists, nurse Susan regarded attitudes as a major cause of abuse – both sexist attitudes and, more generally, those attitudes that make violence acceptable. Consequently, together with physician Kate, law student Brenda, police inspector Tom, probatoin and parole officers Mary and Tim, and attorney Harriet, she regarded counselling and education as central to any attempt to reduce or prevent abuse in the Township.

Township Residents and Mainstream Interventions

Surveyed residents displayed weaker support for law enforcement, legal, and medical interventions than for therapeutic interventions. Most doubted that any of these front-line services could be very effective in stopping or alleviating abuse. However, respondents most in need of abuse intervention, those reporting violence, substance abuse, and relationship distress, were likely to value all components of the Domestic Abuse Committee's proposed inter-agency community-coordinated abuse intervention system. (See tables 4, 11, 12, and 13.)

Mainstream Intervenors and the Shelter Process

Interviewed professionals working in enforcement, law, and medicine differed on the emphasis they placed on sexism, and they differed on whether they regarded the Township's population as exceptional. Otherwise, they presented the same account over and over again. These front-line professionals described *domestic abuse* as pathological, usually intergenerational, and usually alcohol related. They generally agreed that women's tolerance of abuse is important to the establishment and reproduction of abusive patterns. They also generally agreed that a coordinated community response system was needed, and that a shelter for women was an important component of this system. None were wearing rose-coloured glasses. All recognized that there was no singular solution to abused women's problems, or to the problem of abuse, generally.

Despite their numeric strength on the Domestic Abuse Committee, mainstream professionals had a minimal influence on the shelter process, especially when their opinions contradicted those of pro-feminist community development workers and woman abuse professionals. When they agreed with the committee's position that attitudinal change was important to preventing and alleviating abuse, and that levels of abuse were exceptional because residents held the wrong attitudes, their opinions were championed. When they asserted that women and men alike engage in violence, that substance abuse is an important component of the problem, and that levels and correlates of abuse in the Township were typical rather than exceptional, their opinions were ignored.

Two mainstream professionals, attorney Harriet and officer Mary, were nominated to the Township shelter board. Attorney Harriet identified herself as a feminist, publicly and in a personal interview. However, she was not ideologically or politically involved with feminism prior to her involvement with the Domestic Abuse Committee. Nor was she previously involved with the issue of abused or battered women. As was true of several members of the Township shelter board, attorney Harriet was essentially a young middle-class professional eager to take an active and influential role in the public life of her community. Her understandings of abuse as simultaneously pathological and rooted in sexism coincided with a disdain for the 'small-town mentality' of Township residents that many of her urban-based colleagues shared. These women's somewhat questionable regard for Township residents was reinforced during struggles to protect the shelter from the influence of interfering 'old boys,' and it was reinforced even more during struggles to institutionalize professional rather than 'naïvely idealistic' standards and policies at the new shelter. In both instances, it was not the intent of attorney Harriet or those who shared her perspective to subvert feminist principles. Attorney Harriet's intent was to promote progressive education and personal competence. Her intent was to help bring the Township out of its social sexist time warp.

In contrast, officer Mary viewed abuse through a therapeutic lens. Officer Mary had been active in community affairs all her life, as a law enforcement professional, as a parent, and as a church member. In all these spheres, she made a point of promoting tolerance and understanding. Officer Mary wholeheartedly endorsed the Township Resource Centre's community development mandate. She agreed that experts can facilitate but not cause progressive change, at individual or at community levels. Officer Mary did not identify herself as a feminist, but she agreed with a number of core feminist contentions. She agreed with the principle that abused women need and deserve support and respect, and she agreed that it was important to include abused women in the development and running of intervention services.

Unlike other core Domestic Abuse Committee activists, officer Mary did not believe it was necessary that her view, indeed that any particular view, 'win.' Consequently, she managed to remain on good terms with participants in both camps during the struggle for ownership over the shelter development process. When a new set of opposing camps emerged during the early months of shelter operation, Mary quietly resigned from the shelter board and redirected her energies to other activities, again without alienating parties on either side. Officer Mary did not aim to save or dramatically restructure the Township or the world. Her intent was to facilitate change in the lives of troubled individuals and families.

Shortly after the opening of the Township shelter, an inherently contradictory pro-feminist/problem population construction of abuse prevailed. This contradictory construction prevailed despite core actors' successful efforts to keep male community leaders suspected of harbouring stigmatizing attitudes from meaningful participation in the shelter initiative. It prevailed because a highly competent and well-intended contingent of middle-class, urban-reared professionals fell prey to an escalating spiral of bad faith and coercion, in which 'interacting at' replaced 'interacting with' (Denzin, 1984). These actors drew on feminist principles, on community development principles, and on professional principles – on whatever principles that worked – to justify their bids to maintain control over an increasingly out-of-control situation. During this, the voices of those promoting a broad perspective, openness, and accommodation went unheard. In the process, the Domestic Abuse Committee's shelter board lost sight of their goals and values; they forgot whom the shelter served, and what it hoped to accomplish.

In the Township, ideologies were allowed to exert influence only when they served to legitimate bids to assert, maintain, and extend control. Participants across the feminist / non-feminist divide were listened to only when their views supported these practices.

7

Victims, Perpetrators, and Survivors

This chapter examines seven personal accounts of abuse provided by women and men who had successfully overcome serious and even life-threatening forms of partner violence, or who were engaged in efforts to achieve this. These women and men were encountered in a variety of research contexts, in a social environment in which everyone seemed to be talking about abuse, and in which everyone seemed motivated to contribute to finding ways to overcome and prevent abuse. None of the seven was a core respondent in the shelter process. All were recruited from the Township's 'audience' of residents, and all had current or previous experience with various abuse interventions.[1]

The accounts are presented as examples of the types of realities that inform the truth-claims of abuse experts who participate in or endorse pro-feminist or *violence against women*, and *family violence* or therapeutic analyses of abuse. The accounts were not gathered, however, in activist or therapeutic encounters. They were gathered in conversations between a researcher who presented herself as someone who had read a great deal about abuse but who had not yet come to closure on its nature, dynamics, causes, and consequences; and individuals who knew abuse intimately as survivors, victims, and perpetrators. As an academic researcher, I was unavoidably in a hierarchical 'expert' position in relation to the women and men I interviewed. However, I was an odd sort of expert. I was an expert who contended that I was in need of learning, and that only people who had personal experience with abuse could teach me. The individuals who shared their stories seemed to embrace this contention.[2]

The seven stories touch on a number of problematic issues addressed in the abuse literature and that come up in account after account of abuse provided by activists, professionals, and survivors involved in the shelter process – intergenerational violence, incest, substance abuse, coercive control, sexism, promiscuity, jealousy, grief, hope, love, honour, and anger. The accounts were not selected, however, because they exemplify these themes. Nor were they selected with the aim of validating either a *violence against women* or a *family violence* conceptualization of abuse. They were selected because they provide insights into an aspect of the problem that Township residents agreed was a primary goal of intervention – survival, a hoped-for or achieved existential state in which abuse is experienced as a past, rather than a current, reality.[3]

My primary analytic stance is social interactionist. This stance is guided by the assumption that abuse is embedded in a complex interplay of emotional and cognitive processes lodged simultaneously in historically given social structures and in personal, or rather interpersonal, experiences.[4] On the basis of these assumptions, I focus on two theoretically related constructs, emotionality and agency. The emotionality of the self is an implicit theme in *family violence* and therapeutic perspectives on abuse. Structures of domination notwithstanding, abuse is analysed as an expressive process, rooted in social stress and social dis-ease.[5] Agency is an explicit theme in feminist or *violence against women* perspectives. Abuse appears as an instrumental process, rooted in male dominance and female resistance. These purportedly 'either/or' constructions frame theorizing on the most contentious of all abuse issues – the gendered nature of abuse.

Emotionality and the Self

In the abuse literature and in this study, alcoholism and domestic violence appear as empirically related phenomena, that is, as phenomena that frequently co-occur.[6] Norman Denzin provides separate but complementary analyses of these phenomena (Denzin, 1984, 1987). He argues that both are rooted in negative emotionality, that both are grounded in power and control orientations, that both escalate through schismogenic processes that exacerbate hostility, resentment, and hatred, and that both are maintained through reciprocal structures of bad faith. He argues that both are solvable through 'authentic' confrontation with the reality of the abusive situation, and through removal of the self from this situation.

Denzin maintains that the meanings of the violent self are given through violence, denials of violence, self-deceptions, projections of blame, and deceit (Denzin, 1984). Perpetrators (usually male) and victims (usually female) both participate in and maintain these processes – both act and react to an increasingly distorted and self-distorting reality.[7] A series of schisms, conflicts, and contradictions lodged in emergent, spurious, and fearful spontaneous interactions take over. These interactions lead to the collapse of the system, or to an awful stabilization of violence. When violence is stabilized, mutual hostility, jealousy, and hatred rule. Initially each spouse, and eventually each family member, sees the other as an object, and sees the self as an object of the other. Possibilities of empathy and mutual understanding are annihilated. Interacting at replaces interacting with. Family members find themselves bound together in a field of negative experience racked by 'inflicted' out-of-control emotions, drunken binges, spurts of insanity, and emotional withdrawals or prolonged absences. Violent and insane thoughts 'grip the entire family,' who live 'together and alone' in 'a nightmare of overt and suppressed violence' (Denzin, 1984: 503).

Alcoholism feeds these processes. Denzin refers to the alcoholic as 'his majesty the baby,' as s/he who must rule the world his own way (Denzin, 1987).[8] Denzin's basic premise is that alcoholics are trapped within inner structures of negative emotionality originating in a childhood of abuse or neglect, and that these traumas produce self-centredness and self-narcissism. Initially, the alcoholic drinks to regain a self that was lost or never experienced. Through alcohol, he produces a distorted image of himself as omnipotent and invincible. Behind this façade is a self trapped in a world of painful self-feelings, painful emotional experiences, and painful social interactions. The alcoholic always blames others when things go wrong. Paradoxically, he clings to the belief that he can overcome adversity by force of willpower, self-manipulation, deception, lies, or economic coercion. The alcoholic clings to the myth of invincibility in a world that is out of control, in a world marked by schisms, emotional paradoxes, and ruined relationships.

Denzin maintains that processes of domestic *family violence* can only be altered when the wife or spouse of violence, or implicitly the adult or adolescent child of violence, breaks free of the prevailing structures of bad faith, especially beliefs that she can control the violence, or that she somehow causes the violence. Neither violence nor passivity facilitates this break. It can only occur through a confrontation with the 'authentic' reality of the situation and a movement out of that situation. A movement out of violence allows the victimized spouse or the adult/

adolescent child to begin restructuring her relationship with herself. This restructuring entails establishing relationships with and to a 'normal' interactive world, a world not mired in abuse. Similarly, a movement out of alcoholism becomes possible when the alcoholic's structures of bad faith collapse, when the alcoholic is forced to relinquish his self-centredness and desire for and belief in control. For this to occur, the alcoholic must confront the 'authentic' reality of his situation; he must surrender to the facticity of alcoholism. Only after the shattering, relinquishment, and surrender of the alcoholic self can a new self, and a new interactive world, be structured.

Denzin's phenomenologies provide a powerful portrait of deviant, pathologically dysfunctional interactive realities, of processes that progressively bind interactants to these realities, and of processes that facilitate escape or recovery. They are fraught with problems, however.

First, there are epistemological problems with Denzin's concept 'authentic reality.' Denzin unquestionably agrees that definitions of situations as authentic or inauthentic are ideologically laden; they are interpretations of reality, not direct perceptions.[9] It is through interactions with others – co-participants in the AA fellowship, abuse counsellors, shelter workers, family members, friends, colleagues, and the media – that actors constantly define and redefine their current and past realities. As John McKendy (1992) points out, it is through this ideological processing that actors formulate cognitive understandings of what they themselves 'know' in embodied, inchoate, and barely articulate ways. What Denzin and McKendy both assert, and what I would agree with, is that 'authentic' embodied reality is something that language, and therefore ideology, fail to fully capture. It is this 'authentic' existentially present emotional reality that Denzin theorizes must be confronted in order to break free of abuse. And it is both cognitively and at this 'gut level' that we assumedly recognize our own and others' 'bad faith.'[10] Unfortunately, interpreting one's emotions, especially one's negative emotions, is as problematic as the notion of authentic reality itself. Consequently, while we often think we 'see' other people's bad faith, it is only in retrospect that we come to see our own.[11]

Second, Denzin's phenomenologies of abuse are problematic because they fail to address the importance of power in spousal or family relationships. Denzin acknowledges the gendered nature of abuse, making it clear that most violence is male-driven, but he does not incorporate gender into his analyses. His phenomenologies imply that partners who resist, tolerate, or accommodate abuse share responsibility, implicitly equal responsibility, for a reality that renders count-less women and children literally trapped, literally powerless. This powerlessness is dramatically evidenced in domestic homicide data, data which demonstrate that leaving an abuser can be lethal (Dobash et al., 1992; Gartner, 1993). In the Township, three of the five highly publicized domestic homicides occurred in the context of relationship breakdown. Abusive realities are interactive, but this does not mean that partners share responsibility, certainly not equal responsibility, for outcomes.

Third, Denzin's phenomenologies are problematic because they imply that agency and emotionality are opposites. Participants appear to assert agency only if and when they leave abusive situations, only if and when they enter 'normal' as opposed to 'sick' interactive worlds. In the realm of lived experience, emotionality and agency are more 'fused' (Johnson, 1977; Stets, 1988). Abusers commonly report that they feel 'out-of-control' during alcoholic binges or violent episodes, but few report being intoxicated or violent all the time. Most appear to choose when and with whom to engage in drinking binges, and when and with whom to behave in a violent or out-of-control manner. Abusers inflict 'out-of-control' abuse both because 'I lost it' and because 'she asked for it.' Conversely, women remain with or return to abusers for a number of 'valid' reasons. Some return or remain because they love their partners, because they value phases of emotional and sexual inti-macy as much as they abhor violence, because they feel the abuser is a good father, because they value family ties, or because they believe that their own actions are provocative. Others remain or return because they fear that their partner will commit suicide or inflict lethal harm if they attempt to leave, because they have limited means of self-support, and so forth.[12] There is nothing inherently distorted, self-deceiving, or inauthentic in these reasonings. Emotionally charged decisions to express, tolerate, or cope with abuse are not necessarily 'bad faith.'

Agency and the Self

Anthony Giddens provides a interactionist theory of agency that facili-tates recognition of abusive men and abused women as responsible agents regardless of whether they inflict, accommodate, resist, tolerate, or flee abuse. As theorized by Giddens, agency refers to the continuous flow of conduct of knowledgeable subjects in the ongoing process of events in the world (Giddens, 1979). As does Denzin, Giddens contends that all participants contribute to the construction and maintenance of

ongoing interactive realities, and, structures of domination notwithstanding, all subjects share responsibility for outcomes. According to
Giddens, actors cease to be agents, cease to share responsibility, only
in situations so pathologically confining that even suicide is impossible (Giddens, 1979: 149). An abuser's decision to inflict out-of-control
emotions and actions, and a victim's decision to remain with him
despite the abuse, consequently appear as authentic, responsible, and
(Giddens insists) knowledgeable choices. These choices are based on
actors' own appraisals of the reality of their situations, appraisals that,
in the current social context, incorporate mutual awareness of women's
increasing insistence upon and men's persisting resistance to forms of
intimacy premised on gender equality (Giddens, 1992).

Denzin's theory of emotionality facilitates recognition of the ways
non-volitional aspects of the self can come to dominate interpersonal
relations. His theorizing facilitates recognition of the possibility that
actors and situations become overwhelmingly confusing, overwhelmingly mired in negative emotions, 'sick.' Giddens's theory of agency
facilitates recognition of the possibility that abusers and victims choose
to behave abusively, and to tolerate or resist abuse, knowing a great
deal about what they are doing, cognizant of the historically constituted but decidedly real insecurities and inadequacies of human gendered existence. His theory facilitates recognition of the normality and
authenticity of 'deviant' interactive worlds.

Stories of Abuse

The stories presented in this chapter rely as much as possible on the
tape-recorded testimony of the seven respondents. As previously
stated, my aim is not to validate a *violence against women* or a *family violence* conceptualization of abuse; most of the accounts support ele-
ments of both. Rather than support or confront ideologies, my aim is to
provide a glimpse of the individuals themselves – individuals who
struggle with the lived reality of abuse in their day-to-day lives. As
much as possible, I allow each interviewed woman and man to say for
herself or himself whether abuse is intentional, whether 'the family of
violence' or the 'self in violence' is deviant or 'sick,' whether women
are also abusive, and whether staying, leaving, or reconciling is a
knowledgeable and responsible action.[13] The data, however, do not
and cannot speak for themselves: I have made minor editorial changes
to protect the anonymity of respondents and the community; I have

selected and organized the quotes; and I have chosen the analytic focus.[14] I have engaged in these interpretive practices with respect, remembering – and I ask my readers to remember – that it was human subjects whom I sat amidst and to whom I listened. It was human subjects who gave of themselves these stories.[15]

Anne

Anne was one of a number of abuse survivors encountered at the 1991 Abuse Awareness Workshop. She participated in a formal taped interview in 1991, and in an informal follow-up discussion in 1992. The interview took place at Anne's home. At the time of the interviews, Anne was in her early thirties. Ten years previously, she had exited a physically and emotionally abusive marriage, an exit facilitated by support provided by her parents and by the Regional shelter.

Anne reported that she grew up in a loving and supportive middle-class family – a family dramatically different from the hard-living, hard-loving, and hard-drinking family of the man she fell madly in love with at age seventeen. Anne erroneously believed that she could recreate the world she grew up in if she loved her husband enough, if she handled him as he needed to be handled:

> I came from a wonderful home. Ward and June Cleaver. I mean we all lined up in a row and waved goodbye to my father, the four of us. We all had names on our lunch bags. I came from, from what I could say, was a perfect home. Too perfect. In that I believed that marriage was wonderful, blissful. My parents never fought. They never raised their voices. They never had any kind of argument in front of us children. I think, this is what I thought marriage was.
> ...
> Ah, but my ex came from a family of abuse. It was totally different. His mother was battered. His father was a trucker. Had affairs. He was a fairly attractive man, and a drunk. Both parents drank, and they would fight. His mum and dad would fight, always ... My ex-husband, he hated his father ... I remember his mother telling me how he got a butcher knife when he was twelve and he was going to kill his father for hurting her. (Anne, July 1991)

For three years, before and after getting married, Anne tolerated physical abuse, psychological abuse, and pathological jealousy. Anne reported that her parents had raised her to make her own decisions, to take responsibility for her own choices. Despite this, Anne allowed her ex-husband to control her and to dictate to her. She tolerated the abuse, not because she thought it was her duty to do so, and not because she felt that she in any way deserved to be abused, but because she loved her husband:

> Our relationship was abusive right from the beginning. He didn't abuse me physically to the point where I was beat. I knew how to stay clear of that. But my safety was always threatened. And he was suicidal, in that he would take bottles of pills, and three o'clock in the morning he would make me watch him kill himself. And it would be my fault. Ah, he would say things like, go ahead leave, leave. Get out, get out, get out. And I would grab my coat to leave and he would stand in front of the door and he would say [taking a towering pose], do you think you're getting away from me? And things like you'll never get away from me ... And jealousy. Like really really really jealous. I couldn't even watch certain people on TV. I remember going to a bar, and I guess the drummer looked at me. We had to leave. Just stupid. I remember sometimes one of his friends came over. One particular friend and I wasn't allowed to come out of my room. I wasn't allowed in the room because I *wanted* this person. And yet he [husband] was the only person I had ever slept with in my life [laughs]. But then, of course, he was out around doing his thing, being unfaithful, so he had to think that I was. He was just like his father.
> ...
> You know, I was young. That has so much to do with it. I was so young, and so impressionable, in my early years of teenage-hood, that I got trapped. Like, I couldn't see past my nose, on my face, I was so in love with him. I couldn't see. I tolerated the stupidest things because I loved him. (Anne, July 1991)

Anne reported that one of the reasons she tolerated the abuse was because she found her ex-husband's family extremely exciting. Anne said her mother-in-law was willing to put up with seemingly anything, from her husband and from her children. There were no boundaries, no limits. Consequently, things always felt 'alive.' For a time, this hyper-reality was irresistible:

> And, you know, his mother was so permissive. She was too permissive, with everything and everybody. Anything was fine, anything was OK.

She encouraged things that, you just don't encourage. Like driving the car before you get a licence. Like sleeping together in her home. She had so many problems in her own marriage that she couldn't make rules for her children because they were the only thing that she had that was stable. If she was fighting with her children, then she had nothing. If her children were mad at her, and her husband was gone, she had nothing. You know, she was a wonderful, wonderful lady, and I still love her dearly, but there are some things you just shouldn't encourage, shouldn't allow. (Anne, July 1991)

Shortly after the birth of her daughter, Anne recognized that she should not and could not continue to live with abuse. She recognized that doing so would destroy her personal integrity. More importantly, she realized that doing so would burden her infant daughter with an intergenerational legacy of violence and abuse:

It was when my daughter was born, that I realized. Gee, is this the life-style I want for my child? All of my parenting, that my parents taught me, came to me. I thought, hey, this way of life has been a lot of fun for two years, because I'm a teenager. But I remember thinking, a light came on, you know. I thought that this was a wonderful way of life and a great family, but do I want to raise my daughter like this? Do I want her to live this kind of life? (Anne, July 1991)

Anne reported that she exited twice. The first time, she went to her parents, who were totally supportive. The second time, however, she went to the Regional Women's Shelter because she recognized that the shelter staff would know about things her parents had no way of knowing. For Anne, the shelter was highly empowering. Shelter staff told her that she must make her own choice, but that if she decided to leave, they would provide practical and emotional support – mirroring messages she received from her parents. Fortunately, by the time Anne went to the shelter, she had already made the painful transition from indecision to decision:

My parents were totally supportive of whatever decision I made. And I stayed in my relationship with him far longer than I would have, out of fear of telling my parents that I screwed up. You know, my father spent all this money on my wedding. And he told me not to marry him. Not told me, but he had suggested that he didn't feel that it was a good relationship, but that it was my decision. So I made the decision, and I screwed up, and I couldn't go to them after six months and say, it's not working ... But my father never said one word of recrimination. Never once.

...

You know, indecision is the worst decision. Living in indecision. The whole time I was with him, I was living in indecision. Once a decision is made, then you can work with it, you can do what you have to do. But when you have no decision at all, you're living in limbo ... I went to the shelter because I knew I needed to learn about abuse. I found it to be a learning tool, for me. When I went in there, I thought that I was, you know, that my life was over. It was so terrible. I was twenty-two. I knew the situation I lived in was hopeless, and I thought I had the worst life of anyone on the face of the earth. And I think I was really feeling sorry for myself. And by going there, I really opened my eyes, as to what I did have going for me. I realized I wasn't as sad as I thought I was. I had a job. I already had day-care. I was young. I realized that I could be assertive. And I knew what direction I was going in. I knew that I was never going back. There were a lot of women there who didn't have all of those, all the things I had. By the end of the third week, I felt guilty staying there. (Anne, July 1991)

In retrospect, Anne saw abuse as a lifestyle choice. She rejected the idea that abuse is rooted in gender roles. She said she had seen too many reciprocally violent relationships to accept the idea that women are always the victim. Anne emphasized that abuse is typically both intergenerational and alcohol related. Anne believed that people born into abusive realities have difficulty seeing how to extricate themselves. Moreover, she believed that they have difficulty wanting to extricate themselves, especially when they abuse substances. Anne based her assertions on observations made in both her first husband's and her current husband's extended families:

My present husband is from an alcoholic family, too, and I know for a fact that one of his brothers is abusive. Why his wife married him, I'll never know, but she came from abusive relationship after abusive relationship and they both beat on each other. No, she doesn't just fight back. I've seen her hit first, because she was angry. And I've seen her goad him and goad him. A lot of it has to do with alcohol abuse ... I tried to talk to her. Why do you choose these abusive relationships. Well, her mother. She was raped by her mother, a single parent. Her father had left when she was four years old. But I don't think she has any idea. She drinks. I couldn't get her to go to the shelter. She says they take your welfare cheque to pay for your board. So you don't have money to go to bingo, and you don't get money to drink. All you get is food and a place to stay, you don't get anything else. She said why go to the shelter, the abuse isn't that bad.

...

I see my ex-husband's brother's wife with black eyes, and I remember her telling me when we were young, 'I don't know how you can take that.' She was fourteen or fifteen at the time. She said, I'd never put up with that. And she's still married to her husband and has three kids. And, it's unbelievable really. There's no question but that she's battered. She was fourteen and then she got pregnant with their first child. And she's living it now. She won't leave, I don't think she'll ever leave, but she didn't grow up like that.

...

To get out you have to be willing to change your life. In that you want to drink, and you want to hang out at the bars, and you want to do drugs, you aren't going to get away from abuse. If you want to do all those things, you're not ready to change your lifestyle. (Anne, July 1991)

Anne described her current husband as a recovered alcoholic. She reported that her second marriage was grounded in a set of mutually agreed upon lifestyle choices that she had insisted upon when she and her husband first started dating. These include sobriety, fidelity, respect, trust, sharing, and autonomy. Anne said it had initially been a challenge to convince her husband to give up drinking and other women, but that when he realized it was the only way he could win her, he had made a commitment to give up both, and that he continued to respect this commitment.

Anne said that she continued to find the charisma of alcoholics strangely attractive. Moreover, she recognized that she was only attracted to men she found challenging, and she identified her propensity to choose abusive or potentially abusive partners as a personal vulnerability. Anne had thought a great deal about her experience. She believed that exiting abuse was largely a decision, and she believed that staying clear of abuse required self-awareness. However, Anne realized that some people are better able to make this choice than others. Had it not been for her sense of responsibility to her daughter, Anne believes she might have chosen to live in abuse:

I can see now how I could stick to a bad relationship. I can see that in me.

And I think that that's the key to a lot of people's relationship, in figuring out why they end up in bad relationships. And why they choose abusive partners. Even this time, I married an alcoholic. Now he's been not drinking for five years, but he still has all of that charisma. I don't know why, but I know that when boring people came around, who were perfect, who liked me, who did wonderful things for me, I wasn't interested. I wanted someone who was a challenge. That's not to say that I wanted abuse. But I just chose a different kind of person. And unfortunately those kind of people come with a different kind of environment, as well.

...

People stereotype women who are abused. Women who stay. Women who live through things. Ah, you think, how could anyone put up with it? But, you know, you just become a part of it. It just becomes a way of life that, you don't know any better, and you don't know. You don't see.

...

I think for some women it takes children to open their eyes. That was the case where my daughter was concerned. It wasn't until my baby became threatened that I realized it wasn't me that was in jeopardy now, it was someone else. And I didn't have the right to make the decision, the decision to live with abuse, I couldn't make that decision, for her. (Anne, July 1991)

Anne's story is the story of a woman who has achieved a desired state of survival. For Anne, survival was a choice, something she called a lifestyle choice. The choice for survival rather than victimization was made despite and against an emotionally overpowering and, for a time, irresistibly exciting charismatic reality. As a teen, Anne voluntarily entered a world she intuitively 'knew' was deviant, pathological, dangerous. She did not enter blindly. Anne made it clear that she knew what she was doing, that she knew that her husband was abusive, that she knew she was playing with danger. Anne entered this world despite and against her own intuitions, and despite and against her father's expressed concerns. For several years, Anne entertained vain hopes that she could manage or change her husband. However, these hopes were secondary to the passion she felt for him, and to the attraction she felt towards the chaotic, anything goes, unpredictable, 'wonderful' world he introduced her to.

Anne believed that she was able to choose to disengage from abuse largely because she was not a child of abuse, largely because she was a child of normality, sobriety, non-violence. Anne knew alternatives other than abuse. However, Anne did not choose to repress her attraction to the world of abuse. Rather, she chose to tame this world. Anne chose to establish a non-abusive lifestyle with an abuser, albeit a non-violent abuser, a recovered abuser. This meant that Anne retained contact with the charisma and excitement of a world rooted in abuse, a world that could potentially fall again into chaos. Anne knew this. She chose it.

Tracy

Tracy's story is based on material she provided in the survey on violence and abuse, and in a three-hour joint interview with her sister-in-law, Yvonne. The interview took place in the fall of 1992 in Tracy's one-bedroom apartment.

Tracy was a young woman in her early twenties. In the telephone interview, she disclosed that she was a survivor of child sexual abuse, perpetrated by her father, her maternal grandfather, and her maternal uncle, and that she had experienced severe life-threatening abuse in a series of adolescent and adult relationships. At the time of the telephone interview, she was trying to hold on to a failing two-year relationship with a man she described as her 'safe haven.' The relationship had taken a decidedly violent turn in the previous week.

In the telephone interview, Tracy expressed a confusing mix of fear, love, and confusion. Her primary love objects appeared to be her estranged 'two timing' boyfriend, her abusive father, and her two-and-a-half-year-old daughter, Jasmine. On the phone Tracy expressed resentment that her Township Family Services counsellor insisted that she was placing the child in danger when she left her alone with her father, whom she was sure she could now trust. She also expressed her belief that an extremely abusive uncle incarcerated for sexual assault had finally learned his lesson and was becoming trustworthy:

> I've been through abuse since I was seven years old, mental and sexual abuse. From age nine to twelve, I was sexually abused by three family members – my dad, my uncle, and my mum's father. The uncle was my mum's brother ... No, they didn't know about each other ... My uncle's in the penitentiary now, for rape, molesting, and buggery. He was sexually and mentally abused as a child. They figure the same for my grandfather. My uncle's been in and out of the pen for years. He learned what to say to psychiatrists and counsellors and when he got out, he would re-offend,

he'd rape and molest. This time he can't get out. This time family members wanted the courts to call him a dangerous offender. But he's learned his lesson now, he's sorry now. I'm going to see him in a few weeks, I trust him now.

...

Different boyfriends abused me in my teens. You know, I could stay out all night as long as I was with this one guy, a friend, and my mum didn't worry. But I didn't go out with him, he was too nice. Niceness scares me. I don't know it. Women go for the type of men they're used to. Difference is scary. I'm used to guys beating me up. One held a gun to my head. You know, my house is always spotless, and he accused me of sleeping around. He's hit me if one glass was dirty. I was made to do sexual things that made me sick. But then this nice guy comes around not hurting me, and I was scared ... Previous boyfriends have done all of it. The guy who threatened me with the gun is following me and watching me right now. When I involve the police, he stops and then he starts up again. I'm very afraid of him. He's an alcoholic.

...

I can wake up in the morning covered in bruises and not know how they got there. This book helped me [*Courage to Heal*]. You leave your body to avoid abuse. For me that's in sleepwalking ... I have one younger brother and two younger stepbrothers that I grew up with and three stepsisters that I didn't grow up with. They're not sexually abused. But I have an alcoholic uncle on my mother's side. He's another uncle, and he supposedly molested a cousin of mine. I don't believe he's like that. I'm not sure ... My counsellor doesn't want me to leave my daughter with my dad, but we worked it out. I trust my dad now.

...

The one time that my [current] boyfriend Tommy hit me, I was pounding him and left scratches on his face, and then he slapped me. You shouldn't be violent when you're provoked, but when he provoked me I just started hitting him. You see red ... He plays mind games, lies to me when he's going to see her, I mean his ex, who he's supposedly finished with. He says, I love you, I want you, and then he goes to see her. It was the same in a past relationship.

...

My boyfriend Tommy is my safe haven. I want to go to sleep curled up with him. In the last week, since I guess we broke up, I've had no sleep. Nightmares. I have to sleep with the light on. In the dark I can't see what's coming. I have to keep the radio on. The quiet scares me. I told Tommy, I need your shelter. I feel safe with Tommy. He's a very big man. I'm a small woman. I feel I'm in a glass bubble in his arms. I want to put Jasmine in a glass bubble, too, to keep her from being hurt. (Tracy: telephone survey, July 1992)

On the phone, Tracy described herself as 'a small woman' in need of protection. In person, she was tall and, seemingly unknowingly and unintentionally, aggressive. Tracy's account is marked by confusions, resentments, and inconsistencies that researchers, and Township counsellors and therapists, associate with child sexual abuse.[16] For instance, Tracy described her father's family as 'not incestuous' but nevertheless reported that as a youth her father was sexually abused by an aunt. She seemed very concerned that her family considered her to be like this aunt, and wanted reassurance from Yvonne and from me that she was not promiscuous. She described her brother as pampered and jealous, her mother as intrusive, non-supportive, and ungiving, and her father as manipulative. Tracy attributed most family problems to 'secret' child sexual abuse in her mother's family. In some cases, Tracy expressed doubts that some of the alleged abuses occurred. In other instances, she expressed uncertainty about what had happened to her. Tracy reported that her mother had blocked out childhood abuse, and she reported that she has also blocked out childhood abuse. Above all, Tracy complained that her mother failed to protect her:

> There was no sexual abuse in my father's family that I know of ... As far as I know, my father was abused by his aunt, a relative, but they didn't tell me, they told Yvonne. But I've heard stories that my mother and father have said about her and she is apparently a real sleazebag. I guess she used to be a hooker. She has gone from one guy to another and she is always going for men everywhere. I am called a slut [by 'everyone,' especially mother, stepfather, brother] because I go to the bar and I dress with these pants on which are two sizes too big with a sparkle top on, you know. But she was apparently a real slut, and my mom told Yvonne that she did it to my father, that's what happened to him. She tells her, Yvonne's not her daughter, and she tells me nothing.
> ...
> I know my mother was a victim [of incest]. She told me she has blocked out a lot of her past. But my uncle and grandfather both raped and molested my aunt, so why didn't they do it to my mother, as well. And she admitted it to Yvonne, she won't tell me, but she admitted it to Yvonne.
> ...

My uncle [mother's brother] who abused me, the one who's in for rape, molesting, buggery. He was badly abused when he was a child. His father and other guys chained him to a fence when he was fourteen. The women kept commenting how good-looking my uncle was, and these two guys stripped my uncle and chained him to a tree and made their wives look at him and said, if you think he is so good-looking, just look at him now, see how little his thing is ... I do know he molested me, I don't know what else he did, I block it out. I can't remember much.

...

My uncle, not the one who molested me but one of my mother's younger brothers, he's an alcoholic and he was charged with molesting my step-cousin, my aunt's daughter from her first marriage, Carrie. I don't believe it happened. It just seemed my cousin didn't like my uncle and that is all there was to it ... I have always done a lot with my uncle, been alone and done this and that with my uncle and he has never, never touched me, never. For me, I don't believe that he has ever touched her. I don't believe it. And I asked her younger sister Suzy if my uncle ever touched her and she said no. I don't believe it ... My brother Jeff told me, he said I am going to tell you something but it is not funny – I messed around with Carrie when I was younger and I am not proud of it. He said she made the sexual advances toward him. Jeff didn't have any idea about any of this stuff, he was totally innocent. Like he kept pushing her away and saying no, no, but it was like he couldn't not do it ... I don't believe Carrie.

...

My mother never abused me as a kid, but she never protected me. My mother never really protected me. (Tracy, August 1992)

Despite numerous allegations of sexual abuse in her family, Tracy insisted that abuse was always a secret. She reported that she feared that her mother would kill her grandfather if she knew he had sexually abused her. She also reported that she would kill anyone who touched her two-and-a-half-year-old daughter, Jasmine:

My father always told me that it is our little secret. You don't tell nobody. So I locked it into a room in my head and it never came out. But if my dad tried to like punish me, ground me and I would want to go out and do something with my friends, I would look at my dad when my mom was in another room and I would just say, well I guess mom will just have to know about my secret. But, you know, nine times out of ten I wouldn't know what my secret was, I just knew I had one. So I always ended up being able to do what I wanted to do because of that.

...

I didn't tell my mother. I confided in what I thought was a friend and she turned around and told my mother because she thought my mother needed to know and then my mother lost it on me and started yelling at me. Why didn't you tell me and this and that and every other thing. My mother had it out with my father ... They're both remarried now.

...

I remember my grandfather would play with me, and I would end up with about five dollars in change to go to the store with. And my grandfather would say, don't tell nobody, it is your secret. It was just like my father. My brother Jeff knows, Yvonne's husband, and as a family member he is the only one that knows about my grandfather. My mother doesn't know. I refuse to tell her because right now my mom does not like my grandfather and she can't wait for him to die, so I refuse to tell her because I don't know what she would do. I think she would go and literally kill him ... Nobody in my family knows about my grandfather, nobody except Yvonne.

...

I feel sorry for anyone who touches Jasmine because I would literally kill them; I would end up in jail because I would kill them. I'd torture them, I'd castrate them and let them bleed. (Tracy, August 1992)

Tracy elaborated on the abuse she experienced in dating relationships, a phenomenon she regarded as a direct consequence of the abuse she had experienced as a child. In the first passage, Tracy describes how she responded to the provocations of a severely abusive partner, a partner who still stalks and harasses her. In the second passage, she describes her reactions to the blatant infidelity of a previous boyfriend. In the third passage, she describes how she 'tested' a non-abusive man whom she regarded as a friend rather than as a lover, though she shares sexual intimacy with him 'fairly regularly':

Frank was very, very abusive. He used to punch the crap out of me all the time. It was in the middle of the summer in the middle of a heatwave and I use to wear long-sleeve shirts and pants because I didn't want anybody to see my bruises. He held a gun to my head and said if I ever fooled around on him he would shoot me ... One day he came in and held me by the throat up against the wall, and I was on my tippy toes and I just got enough air in to let out one good scream ... My brother actually heard me and he came out and grabbed a hold of this jerk and said if you ever do that to my sister again I will kill you. So he let me go and went back to his drinking binge ... One night we were lying in bed with a pocket knife out, a paramedic knife that was very sharp, and he was holding it to his stomach. He was holding on to the blade, the stupid idiot, and he said, I know you want to kill me, just go ahead and stab me. I said, if I really wanted to kill you I would take the knife and slice your throat, I would do a really good job because if I stabbed him in the stomach, the worst is going to happen he is going to bleed and go to the hospital and he'll be fine. Why the hell would I want him to live if I am trying to kill him. So I took as much of his nattering as I could take, and I rolled over and grabbed the knife and heaved it out of his hand and sliced his hand open, and he should have gone to the hospital and got stitches but at that point in time I wouldn't have cared if he had bled to death. So I grabbed some gauze and I wrapped his hand up, and I said, you go to sleep and I don't want to hear a word out of you.

...

Another guy, Billy, he would abuse me mentally, like Tommy. He would break up with me and go with someone else and come back to me and say, I love you. As for sexually or physically, he never did anything like that, just mentally ... Some of the things he has done to me, like bringing another girl home. I lost it and was ready to pound the piss out of her just the way she looked at me because she wasn't supposed to be there and she knew it. I didn't see him for the longest time.

...

This guy Dave, he's basically a friend. The first night he was here we were talking and talking and talking, and I said I am going to tell you something but I don't want you to tell anybody and I want you to listen, I want to get this out. He said, OK ... I told him how I was feeling and everything. That night he spent the night and he slept with his pants on. I am thinking, wow, I never met a guy that has done that; any guy that has slept over at my place has slept with me, they have tried something. He was such a gentleman. He wanted to kiss me, and I said OK, because I had already kissed him before. So we kissed and that was about it, and I said, I can't do anymore, I am sorry. He said, OK, no problem. So he cuddles me all night, which makes me feel really good and really safe. The second night he stayed here, he again slept with his pants on and fooled around a little bit more than what we had the first night, and then I said, I am sorry, I can't do any more, I am not ready. He says, OK, whenever you are ready we will continue. Again we cuddled the rest of the night. The third night he stayed here, I teased him to the point where most guys would say, forget it, I am going to anyways. And Dave, when I pushed him over that line, I turned to him and I would say, no I am sorry but I can't do anymore, and he said, OK, no problem, and he slept with his pants on again. The fourth night he stayed here, I said to him, you know, you don't have anything that I haven't seen before. If you want to sleep without your underwear on, it doesn't bother me, because that is how most guys sleep. He took them off, and I teased him past that point, and I said, no, he said, OK, whenever you are ready. That night he looked at me and said, you know, what they say is wrong. They said you were a real slut and you were easy and all this stuff. Well, obviously, you are not a slut ... He said, I think you are having a lot of problems that you are working out and you are doing a really good job of it. And I said, thank you. He ended up being really understanding, and the fifth night that we stayed together I ended up sleeping with him because I felt that he understands. But he's just a friend, he doesn't mean anything to me. (Tracy, August 1992)

Tracy expressed considerable anger at sexist and sexualized denigrations that she had experienced in myriad intimate contexts. She reported that she especially resented family members' claims that she was sexually promiscuous. She said that although her family maintained her sexual behaviour was proof she was crazy, she didn't really behave in a manner that justified her family's allegations:

A couple of years ago we got into this big humongous fight one night, and my stepfather said I was crazy and needed to see a counsellor or psychiatrist. I was standing in the doorway with my head against it, just waiting, and then my mother started beating the crap out of me. My head started bleeding, and I said, to hell with this, and took off running and my stepfather caught up with me. I locked myself in my room and cranked up the music so I couldn't hear them. Finally I fell asleep, and the next day I seen Billy and told him what was going on, and he said, no, honey, you are not crazy, don't listen to them. He did at that point know about my dad. That's why he told me I wasn't crazy. (Tracy, August 1992)

Tracy maintained she was not promiscuous, and that she never had been promiscuous. She said that she had only 'slept' with 'two guys' over the past two years other than her estranged boyfriend Tommy, who had been driving her mad with jealousy, and whose ex-wife she had physically assaulted about a month prior to her recent fight with Tommy. These 'two guys' were an ex-lover of Tommy's ex-wife and the friend Tracy 'tested' over a five-night period. Yvonne reminded her that she had also had a recent affair with Yvonne's bother Ron, and Tracy agreed, 'Oh yea, Ron.' On the other hand, Tracy admitted that she tended to flee her troubles through sex, and enthusiastically offered to show me her lingerie collection. She said she had a large collection because she always bought something new when she's seeing 'a new guy.' Tracy said she currently had her eye on 'a cute cop' who had intervened in a neighbour's domestic violence incident a few days previous to the personal interview, a cop who had reportedly reciprocated her flirtatious overtures.

Tracy devoted considerable attention to sexuality. However, she stated that what she most wanted was to be pampered, to be protected, to be loved. Tracy appeared to see pampering as evidence of a willingness to protect, and a readiness to love. She maintained that her mother had always pampered her brother Jeff, that no one had ever really pampered her. Tracy's descriptions of family interactions were marked by a confused mix of loyalty and resentment, love and jealousy, distrust and misplaced trust. Tracy said that she 'firmly believed' that sexual abuse runs in families. However, she furiously resisted suggestions that she was passing on an intergenerational legacy of abuse to her daughter, Jasmine. Tracy insisted that her Township Family Services Counsellor was wrong to constantly confront her with the danger her father posed. She brought this issue up on the telephone and again in the personal interview:

> I hate these counsellors that are giving you advice on a subject that they know dick all about. I am sorry but reading it in a book and experiencing it is two different things. When you have experienced it, you know what you are feeling. You know how it feels, so you can give advice better. I don't like being told, eight out of ten men that have sexually abused their daughters will abuse again. Excuse me, what happened about that other two per cent here that didn't abuse again. Could my father be one of those two? ... Stuff your statistics up your ass because I am not a statistic. I am a human being.
>
> ...
>
> I have been asked if I have ever left Jamine alone with my dad. So I say it. My dad has taken Jasmine to the store by himself, which I don't have a problem with because I've worked things out with him and I know I can

trust him. And, anyway, Jasmine knows you don't let anybody touch your daisy ... I don't think my father will touch her. I have no fear of my father. I trust my father. Ask Yvonne, she can tell when a man's like that. (Tracy, August 1992)

As in discussions about whether of not she was promiscuous, Tracy sought reassurance from Yvonne and from me that she could trust her own intuitions, and that she was behaving properly. Ironically, as the following exchange demonstates, Yvonne tended to disconfirm rather than confirm many of Tracy's assertions, including Tracy's assertion that her father could be trusted with Jasmine, and her assertion that Jeff got all the preferential treatment, all the pampering. Tracy chose not to respond to Yvonne's claim that her father displayed a 'difference' typical of child sex abusers. Rather, she focused on the rivalry between herself and her brother, and on ways her family slighted, excluded, and denigrated her. Yvonne confirmed that this rivalry was intense, and she confirmed that Tracy's family habitually scapegoated her. This appears to relate to the extent to which the family carefully guarded its secrets. Everyone, including Tracy, wanted to protect Jeff from knowledge of what his father had done:

I [Yvonne] knew from the day that when Jeff first took me to meet his father, I knew there was something different about his father and I knew his father had sexually assaulted somebody. I didn't know who but I knew he had done it ... Because he would be as exactly as my father was. The way he acted. He was nervous around Tracy, he was edgy. He was always doing things, he was catering to her every need. It was like he wanted to show her that he was grateful that she forgave him ... Jeff didn't understand why her father is doing it and he got pissed off with Tracy because he feels that Tracy is trying to take her father's attention away. If they would have just out and out told Jeff what the hell was going on there wouldn't have been all these fights. (Yvonne, August 1992)

If Jeff and Yvonne go up and see my dad, I won't go up there at the same time. Tommy told me that I was being stupid, selfish. But I am driving seven hours up to see my dad. I want to spend time with him. If my brother is up there I won't get any time because my brother is the one – he is the man so he gets to help in the bush – and my brother tells me, you are a girl, you can't go into the bush, you can't work on the tractors. (Tracy, August 1992)

> I [Yvonne] use the chainsaw. I go into the bush to get firewood. Jeff uses this [sexist] stuff on Tracy but not to me ... They think that something is wrong with her. The whole family. In her family's eyes, I am a saint and she is the devil in disguise ... The one thing I dislike about the family is that they went through all these years after it came out in the open and everything and nobody ever told Jeff what happened. All of a sudden I come along and everybody is telling me these stories and I am telling him because they are asking me to tell him, and now he is really upset and hurt because it is like why didn't they tell me themselves. (Yvonne, August 1992)

A striking characteristic of Tracy's physical world was her exceptionally clean and tidy apartment, which appeared completely free of toys. When I asked if Jasmine had anything to play with, Tracy assured me that Jasmine had a toy chest in her room but that she was not allowed to 'clutter up' the apartment. Tracy made it clear that the living room was her room.[17] Throughout the interview, Tracy subjected Jasmine to a seemingly constant stream of admonishments and threats. At one point, Tracy threatened to lock Jasmine in her room if she took a third cookie from the plate on the coffee table, a threat that proved more effective than a previous threat: 'Mummy will slap your hand if you don't stay away from those cookies.' Other admonishments were to not make a mess of the magazines (that is, not to disturb them), to not make noise, to not interrupt, and to not even think about biting. In the midst of describing an alleged biting problem, Tracy turned to Jasmine and asserted that she would have all her teeth pulled out if she ever bit anyone again. Tracy told me that 'actually' Jasmine hadn't bitten anyone recently but that this problem was a major reason Jasmine had been assigned priority on the daycare waiting list as a 'high risk child.' Tracy said that one good thing about that was that she was going back to school to finish her grade twelve and that this would prove to her family that she wasn't stupid. She said she planned to study business, and eventually she planned to open a country and western bar, not because she liked drinking, which she said she didn't, but because she loved country and western music.[18]

Tracy's story is that of a young woman who appears to live, not simply in violence or abuse, but totally in emotion. Tracy's story is about an all-encompassing, recurring, serial, and ongoing experience of emotional, physical, and sexual victimization. It is the story of a self trapped within and utterly haunted by negative emotionality rooted in childhood memories, relationships, and feelings. Tracy authentically believed that this past caused her to seek out abusive partners; and that it caused her to experience non-abusive men as scary, and men who assaulted her with knives and guns and sexual denigrations, as safe and familiar. Tracy believed that this past caused her to be a victim of adult relationship violence. Tracy did not report, however, that she experienced physical violence or forced sex as a child.[19] On the other hand, Tracy wasn't sure exactly what she experienced she reported that she had blocked out painful experiences. Consequently, Tracy wasn't sure what lay in her past. She was sure, however, that she craved protection and recognition in the present. She sought safety, and she conceived of safety as an encompassing embrace which made her feel that she was in a glass bubble. Tracy dreamed of being rescued by a white knight, an overwhelmingly attractive and overpowering male who would pamper, protect, and shelter her.

Tracy made it clear that she experienced her world as painful, but it is not clear if she experienced her world as deviant, pathological, or sick. Rather, Tracy appeared to experience herself as sick, as having been made sick by abuse. However, Tracy insisted that her family was wrong; she insisted that she was not crazy. In the abstract, Tracy wanted 'to heal'; she wanted an end to victimization, and she wanted to see or experience herself as good, as safe. These desires had led her to contact a Township Family Services counsellor. However, Tracy vehemently resisted and resented her counsellor's attempts to assist her towards wellness. Tracy insisted that she knows better than the experts about how she feels, that her personal experience is a true guide both to how she feels and to whom she can trust.

Tracy exhibited a self-centredness and self-narcissism that Denzin associates with the alcoholic and/or the violent self.[20] Tracy's discussion of her father's childhood victimizations was less a discussion of what had happened to her father than an opportunity to argue that she was not 'a slut' like her aunt. Her discussion of her father's obvious 'difference,' and therefore non-trustworthiness, was transformed into a discussion of her father's preferential treatment of her brother. Similarly, Tracy's discussion of her cousin's claim of sexual abuse was dismissed because the alleged abuser had never sexually approached Tracy. Finally, Tracy's own personal needs for cleanliness, order, and parental love blinded her to her child's needs for play, companionship, and protection.

As in the case of Denzin's alcoholic and/or violent self, Tracy always believed that it was someone else's fault when things went wrong. It was her estranged boyfriend's ex-wife's fault that he was not faithful. It was his fault that Tracy physically assaulted him for lying and for then admitting that he had lied. It was her child's biting behaviour (and not her own disclosures of irresponsible parenting) that was to blame for Jasmine, and therefore Tracy, being labelled 'high risk' by abuse intervenors. Most importantly, it would be her two-and-a-half-year-old child's fault if Tracy's father or anyone else sexually abused the child, since Tracy had taught Jasmine not to let anyone 'touch her daisy.' Tracy blamed her mother for not protecting her, but she was not able to take responsibility for exposing Jasmine to possible and even probable victimization.

On the surface, Tracy's story is a story of rationalizations, of 'bad faith.' However, it is more a story of hurt and confusion than of bad faith. Tracy appears too hurt and too confused to act responsibly, as this term is conventionally understood. She doesn't seem able to recognize that she must protect herself and that she must protect her child. She doesn't seem able to recognize that white knights and glass bubbles are illusory. Tracy doesn't seem to have a concept of responsibility. Her choices appear almost completely rooted in emotional processes. Cognitions appear as separate from emotions, and as utterly irrelevant to action. This is surely, however, not Tracy's fault, or Tracy's 'choice.' To judge her as 'responsible' for her hurt and confusion would be the epitome of victim blaming.

Yvonne

Yvonne, Tracy's sister-in-law, was a petite and attractive young woman in her early twenties. As had Tracy, Yvonne had survived incest at the hands of several male family members, as well as serious, life-threatening violence at the hands of a male partner.

Yvonne's family was perhaps even more abusive than Tracy's family. Yvonne said that in her father's family, incest was regarded as normal, as something families do, and that while intercourse was supposedly reserved for spouses, other family members were expected to sexually touch each other. In contrast, incest was a shameful secret in her mother's family, where physical abuse was overt. Yvonne said that in her mother's family no one dared disclose that they had been sexually abused since this was likely to elicit even more severe violence:

My dad was taught as a child that sexual intercourse is only meant for your wife, but when you love somebody else, like your daughter or your sister, a family member, going beyond 'I love you' is showing yourself to them or fondling them. Sexual intercourse is just kept for your wife but you can touch your sister and your daughter, you can have them touch you, there's nothing wrong in that. My father was very sexual with his sisters, to this day, and my mother can't stand it, and to this day my dad say's there's nothing wrong with it ... Like I heard my father defend that his sister had intercourse with her son to show him so he wouldn't feel stupid on dates. My mother was saying, don't you realize, but in his mind, he grew up secluded in the bush, he didn't really hear about the news, he didn't really hear about things going on, he didn't see what was wrong. He had created his own world.

...

My mother was assaulted sexually in her family, too, but she never will admit it to you; but she admitted it to me once. Don't ever tell her that you know because she will kill me. Nobody else knows. My father doesn't know. Nobody else knows. My mother has blocked it out; to this day, she refuses to admit it. But she did admit it to me. It was in her family by her brother. He is a violent person to this day. I never doubted he would do anything like that because he has always been a very assualtive person. He always beat up my mother physically, before my dad came around. He would put my mom's head through a wall or he would punch her or knock her teeth out. He was always beating her up and she was always having broken arms. And she can hardly admit it, but he raped her, too. My mom has never told my dad about the sexual assaults. He knew about the physical, and I think if she would have told him, it would have made him realize that what was happening in his family was wrong, because my father didn't know it was wrong.

...

I don't know if my mother's sisters were abused when they were growing up. But my mom's older sister, my Aunt Marie, she met my uncle and he was a real wingding, this one here. He told her that if she didn't marry him, he was going to kill himself. She said, no, she didn't want to have anything to do with him, and he made himself get into a car accident and ended up in the hospital and almost killed himself. His parents begged my Aunt Marie to marry him, so that he could survive and she did ... stupid, stupid, stupid, stupid. He beats her up all the time. When they were first married, my aunt was pregnant and my uncle abused her and my cousin was inside her stomach, and he really beat her. And my two uncles went over there, and he put both of them in the hospital. The uncles were my mother's brothers. They went to protect her, and my uncle put both of them in the hospital.

...

It happened to my Aunt Marie's two daughters, too, by her son, and she totally denies it. Her son's a fruit loop. His father did it to him. But to my Aunt Marie, her son could do no wrong. He broke his sister's nose with an axe. He was trying to sexually assault her, and they were chopping down firewood ... She wouldn't and was fighting back, and he grabbed the axe and hit her with the back part and smashed her in the face with it and broke her nose. He beat his sisters to a pulp and broke their arms. He sexually abused both of them. Someone reported him to Children's Aid, but there was not enough evidence. My aunt denied it. To this day, she won't admit it. (Yvonne, August 1992)

Yvonne reported that she was subjected to both kinds of sexual abuse, her father's seductions and her mother's sister's son's violent rapes:

I was abused by my father. My father was a fondler, mainly. But I was also abused by my Aunt Marie's son and his two friends. He was five years older than me. He was a fondler, a toucher, he was an intercourser and he didn't think he was happy with just him and so he would go and invite his friends. They were the types that would put knives at your throat and that's when they forced my older brother Ron on me. He was crying and he would fight them and he was bawling his eyes out, and after that day my brother could not look at me, until this day. Thank god, that only happened once.

...

Aunt Marie's son used to baby-sit us, and he would beat my brother up until my brother could hardly walk. He would take him into a room and sexually assault him, and after him he would take me. My aunt does not believe it happened until this day. She denies it totally.

...

And here were these people who were just showers. My mom's younger sister used to baby-sit us ... and when she would baby-sit us, we would visit her friends and their fathers would show themselves to me. I had no idea who these men were, but I remember two of them showing themselves to me. And my uncle, my mom's younger sister's husband, he was a shower too. He was also very abusive with his daughters. I don't know if he sexually assaulted them, but I know everything they did was wrong

... If they looked at a guy, they were whores and for punishment they had to write hundreds and hundreds of lines of repentance on brown paper bags. (Yvonne, August 1992)

Despite all the violence and shame associated with sex at the hands of cousins, uncles, and acquaintances, Yvonne reported that it did not really occur to her that sexual fondling between father and daughter was wrong until she participated in a sex education course at school at age nine. Despite not knowing that it was wrong, Yvonne tried to hide the abuse from her mother. Her parents' frequent arguments made it clear that her mother believed that sexual closeness between father and daughter was shameful. Moreover, Yvonne was well aware that her mother suspected that abuse was occurring. Yvonne said she didn't tell her mother because she feared that if her mother knew what was happening, the family would be destroyed. Instead, she adopted her father's interpretation that her mother's attempts to intervene were displays of jealousy:

As far back I remember, regardless of what was happening, I was daddy's little girl. My mom was always jealous of that because – they would go to these Christmas parties and family get-togethers – instead of my father wanting my mother to sit beside him, he would want me. On the way home, all I ever heard was how come you wanted her to sit with you and not me ... I am your wife. She is not your frigging wife. She is your daughter. He'd say he didn't see anything wrong with it and they would fight. I always felt it was my fault they were fighting, and then my two brothers didn't understand either so they said to me, if you weren't here mom and daddy wouldn't fight. I think my mother knew that my father was fondling me. She had a feeling, but every time she asked me I would deny it because I was so afraid that the family was going to fall apart and I was going to be blamed.

...

I didn't realize it was wrong until I was about nine years old, and then you start going to these sex classes in school and then they start telling you about molestation and all this stuff and I am just sitting there baffled. All of a sudden there is a ton of bricks that just falls on you. You've been taught that there is a special bond with your father – this is what he was teaching me. They say, no, it is not a bond, it is wrong. At first I didn't know how to feel ashamed. That's why I had problems, too. It is not that I liked it, but I was indifferent about it because I didn't know if I should like it or not. After I found out it was wrong, I started feeling ashamed about myself.

...

It didn't happen all the time. My father went in spurts. With my father, usually it was when he was drunk or when he didn't feel like my mom loved him. My father would do it three times a month, and then it would stop for four months. He would do it continuously for two or three times a month for a year, but then he would stop for a year. When I was in grade five, we moved to a smaller town for a year, and I remember that whole year he did not touch me. When I was in grade five, nobody touched me. My room was totally on the opposite end of the house, and if my father was at the other end of the house, my mother would ask him what the hell are you doing on the other end of the house. That whole year I got to be me. Nobody bothered me that whole year. Then we moved back to where all the family was, and it all started again. Just for that year, nobody touched me. (Yvonne, August 1992)

It was not until Yvonne was thirteen that she found the strength to resist her father, and to confide in her mother:

When I was about to turn thirteen, my mom said we couldn't go on living like this anymore because I was getting too old to be in the room with the two boys. She said we have got to build another room, and I don't care if we have the money or not. They started building an addition to have a new bedroom. While we were wallpapering, she had to go to town because my father had come home early and he needed some parts for his equipment, and she asked me if I would finish wallpapering the new room for her ... So my father was in the bedroom, and when I walked by, he wanted me to hug him and I said no. He went to grab me and I punched him, and that's when he said, you are not going to punch me, and he grabbed me and said, I want a hug and you're my daughter and you are going to give me a hug. And it scared me and I just hauled off and decked him one right between the legs, and he hunched over and fell on the bed. I ran in the bathroom and locked the door. I had the wallpaper there and I took a piece of the excess wallpaper that we were cutting off and I wrote on it. I wrote, you are not my father. My father wouldn't do this to me. I don't want you to ever call me by my name again. I am disowning you as a father. What you have done is wrong and this is not how you treat a daughter. I was taught in school that this is bad. I slid it under the door, and I told him to call me Mary and I told him I was changing my last name and I didn't want his last name anymore and I didn't want to ever see his face again. I was going to leave home. He read it and started bawling his eyes out, and it was the first time I had seen my father cry. That letter hit him like a ton of bricks and made him realize what he was doing was wrong. Until then he had no idea. That is when it stopped ... After, I would come to him if I wanted a hug and it was a hug in front of my mom where I knew what it would be like. I wanted to say, dad I don't hate you, I still love you regardless of what you have done to me, but you are never touching me again.

...

I never could talk to my father. I talked to mother, but I have never talked to him. I won't be in the same room with my father alone, because I know the way he looks at me; not like the way he supposed to be looking at me. My father is looking at me with love in his eyes like you do for a woman. To me my father is still in love with me, but not in the right way. This bond that he was supposed to be developing got out of hand for him, and all of a sudden he started getting deeper feelings than he was supposed to and feelings he did not understand. I think my father fell in love with me as a person, not realizing I am his daughter. (Yvonne, August 1992)

Yvonne reported that her mother never blamed her for what happened, that her mother blamed her father. Yvonne reported that her mother was unlike the other members of the extended family. Her mother believed that she was telling the truth when she said she was being abused. For years, Yvonne's mother had been trying in vain to intervene to protect her children. However, Yvonne said that neither the police nor the Children's Aid Society were willing to press charges:

When my cousin was abusing us, my mother started noticing that things were different with my brother Ron. She didn't notice that there were things with me. He was a more drastic change than I was ... She took him to counselling at the old MacDonald's house they had. It didn't help because they couldn't get through to him. He wouldn't let them through, and to this day my mother doesn't know what happened. Even I don't know exactly what happened, but I do know from him insinuating it that it must have been something really bad because my brother has been fighting with his sexuality all these years. He has been fighting with guilt. He has a real attitude problem. I know my brother and it is a big cycle now. He always looks for an abusive relationship. Everybody who has been sexually abused does.

...

When it came out that my father molested me and that my cousin did, most everybody believed me that my cousin did, but nobody believed me that my father did. They all accused me of being a liar and stuff. Not my mother but my aunts did, my mom's sisters. My mom's sisters were madly in love with my father, my father could do no wrong. But my mom believed me. She doesn't blame me, she blames my father. She would love to kill him to this day. My mother has stayed with him by choice, but she is afraid she wouldn't be able to live on her own. My mother has a handicap, one leg shorter than the other. When she was born, they dislocated her hip and didn't realize it and it grew that way. Now she has problems, a really bad back. She is a cook right now and she isn't supposed to do that. When she comes home from work, she can't walk. She doesn't have grade twelve. She doesn't know if she could make it on her own.

...

My cousin, of course, denied everything to do with anyone to the Children's Aid. My father denied it happening, too, so the cops didn't believe it. I said to them, what's going to happen? They said, we are dropping the charges because of insufficient evidence and no witnesses. I looked at the cop and said, you son of a bitch. And he said, there are no witnesses. I said, you fuckin asshole, if there had been a damn witness, it wouldn't have happened. (Yvonne, August 1992)

Yvonne also described her experiences with abusive relationships as a teen and an adult. As had her sister-in-law Tracy, Yvonne admitted that she could be both self-abusive and abusive:

I moved away from home when I was fifteen years old, and I moved in with a guy, Steve. I thought he was the greatest in the world, and at first he was until he started using me as a punching bag if I didn't want to do what he said ... I moved in with him in June of 1987, and I was pregnant in February and he accused me of sleeping around on him. It was him sleeping around on me, although I didn't know it at the time. Anyway, he got mad and beat me up ... One of the ladies I worked with told me about this place you go to and you go on welfare and it pays your rent and you have your baby, and nobody will be able to get to you. It was my only chance and opportunity. I had everything packed in five minutes and was out of there. I left him no note. I left him nothing. He had no idea where I was.

He looked for me everywhere ... One night after school I didn't realize he was behind me and I turned around and there he was and he beat me up. I almost lost my son. That time I sent him to jail. I pressed charges and he went to a correctional home.

...

I went through a period of time where I felt really bad about myself because of what happened with Steve, because he was the first person who I had confided in about what happened. Then I found out he was a molester himself, because he had molested his cousin. It tore me right apart. It was like how could you be such a hypocrite and I not notice it. I cried on your shoulder and you called my father all these names, you called my cousins all these names, and you are the same type of person. I went through a period of time where I thought I didn't deserve anything better, so I was promiscuous for about three months. I went out with one guy who I had known since grade nine, and I had a sexual affair with him for about a month, and then after that I went out with another guy for a week and then I broke up with him and then I went out with another guy and I had a sexual affair with him, too. It was one after the other. Until I met Jeff. (Yvonne, August 1992)

Yvonne reported that her husband, Jeff, was possessive, intrusive, and controlling, but she described herself as the abuser. She reported that she sometimes thought of leaving Jeff, despite the fact that she loved him, that he was a good father, and that he had never abused her or the boys, physically or sexually. She said she simply got fed up with his immaturity. She said that she especially resented his intrusions into her personal thoughts and feelings, as when he read her journal and complained that it was obvious she didn't love him since she portrayed him so negatively. Jeff called at least three times during our interview to 'check on things.' As I was pulling out of the drive, he drove up. Jeff was apparently unable to heed his wife's repeated request that he wait until she called him.

Yvonne reported that she had just enrolled in a counselling program at Township Family Services. She said that she had participated in counselling before, but that it had never been very useful. As did her sister-in-law Tracy, Yvonne resented professionals who emphasized statistics and risks. Yvonne had her own personal theories about abuse. Like Tracy, she believed that people who grow up with abuse become habituated, and that they seek abusive relationships as adults. She made it clear that she was looking for psychotherapy, not re-education.

Yvonne had worked to educate herself for years, so that she did not theorize in a vacuum. Yvonne read, and she attempted to incorporate what she read into her personal theories:

> Our theory, on this, my personal theory, is that you grow up seeing these abusive things, from somebody that is going to love me, so subconsciously you are looking for somebody who is going to yell at you and hurt you and throw dirt at you and punch you. Those are the stronger points that you have seen when you were growing up, not the understanding and not the love ... It's different with my husband. I get fed up with him, but he wouldn't be abusive. He's very gentle. With my husband, I'm the one being abusive. I know I am being abusive of him, and I don't mean to, and that is why I am seeing a counsellor now, so that I can stop doing it to him, because otherwise he is going to end up a fruit loop.
> ...
> I have been reading books myself. Just articles I found here and there. And I take notes on myself. I have still got the ones from when I was in the home for unwed mothers. I keep them in my Bible. I decided I would always write, for instance, before I made a final decision. I would check and I would list all the possibilities. I would consider pros and cons for each and then I would make a final decision ... I would leave the notes in my sock drawer and every morning and I would open my drawer and there would be this note and I would read it. While I stayed focused on those things, I found Jeff. Once I married Jeff, I put all the notes away. I had thought I had done it. But I still haven't quite subconsciously computerized it in.
> ...
> I want a therapist who is going to understand me or try to understand me, listen to me, not pretend to listen to me, but somebody who will actually hear what I am saying ... I told this Township Family Services counsellor on the phone right off the bat, don't tell me what I feel or I'll never come back. I told him, I'm going to tell you some stuff, I don't mean to be rude but this is the way I am. This is what I like and this is what I don't like. I told him I know why I am doing this stuff, but I can't figure out how to stop doing it. (Yvonne, August 1992)

Yvonne's story includes accounts of incredibly severe physical and sexual violence, experienced as a child and as an adult. Unlike her sister-in-law Tracy, Yvonne recognized that she needed to move out of a life of abuse, and she recognized that she must personally assume responsibility for achieving this. Yvonne reported that she had gone through periods of promiscuity, that she had participated in severely violent relationships, and that she had a tendency to be emotionally abusive. She believed that these experiences or proclivities were directly related to childhood victimizations. However, Yvonne did not see these as fixed or permanent features of her reality. She saw them as inappropriate and self-destructive responses. Yvonne labelled abusive realities as unequivocally pathological, and she regarded herself as basically capable, basically responsible.

Yvonne did not appear mired in the emotional and moral confusions that seem to have paralysed Tracy. Nor did she appear mired in the same sort of self-centredness or self-narcissism. Instead, Yvonne was assuming responsibility. She was wary of professional constructions of abuse, but she was cognitively involved in a reflexive attempt to understand and cope with her experiences. In the present, this included efforts to authentically engage with a therapist. Yvonne was 'very theoretical' and highly introspective. She did not have difficulty establishing who was to blame for her abusive childhood, and she valued the trusting and mutually respectful relationship she had established with her mother. Yvonne was confident that she would never again tolerate physical or sexual victimization. However, she was concerned that she learn how to curb her tendency to be emotionally abusive. She didn't blame her obsessively insecure husband for her behaviours. She recognized that she might eventually decide to end this relationship, despite the fact that her husband had positive as well as negative characteristics. Yvonne was prepared to examine her alternatives and to choose. However, she did not delude herself that she could solve her personal problems solely by exiting. Yvonne's story is the story of a young woman moving towards or reaching for survival.

Kim

I've adopted the male attitude. You know, the egotistical-me-first kind of attitude. The I'm-not-taking-any-shit attitude. (Kim, August 1991)

Kim's story is the story of a young woman about to enter her second year of university studies who proudly proclaimed that she had adopted 'the male attitude,' who reported that she did and would 'pound' any male who dared affront her dignity, and who had been expelled from high school for assaulting a teacher. Kim reported that she regularly drank tequila by the litre. In my presence, she drank beer by the case.

I first encountered Kim at a Friday evening party that I attended with a co-op friend, Jocelyn. The party was held in a dilapidated cottage inhabited year-round by two males in their mid-thirties who appeared to value motorcycles and beer more than creature comforts like indoor plumbing. Initially, Jocelyn and I had difficulty approaching the cottage because of a large menacing dog. We were about to give up when Kim arrived. Kim, who was over six feet tall, easily intimidated the dog into allowing us to pass. I asked her how she had learned to handle dogs so well, and she responded: 'I don't take shit from any living creature.' I introduced myself as a researcher interested in the problem of abuse in the Township. Kim expressed interest in my study and enthusiastically shared her story, informally at the party and later in an interview at her grandmother's house in one of the smaller towns.[21]

Kim reported having witnessed frequent, severe, life-threatening mutual assaults between her alcoholic parents from early childhood. She reported that these assaults only stopped when her financially successful father abandoned the family for another woman a few years prior to the study:

> I was never abused, but until my father left, I'd see my mom chasing my father around the house with a knife, and I'd see her swing a telephone around by the chord and bump him on the head with it ... My dad had the upper hand and my mom fought back ... My mom would provoke him, and then he'd hit her and she would hit back. It was all about money and alcohol. After my dad left, my mother lost the house in alcohol because she spent a lot of money on drinking. (Kim, August 1991)

Kim said that aside from mutual physical 'fights' with her mother as a young teen, she did not experience physical abuse while growing up. She knew very little about her father's family, but reported that, as she herself did, her brothers and father engaged in extra-familial violence. She described her mother's family as non-abusive:

> My dad is a mouthpiece when he is drinking. He'll provoke people into fighting ... I know there was one time when the bouncers had four guys hold down my dad. My dad is always saying what would the neighbours

think, meanwhile he is always the one getting caught in uncanny, uncanny, humiliating, embarrassing situations.

...

My brothers are all very violent. For them it's something to do. They fight without provocation. My brother took his girlfriend out and some guy at the next table said, look at that fat cow, and my brother wasn't even positive if he was talking about his girlfriend or not, and he jumped on him and started pounding him. (Kim, August 1991)

Kim reported feeling emotionally rejected by her father, who refused to provide support or to assist her in any way with her with university expenses. She also felt emotionally neglected by her mother, who made no attempt to provide supervision or guidance during Kim's teens:

My dad's got money, he's got property. It all goes to his step kids. He has bought them both cars and they don't go to school or work and they each have illegitimate children. He has bought them both cars. And me I'm going back to school, I'm doing great, I don't have any kids, I got myself out of a shitty relationship and he's done nothing ... I went and begged my dad to pay my car insurance. My mom's given me a thousand bucks for university next year, plus my boyfriend has given me a car. I'm paying for my tuition and my living there, I saved that from my summer job ... I can't wait until he's old and needs someone to take care of him. I'll do it, but I'll rub it in.

...

My mom was always drinking, like I said. And I would go away for weeks at a time and come home and she would stuff all these responsibilities on me. I would retaliate and she would smack me. It pushed me more towards it. It pushed me right into being more wild because I would leave more often. I was always in trouble. I was kicked out of school three times. (Kim, August 1991)

Kim reported having no permanent place of residence through most of high school. She was expelled once for truancy, once for alcoholism, and once for assaulting a teacher. Nevertheless, Kim maintained an A average:

I wasn't really a street kid, because it was a small town, you know, and I could always crash at a friend's house or crash a party and stay. I did that from about age thirteen ... I'd spend a couple of months with my dad and a couple of months with my grandmother and just move around, until I moved in with this jerk at age fifteen, that is.

...

I need very little sleep to function. When I was in grade thirteen, I was going to school from nine until three, and then I worked from four till twelve. And every night, I would hit the bar for last call. I would some-times party after and sometimes I would just do an all nighter. I still kept my A, at least at long as I kept attending. Like I said, for spells I didn't attend. (Kim, August 1991)

Between the ages of thirteen and fifteen, when Kim was 'not really a street kid,' she engaged in extremely dangerous behaviour, behaviour rooted in drugs and alcohol. She reported that she experienced gang rapes, and that she had experienced two miscarriages by the time she was fifteen. At age fifteen, Kim moved in with a twenty-two-year-old drug dealer who saved her from the life of 'not really a street kid' only to subject her to intense domination and control, sexual denigration, and severe violence. It was in this relationship, terminated two years previous to the study, that Kim had learned to fight back. According to Kim, the violence was mainly the result of alcohol. Kim reported that she had been publicly pulled by the hair from places of employment, that she had been pounded against walls, and that she had had her fin-gers broken. However, she maintained that her boyfriend 'never phys-ically really hurt me.' She said she basically took the violence for three years, but that she began to reciprocate in the last year:

I moved in with him when I got pregnant ... I had a miscarriage. Actually, I got pregnant once before and I had a miscarriage then too ... We were into like acid and hash and stuff like that, not so much cocaine ... The same old shit. He was obsessive. I was raped when I was going out with him, by a group of people. He got really scared to let me out of his sight and it wasn't really bad at first but it got progressively worse. He would follow me and quit jobs on me. He'd call in and say Kim isn't coming back to work. I would go back in and get bawled out by my boss ... It got to the point he didn't want me to go to school. He wouldn't let me off the property with-out him. He was also really paranoid. He thought what happened to me was an effort to get at him. He did acid all the time. And he would black out if he had too many drinks. He would drink all the time. He would black out every day. He would go about his actions but have no recollections.

...

He came home from work one time stinking drunk. I worked in the dining room at the country club, and he walked in reeking of alcohol and picked me up by my hair, right out of my seat, and dragged me out by my hair in front of everybody I worked with ... It was more humiliating than anything. He never physically really hurt me. He broke three fingers once, but I'm not talking about broken jaws or broken nose. He liked to push me up against walls. It is more humiliating than anything ... He said that sometimes a woman deserves it, but I don't buy that at all.

...

I decided I was going back to school. I told him, you're not going to stop me, and he grabbed my head and knocked me against the shower a couple of times and then he went to work. I got the message and caught the bus to school, talked to a friend, and she said, you're coming home with me tonight. The next day I called my grandmother to come and get me and there were five teachers and three guidance counsellors. He was a raving maniac ... He still tries to get me to go back with him. (Kim, August 1991)

Kim was opposed to the idea that you could classify or theoretically explain violence. She described educational initiatives at her university as largely 'off-base.' She reported that people had made a 'big deal' about the likelihood of being raped while going back to your dorm after dark. She said the problem was not being raped on the way back to the dorm, it was date rape. She said that anyone who had ever been date-raped would tell you that date rape occurs when you've been drinking. Kim said it's not that the guy is bad or mean; rather, alcohol lowers inhibitions and makes people extremely selfish. Kim saw alcohol as the major reason for abuse, generally, and for abuse in the Township, in particular. Kim expressed strong objections to what she termed 'psychological theories.' She also objected to gender theories. Kim said she didn't 'buy it' that women ever just submitted to violence, and she said that if it was true in the past it certainly is not true in the present. More than anything, Kim emphasized the centrality of drinking to violence:

As I said the other night, alcohol is the biggest factor of violence in this town. I see a lot of theories about why a father will abuse a mother. A lot of theories. But the most common, common reason for any violence is alcohol. The most common line I've heard between my friends and their boyfriends and their friends' parents and my parents is, I'm sorry I struck you, it will never happen again. That is the most common, common reason. They're drunk, that's all, they're drunk.

...

You can't make theories. Every case is different. Like they say, violence is cyclical. You know, they say there's phases of violence and of making up and it keeps building. I saw this program. Well, I don't find violence cyclical. What I see is that violent relationships don't last. Around here I don't know many people that are in chronically violent situations because people around here tend to break out of it. I know lots are like my one friend, she kicked her boyfriend out of the house because he was always beating her up. In this town, relationships are quick and frequent.

...

I know with a lot of the stuff going on now is, well, I know there is a lot of reciprocal violence among young people. I think as time goes on you're less likely to take it. And I think that in a second violent relationship the woman is less likely to be passive from the start. She realizes she doesn't have to stand for it ... Women fight as much as men. And, except for alcohol, I would say cheating creates more violence than anything else and women are just as jealous. Finances will create trouble between a husband and wife, but cheating, the girlfriend going after the other girl and the guy after both girls. This whole town wars over shit like that. (Kim, August 1991)

Kim firmly believed that violence is alcohol driven. However, she also regarded violence as a learned response. At the party, she told me that violence works.[22] She said the fact that violence works means that it is a 'self-reinforcement.' Kim said that for violent people to break away from violence, they had to have negative reinforcements, and they had to develop insight in order to see where the violence was taking them. Kim said she realized that she was unlikely to avoid violence as long as she kept drinking. She said that she usually managed to contain drinking situations by avoiding rye, which made her 'crazy violent.' She said that, except when drinking rye, she was not violent unless provoked. However, Kim reported that she drank rye fairly often, and that, regardless of what she was drinking, she was frequently violent:

The only time I get truly violent without being provoked is when I hurt myself and then I'll lash out at anyone. And, like I told you the other night, I can't drink rye. If I have four or five shots of rye, I punch out the person closest to me. I know I do, I've done it. I did it the other night, after the party we went to Joe's and I had a few rye. It happened then. But when I really beat someone up, it's for something different. It's when I'm provoked. Like when I fell asleep after another party and I woke up with this jerk trying to take my pants down. I pounded him good ... My favourite drink is tequila. I can handle twenty-five tequila. Last time I tried twenty-five tequilas, I got in a fight with a five-hundred-pound bouncer. You know the bouncer at the bar. That wasn't usual, though. Usually I can drink tequila with no problem. (Kim, August 1991)

Kim described herself as an avid reader. She reported that she had a gift for academic studies since early childhood. Kim enjoyed fiction, philosophy, and political science. She described study as 'almost an alternative to the bottle,' and enthusiastically discussed Plato, Kant, and Descartes. She planned to use education to achieve power over herself. However, Kim also planned to use education to achieve power over others. After completing her BA, Kim planned to study law. She also planned to write fiction. However, Kim said that her ultimate goal was to be prime minister of Canada. Kim said that she realized that at some point in the future she would have to consciously step away from violence if she was to achieve these goals. She saw university as a step in this direction:

People make an effort to get out of it around here, but it seems like every time you get out of it you get into another one, because everybody drinks. This place [the Township] really sucks you back, because everybody drinks. I think I made my break when I got to university and I vowed never to come back. Course, I partied there too. (Kim, August 1991)

Kim's story is the story of a young woman struggling to create a positive possibility of herself. It is not, however, the story of a woman ready to repudiate abuse. On the contrary, it is the story of a woman who enjoys power, physical and mental. Kim stated that she believed that she could make her future happen as she progressively learned how to 'manipulate' reality. Kim likened reality to a piece of fiction. She believed that she could control outcomes through insight and action. However, she appeared unready to apply her insights, unwilling to curb her propensity for violence, and unwilling to curtail her use and abuse of alcohol. Kim's story is the story of an invincible 'in control' self navigating through an 'out of control' world. It is the story of a self equipped with intelligence, insight, and a hunger for knowledge, but mired in alcoholism and violence:

> You know how you can tell the way a story is going to turn out, you can generally see it. That's how we manipulate our own stories. There are a lot of openings, and there are a lot of closed doors ... I already know something about just about everything, but you never really see it, anything, even firsthand. It always comes around in a roundabout way. There is a lot more that goes on that we just don't know about ... We have to learn how to see, we have to learn to make things happen. (Kim, August 1991)

Keith

> My life has had its ups and downs, but it is mostly downs as much as I can remember ... I talk to my counsellor and I always told him I felt there was something better around the corner for me. But I never knew how to make it happen. I knew I was doing all the wrong things at all the wrong times. But I always knew that some day I would be OK, someday I would be a better parent, someday it would be all right.
>
> ...
>
> I used to have a real anger towards life and carry it with me all the time. I still have a chip on my shoulder, but I feel it's not as big a chip anymore. But I still have an ego, I'm still riding motorcycles and thinking I'm as tough as everybody else. (Keith, July 1991)

Keith was a voluntary Regional Woman Abuse Program client who participated in a conjoint interview with his wife, Cathy, in the summer of 1991, and in a follow-up interview in the summer of 1992. Both partners were in their early thirties. Both were child-abuse survivors who maintained strong emotional ties with a non-abusive parent. Both had participated in previous relationships marked by severe violence. The interview took place in Keith and Cathy's rented house, located in one of the Township's villages. At the time of the interview, Keith and Cathy both participated in individual counselling through Township Family Services and group counselling through the Regional Woman Abuse Program. Cathy also participated in Regional Sex Abuse Program counselling.

Keith reported severe physical child abuse at the hands of an alcoholic father, who physically battered his wife and youngest son, and who sexually abused his daughter. Keith reported that his sister had recently attempted to kill her first husband, a 'really abusive man,' and that his older brother, whom their father chose not to batter, was 'weird,' 'gross,' and sexually 'inappropriate.' Keith reported that he always loved his mother and he had always known that she loved him, despite her inability to protect him or his sister:

Both my parents were alcoholics ... Oh would they fight! My dad would throw TVs through the door ... My mother wasn't violent, she was like a scared rabbit, really scared. There was lots of times when she would get beat up and hide it from us.

...

I was in the middle of the family, so I was always the one that got beat up by my dad, maybe 'cause I looked like my mother ... And I think he molested my sister ... My dad, he was always, he says he loves me, but I take it as it comes. I never really felt loved, not by him. I felt more like he was angry at me. I always felt, like, why are you always angry at me? Why do you always beat me up? What does it all mean? (Keith, July 1991)

Keith's history since leaving home at age fourteen centres on juvenile criminal behaviour – theft, drug trafficking, vagrancy – and juvenile and adult violence and substance abuse:

I was 14 when I first left home ... I was bumming and living off the street, buying drugs and selling them, things like that ... When I was sixteen I was in jail, car theft. Stole a car and did three months for that ... I ended up in jail a second time after that. There was a truck with a whole shit load of leather clothes – leather jackets, leather overalls, leather skirts, the whole shebang. We walked out of there with $6,000 worth of leather clothes in garbage bags, and we got caught. I got six months in jail for that. I was seventeen, going on eighteen.

...

I went coast to coast. I came to Toronto and learned to bum the streets in Toronto, and one day me and a friend go up Yonge Street. I had this old man's hat, it was really cool, and I had platform boots, the whole thing, and most of the time, snook boots, but my snook boots were wore out, but I had platform shoes. Snook boots are like cowboy boots, but they've got a square toe and they used to have the rings here where the straps went around ... A cop car came by, and the cop saw me and this friend ... So we walked two blocks up and waited there and stood on that corner and they got us in the car. They asked if we had any drugs, and I said, no. Then they conspired in the front. They said, we don't like your kind here. What are you doing here? I said, I was visiting a friend. He wanted the address and I wouldn't give it to him. I said, if I don't give you an address, are you going to put me under arrest? So they had the guns in our faces and kicked us out of town, and I was on the bus the next day and took the bus to Sudbury and got out on the highway and hitch-hiked to B.C. from there. Went out to Vancouver for a while and got in a lot of trouble ... I was in jail there for a little time ... I left there and went back East ... I still wasn't nineteen. (Keith, July 1991)

Keith was involved in a series of violent relationships prior to meeting Cathy. His violence was related to a number of issues – jealousy, depression, feeling taken advantage of, feeling threatened, substance abuse. In most instances, Keith described himself as the sole or prime perpetrator. In other instances, he described reciprocal, even female-instigated, violence. He described two previous relationships in some detail, his relationship with his first wife, Liz, and his relationship with a 'live-in' girlfriend, Nadene:

I was twenty when I got married to Liz. We already had Todd, she was pregnant for a second time ... A month after our first anniversary, she was leaving, going out the door. She left me with the babies ... Todd wasn't much over two, and Arial was really a baby.

Before she left there wasn't physical fighting. There was physical fighting when she left. When Liz left, I was really depressed. I went out and broke somebody's window, and I went over to her house and actually popped her in the nose once and walked home. I walked into a bar and she was with this guy ... She later came home and said, I'm leaving you, and when she did that I said, your leaving through that wall ... I pushed her head into the wall. I booted her in the ass. It was a good boot.

She came back once ... I looked to the end of the walkway and I seen him, and I thought I was seeing things. They were playing tricks on me, eh? And I said, correct me if I'm wrong, Liz, is that your boyfriend I see standing down at the end of the road? And she said, you must be seeing things ... I saw him behind the garbage can and said, you are an asshole for coming out here today. I followed her back to the house and she kept saying, I want to stay here, I want to stay here, and I just grabbed her by the seat of the pants and drug her down the stairs and threw her out the door, she fell down. I said, go with your lover, I've had enough of your bullshit. That's enough.

...

When I was living with this one girlfriend, Nadene, this one [pointing to a tattoo on his forearm], I ended up getting real sick. We were at this bar and my guts were just killing me. I was doubled over in pain, and she was all pissed at me because we had to go home. I said then, you stay. I went home. I think I took a cab, and she didn't come home till real late and by the time she come home she was drunk. I wasn't drunk because the pain started happening. I was sitting on the couch, we had this babysitter there, she had a kid and I had mine. I was holding myself, I was doubled over. My guts were being ripped out as far as I was concerned.

Nadene come over to me and started kicking me in the face, while I was bent over. I told her I wasn't in the mood for this. She was physically violent all the time. She grew up that way. If she drank, she was nuts, total nuts. You couldn't reason with her, talk to her at all. I was doubled over in pain. She was kicking me in the head, two or three times. After the third time, I said, don't do this, I'm in too much pain. I asked the babysitter to call an ambulance, I said, I'm in a lot of pain and I need an ambulance. I said, I feel like I'm going to die. She stopped kicking and the babysitter went out of the room and started to use the phone to call an ambulance. Then she was grabbing me by the hair, trying to lift me up to punch me. I come right up, I grab her behind the throat, and I just went pow. I drove her so hard, she flew over the couch, knocked the whole couch over, and slid under out dining-room table, and she was like this, knocked out cold. I couldn't believe I hit her that hard. I was in so much pain, I just reflected all my pain out and struck out at somebody and probably could have killed her that night if I kept going, but one punch was enough. I was lucky I didn't kill her.

...

Another night, I left Nadene in a bar because she was freaking out, she was threatening me. She had this table full of guys and said, you see those guys over there, I'm going to have sex with all of them. I said, good for you. She said, how do you feel about that? I said, you want to know how I really feel about that, and I picked up my beer and dumped it on her lap and I get up and walk out of the bar after her, eh? She is there looking at her pants and looking at her pants and looking at me. I walked out of the bar and left her there. There were a lot of times when I think I acted logically, but there were times when I acted logically for only a short, short time. I have a real short fuse, eh? I bought a case of beer and went to a friend's place, and sat and drank half a case of beer with him. I had about three beers, his wife had a beer, and he had about three beers, and I said, I'm going to go back and pick Nadene up. I found her in a gas station. We're driving down the highway, and she grabs me by the hair and starts yanking me across the car as I'm trying to drive. So I pull the car over on this median and I drag her out of the car, and I leave her in the middle of the highway. I drive down and take the kids to the babysitter, and I say to myself, I'm leaving her there, that's it ... The cops end up bringing her down to where the babysitter's was. What saved my ass was that she was so rowdy, she was standing up on the steps calling the cops names and was spitting on them, so they took her to jail, not me ... She was calling them pigs and everything under the sun and going [pig sound]. (Keith, July 1991)

Keith's decision to change was rooted in his love for his children, Arial and Todd. For their sake, he decided to cease interacting with wild and abusive people, and he decided to give up his addictions. Keith was forced to acknowledge that criminality did not fit with parenting. For Keith, leaving abuse also meant leaving Nadene:

My kids had a lot of impact. I wanted their lives to be better ... When I was in B.C. and heavily into alcohol and coke, I lost the kids for a month. I drove a car through a house. I was trying to get some people. I was really mad. Before I even got in the car, I took a stick to one guy and broke a few of his ribs, and I went into the house and punched out Nadene's cousin and punched out her brother. This was all over a $900 phone bill ran up under my name. The car I tried to run through the house was almost totally wrecked ... They kept me in jail overnight and then they let me out, but they took my kids from me for a month. I lost both of my kids.
...
That's when the major change came in my life ... I was blaming other people, but I took some responsibility on myself, too. At that point, I felt that no matter who I am with, no matter what I do, the kids should always come first. At that time, I sat down, I was watching the fire burn, and that's when I came to the conclusion that I've got to get the hell out of here. I left B.C. and I came here and met Cathy. (Keith, July 1991)

Keith and Cathy met at an Alcoholics Anonymous meeting. Their six-year-old relationship had been marked by episodic relapses into substance abuse and violence. Both partners maintained that they had 'addictive personalities,' and both maintained that they felt good when they were high, especially when they were high on cocaine. Unfortunately, relapses into substance abuse coincided with relapses into violence. Violence typically took the form of Keith's verbally abusing Cathy over imagined infidelities, throwing and smashing things, and coercing or intimidating her into sex. In 1989 Cathy sought refuge at the Regional shelter, and Keith enrolled in the Regional Woman Abuse Program. Keith reported that this last relapse into violence coincided with his relapse into alcohol abuse, and that he had now 'pretty much totally' given up drinking:

> I think that men feel that underestimating the damage they have caused is easier than admitting to themselves the amount of damage they have caused. I think a lot of it is remorse. I had to go through a lot of remorse about what happened between Cathy and I. We went for a couple of years of really bad times. We were on the verge of splitting up. She went to a shelter because I was so abusive, eh ... Always verbally abusive. Sexually abusive. I wanted to have sex when she didn't really want to have sex. I'd push her into it, which was wrong. She would want space and I wouldn't give it to her, I realize that now ... I felt she was being unfaithful to me, she was having sex with somebody else. Without a real reason, eh. A lot of my jealousy stemmed from my ex-relationship ... Violence is what I had learned before and knew how to do best. It was the way I dealt with it. It wasn't fair to her. It wasn't fair to me either. (Keith, July 1991)

Keith and Cathy both expressed commitment to overcoming violence, and to maintaining their relationship. Both accepted that Keith was fully and solely responsible for past abuse, and both endorsed a gender-based analysis of *domestic abuse*. Moreover, both believed that the model of equality and respect that guided their current handling of domestic responsibilities and decision-making would prevent a relapse. Finally, both viewed their past struggles as learning experiences:

> I think, back when I was a kid and my parents were going through that, my father was allowed to come home and do that to my mother because it was justifiable. He was the father, the breadwinner of the house, and if he got a little pissed off, he could take it out on her because she was married to him and she was supposed to take it. And that was my understanding when I was a kid, although I have a better understanding of it now.
>
> ...

Men think that women are like household items that are there to do the cooking and cleaning and looking after the children ... We decided that when Cathy went back to work that we'd share the housework. It makes sense that I do more now because I'm home more. (Keith, July 1991)

I think a lot of men would break their own habits if they knew how to ... I think a lot of it is attitudes. (Cathy, July 1991)

You can only do what you can do, and you can't look back and blame yourself for things that you've done. You had to go through them to learn. For me it's all a learning experience. I had to go through what I went through in order to get where I am today. (Keith, July 1991)

In the summer of 1991, Keith believed that he had achieved survival status that, with the support of Cathy and Regional Woman Abuse Program and Township Family Services counsellors, he had taken a number of steps to put an end to violence and abuse. He had broken off relationships with his wildest and most abusive friends; he had accepted personal responsibility for his actions; he had worked through guilt and remorse; and he was actively working to transform sexist attitudes and behaviours. However, he continued to delude himself that he could use substances responsibly.

In the summer of 1992, Keith and Cathy relapsed once again into addiction and violence. As in previous episodes, the violence was fuelled by Keith's jealousy. I saw Keith briefly before he and Cathy left the Township to participate in separate detox programs. Visibly 'strung out' on cocaine, Keith blamed his 'paranoia' and violence on the drug. With Cathy, he hoped that this time they would succeed in giving up all substances for good, and that the cycles of violence would stop. Cathy's hopes fed his; his fed hers:

I've been sober before. I know I can be sober again. I'll do it. I'll do it for Cathy, I'll do it for the kids. (Keith, October, 1992)

Keith's story is the story of a male who wanted to take responsibility, who wanted to 'stop doing all the wrong things at all the wrong times,' but who kept doing the very things that led him, again and again, into cycles of abuse. Keith's story is the story of a male reaching again and again towards survival. Despite repeated failures, he continued to believe, or hope, that someday he will be OK, that someday he will be a better parent and a better husband, that someday he will stop being abusive.

Sam

> I was a real nut, so I figured I'd better get into counselling. But it was mainly her giving me an ultimatum – either you change or you're out. (Sam, September 1991)

Sam's story is the story of a twenty-six-year-old court-mandated Regional Woman Abuse Program client who, in his own words, was 'seriously, dangerously violent.' Sam recounted driving other motorists off the road because they were driving too slowly or because they tried to cut him off, kicking and beating his dog, and terrorizing previous and current girlfriends with weapons. Sam reported that he still longed for reconciliation with his first girlfriend, 'the love of his life.' He also reported that he was ambivalent about his commitment to his current girlfriend, Florence. Nevertheless, he had cut the wires to Florence's car so that she couldn't leave him, and he had smashed the phone so that she couldn't call the police.

The interview took place in the fall of 1991 in the bungalow Sam and Florence shared. Florence participated through the first half of the interview. Both partners described themselves as children of 'dysfunctional' alcoholic families; both abused substances; both had participated in a series of abusive dating or spousal relationships; and both were currently working to 'break the cycles in our lives' through participation in various counselling programs (Florence, September 1991).

As in the case of the majority of admittedly violent men who abused substances in the survey, Sam did not attribute his problems with anger and violence to substance abuse. He maintained that alcohol and other drugs shortened his fuse a bit, but that his problems were inside him.[23]

> Alcohol is part of my problem, but it's not a problem with my temper, though. My temper is just as bad whether I am drinking or not drinking, just as violent, just as dangerous, just as destructive. The only thing alcohol will do is the fuse is shorter, that is all, or maybe no fuse ... I am basically the same guy that I am, whether I'm drinking or not. It is just that the fuse is way shorter that's all. All the paranoia and insecurities are there just like every day, they're inside me. (Sam, September 1991)

Sam attributed his insecurities and destructiveness to the 'weird,' secretive, emotionally isolating, and reality-denying practices of his middle-class alcoholic parents. His mother surreptitiously added alcohol to her morning coffee, and maintained a 'glow' throughout the day. She used alcohol to mask awareness that her husband might carry through on his periodic threats to leave her. His father, who held an administrative position with a large corporation, used alcohol to cope with a marriage too disappointing to face. Publicly, he contained his drinking and disappointment behind a smooth professional façade. Privately, he vented his anger through object aggression, and then denied that anything was wrong. Neither parent would admit that their son had problems. They regarded his present participation in therapy as a way of blaming them for problems he only imagined he had:

> Everything is secret in our family. Everything is denial secret. Nobody knows anything. We don't know anything about each other. (Sam, September 1991)

> You would never suspect Sam's father is anything like he is. (Florence, September 1991)

> I never knew my sister. She's three years younger, but I never even talked to her till three years ago.
> ...
> My parents deny that I'm like I am. If I had normal parents, they would have known how to deal with it. They don't deal with anything. My mother threw me in jail one time. She says now I am making that up. I can't even comprehend how you could deny something like that. It is unbelievable ... They don't like me going to therapy because they have this fear that they are going to be blamed for everything. (Sam, September 1991)

With the help of Regional Woman Abuse Program and Township Family Services counsellors, Sam was in the process of exploring childhood experiences that he believed fed his violent behaviours. However, it is not violence that marks Sam's childhood accounts; it is an intense sense of emotional neglect, isolation, and loneliness. As Sam expressed it, abuse in his family was 'more mental trauma than anything.' His descriptions of traumatic events centre on needs that went unrecognized, on things generally 'not right,' on things generally 'not good':

There was a very significant thing in my first year in school, in kindergarten. I remembered coming home with some kind of art that I wanted to show my mother, and two bullies threw me around and ripped up my art and stuff. I remember clearly, to this day, how I felt, how upset I was, how scared I was and everything. The therapist says, what happened when you got home? And I don't know what happened. I guess nothing and that is very significant. Obviously I didn't get the nurturing that might have been necessary for something that dramatic.

...

I still haven't clarified it all. I don't know if it is rejection. It is strange, this severe loneliness. I quite don't know why that happened ... There was nobody there to comfort me the way I needed it. Here I am seven years old and I was forced to play the piano, and I would sit and pound the piano as hard as I could, I was hoping I could break it. I pounded and pounded and pounded. There was nobody there that came around and said, jeez you really don't like the piano, eh? It was you're going to sit here a half hour until you play. Now sitting back looking at this, I say, jeez, that wasn't really right.

...

Grade six was the most critical year of my life. It was when I turned twelve to thirteen and realized, hey, my parents aren't happy. I overheard a fight my parents had in which my father said he never wanted to have us and I found that very devastating. I had no idea that that was the situation in my family. I was totally naïve to it all, and it hit me that night ... wow, this isn't good. (Sam, September 1991)

Sam's generalized feelings that things were not right were complemented by his father's occasional bouts of object aggression. These acts of 'minor' violence provided Sam with a model for how to assert and experience power. At the onset, Sam experienced violence as instrumental. His goal was to instil fear:

I used to see my father throw something, or smash something and growing up, well, wait until I get big enough. When I did get big enough, I got bigger than him and I really took it to the extreme. I made sure everybody was scared of me then ... My objective was I was going to scare my father, instead of him scaring me. He was shocked and I said this is good, it works good. (Sam, September 1991)

As an adult, Sam takes object aggression to an extreme. He throws

Florence against walls. However, Sam insisted that this violence is aimed at self-destruction, not at intimidation or coercion At the same time, instilling fear gives Sam a sense of power. This attraction to power is epitomized in Sam's obsession with weapons. Sam maintained that weapons were expressions of his contradictory needs for self-assertion and self-destruction. Obsessoin with power, and the destruction of objects and others, appear as by-products of self-processes that leave Sam feeling that others will only take him seriously if they know he will carry through on violence:

> This kitchen had holes all around it a few months ago. I get super violent, very dangerous. I throw Florence ... I always felt that if I punched her, she doesn't stand a chance ... I feel very bad when she gets a bruise from me holding her. That was not part of the plan ... The plan is mainly to hurt myself, to destroy everything that I value. I totalled my car. I used to have a Dukes of Hazzard car that my ex-girlfriend and I worked on together, and it meant a lot to me. I totalled it, and it couldn't be driven again. I took a jack and walked around the car and just wrecked it. (Sam, September 1991)

> I would get scared and he would get the gun out and I would say, oh no, he is taking it out on himself now, or he has threatened to kill himself or he has threatened to take an overdose ... I'd be scared to come home: Oh no, now he has ... I can't leave the house if I'm angry because he blocks my way. I am a hostage in my own house ... He has got his firearms, and one little decision, that is it. He could blow my head off, too. (Florence, September 1991)

> I have always known that my temper is really bad, and any of my friends that have seen it have said, holy shit, man, that is major, and they know if I have a gun in my hand, call my bluff. And I hope nobody calls my bluff, but if they do, I'll have to carry through. If you're going to go that far and are standing there with a loaded gun. You're hoping that nobody makes me do anything with this. I hope nobody calls the police, because if they do, I am going to have to go out shooting. I would, because I am not going to look like an idiot now.
>
> ...
>
> That is just standing your ground and holding your honour and pride – you stand up for your style, nobody screws around with me in my own house, no matter what the cost. I guess I am fortunate to realize that, holy

cow, I am going to shoot myself one night because I am going to have to follow through. I am always threatening, I am going to do it one of these days, I am going to do it, whether I am going to want to or not, just so I don't look like an idiot ... You're freaking right out, and you have to carry through, you have to. If you keep doing these things, nobody will take you seriously. You have to let everyone know you are serious all the time, and I am getting really tired of getting serious all the time. It gets very hard to play that act all the time. (Sam, September 1991)

Sam's account of his relationship with his high-school sweetheart, whose father was also violent and alcoholic, demonstrates how Sam operates when he feels most threatened. In this account, substance abuse exacerbated violence rooted in Sam's insecurities, and 'weird' messages from his father fed obsessions about whether others would recognize his personal power:

I lost the love of my life. All that is gone ... I was abusive. But what she really hated was me smoking up, because my personality changed drastically. I get very quiet. You don't know anything about me when I am stoned. I get really weird. I get very closed and she hated that. The two years we were together – we were together five years in total – I was very violent and very abusive and controlling, with temper, choking. I drank like crazy. With booze I get violent. That is when the violence is worse, when you are drunk, because you are really upset when someone is ruining your good time.

...

I remember once she was taking her clothes off, hoping I would stop ... I found out she was seeing another guy a bit, nothing sexual, but I was intimidated a relationship was starting with somebody else. The cat was let out of the bag, I was flipping. She just started taking her clothes off to get me to stop. She must have went home then or something. Anyway she left. That is when I had the gun thing. I flipped, lost it. I went looking for her all over town. I threatened her father and threw him around the yard. I found out where she was with this guy, and I tried to kick in the hotel door and I couldn't, and the police came and they should have arrested me, but they didn't, because the rampage continued.

...

I went home and my father dared me to get my gun, which is weird. I was all stoned and juiced and really upset, crying, and I came in the house. I went home and my father is freaked out at me about being stoned and was saying, why don't you get your gun and show us what a real hero you are? I say, OK, and so I did. It was weird.

...

So I am standing in the driveway with my rifle, and everybody can see me and I am going like this – come on, who is first ... Her father came out and talked to me very calmly, and she talked to me. She came out and talked to me, and I just went in my truck and I figured that this is pretty screwed up, I'll just crash in the truck. I woke up with the police breaking out my windows and there she is hiding behind a bush. They called the cops because they thought I was going to shoot myself, eh. That's what happened. That was the end.

...

I don't know why, but I always prayed to god that she would come back to me and I am going to be different. She came back after a period of a year, and I figured I would be different and I was. I got my commercial pilot's licence and I quit drinking. I quit booze for a year and drugs for a year-and-a-half. Then she left again ... I don't know why. She didn't really say. She just said, she made a mistake. She thought it might be right, but it was not. I was devastated ... I always felt that it was because no matter what you have done you can be forgiven, but it is never forgotten. All this abuse that you've done ... If you hurt somebody, for what you do against them – you're screwed. (Sam, September 1991)

For Sam, breaking violent patterns was incredibly difficult – in part, because Sam experienced violence as an addiction, as a rush of power. This rush provided temporary refuge from the pain which prevents him from believing that anyone might love him. Sam reported that he frequently felt like giving up on his relationship with Florence, whom he experienced as emotionally cold, detached, resentful. Even more, he felt like giving up on his struggle to put an end to violence:

You're violent mainly just to relieve that pain – someone is hurting you, they are not listening, they are not understanding you. Then you're violent, wham, now everybody understands, Sam is upset.

...

It is that instant rush. I guess it's an addiction. It is the only thing you know that works well. .. The rush while you are doing it is unbelievable adrenalin and power, you know. And after it is over it is, wow, why not do it again? ... It's like alcohol, it's an addiction ... It is a major rush. It is

super hard to control. You are addicted to that rush ... The depression comes immediately after, but at the time, at the instant, it's the rush.
...

Sometimes I wonder, what am I trying for? It is very easy to be violent, it's the easy way. It is the easy way to hide the hurt, it's easy ... Familiarity breeds contempt too, you know. You get into this, it happens again, it keeps working. You are letting yourself go and getting the control you are looking for. (Sam, September 1991)

As was Keith, Sam appeared to be reaching towards a possibility of himself as a survivor, but was finding it a difficult reach. Unlike Keith, Sam did not attribute his problems to something outside himself, that is, to substance abuse. Sam believed that his problems were 'inside him,' and he recognized that he did not fully want to give up the feelings of power and control that he gained, however temporarily, through violence.

Sam's story is more a story of defeat than it is of bad faith. Sam recognized and accepted that he was 'screwed' because he had been abusive and that nothing he did would eradicate his past abuses. His ongoing abusiveness was rooted in an intense need to experience himself as 'serious.' For Sam, anything, even his own death, was preferable to not being taken seriously.

Hank

I still feel that my wife deliberately provoked an assault, and I was stupid enough, violent enough. I believe if she didn't provoke it, she engineered it. She definitely did. (Hank, September 1991)

Hank was a court-mandated client of the Regional Woman Abuse Program who had previously participated in counselling through Township Family Services. He also participated in Alcoholics Anonymous. The interview took place in the fashionably furnished apartment Hank established subsequent to his recent court-imposed separation from his wife, Vicki. Hank was forty-two when Vicki and their older daughter, Melissa, charged him with domestic assault.

Hank reported that he grew up in a 'dirt poor' rural family, the fourth of ten children. The family was ruled by an authoritarian father who insisted that his wife, daughters, and young sons eat only after he and the older boys had finished, who severely teased and physically abused his young sons to make them tough, and who insisted that his sons settle their differences by 'pounding' each other to the point of exhaustion.

Hank reported that, as a teen and youth, drinking and brawling were his 'primary entertainments.' These activities resulted in three assault charges, one at age eighteen, one at age twenty-five, and a third at age thirty-two. Hank described 'conquering women' as a second, and apparently less important, form of entertainment. He reported that his wife, Vicki, the daughter of an abusive alcoholic, had been 'as easy as most.' He reported that he had reasons to believe that she was an incest victim, and he maintained that she had had at least one affair since he married her.

Hank acknowledged that he had a 'jealousy problem' and a 'drinking problem,' and he freely admitted that he had been violent with 'everybody' for as long as he could remember. However, he denied that he had been violent with Vicki or their daughters prior to 'the incident' that led to the domestic assault charge and his forcible eviction from the marital residence. At the same time, he acknowledged that Vicki had been trying to end their relationship for some time.

Hank reported that several months prior to 'the incident,' Vicki had insisted on separate bedrooms, and separate social lives. She had presented Hank with a legal separation agreement, which he refused to sign. She had also instructed their thirteen-year-old daughter, Debbie, to call the police should Hank assault her. Hank maintained that Vicki manipulated him sexually, and that she intentionally provoked him, 'knowing what buttons to push.' Hank was convinced Vicki 'engineered' or even 'staged' his assault of her as part of a 'plan' to get rid of him and obtain sole legal possession of their house:

> The night she announced it ['that it was over and done with'], she brought her brother in with her. She didn't present me with that separation agreement then, but when I got it, it was dated prior to her mentioning it. So she brought her brother. Her sister-in-law had already taken Debbie and they had gone. I really didn't like that brother, but I felt she brought him thinking she might provoke me, and then she told me it was over and they left.
>
> ...
>
> The next day I tried to convince her that we shouldn't separate. I said, I will quit drinking and do all these things and we should get some family counselling. She said, I don't have a problem, you have a problem, you

look after it. And that would just annoy me to no end. All these insults she would give me ... Like that I'm a liar and she don't trust me, that she don't want the kids to grow up around me, that kind of thing ... I told her, look, that's over [an eighteen-month-long affair with another woman]. If you want, I will even arrange a meeting, anything if that will help. She wouldn't go along with that, but she would keep making these visits to my room when she felt like it, you know, for sex. And that gave me a tremendous amount of hope. (Hank, September 1991)

A Saturday morning incident that preceded 'the incident' demonstrates Hank's reasoning. This incident originated in an argument over whether thirteen-year-old Debbie would go to a baseball game with Hank, or to a picnic with her mother and her mother's friend, a woman Hank characterized as a 'slut' and a 'lesbian bitch.' His account centres on the ways this pre-incident incident fed his wife's 'plan' to get him out of the house for good:

I said, Debbie, I thought you were coming with me today. She wouldn't answer; she looked at me and her mother, the poor kid. Anyhow, they continue to cart stuff. I was cursing and Vicki just wouldn't respond. Just knowing which buttons to push can drive you around the bend. And, of course, her purse was there, and I kicked it out the door and all her stuff was in it and it went everywhere. And she said to Debbie, get Cricket, that's our little dog, and get in the car. So I got in the car, too, and she drove right up to the police station and we went in. She went up to the policeman and said, I want to know what I can do to get rid of this guy, I can't take it anymore. The policeman says, if he does this stuff [throwing and smashing objects], we'll come down there and watch him, but the only way you're going to get him out of the house is if he starts hitting you or one of the kids, and then we'll arrest him and he'll be out. That is when I think the plan started. (Hank, September 1991)

Hank complained that Vicki manipulated him, especially in the bedroom, and that she had intentionally implemented a 'plan' aimed at ensuring that he would have no choice other than to vacate their residence. His account demonstrates that, in fact, Hank attempted to use sex to manipulate Vicki, and that he had a 'plan' of his own – one aimed at subverting Vicki's attempts to negotiate a legal separation:

I said to myself, well I am not going to live in limbo, the next time this woman friend of mine calls me up I am going to be nice. And I went and told my wife that this is not a threat or anything but, but I am going to do this. I was getting a few things ready to go away for that weekend. She came crying and upset. I said to her, look I am probably not going to sleep with her or anything like that, but I was going to go. All you have to do is tell me you don't want me to go and I won't go, and she wouldn't tell me not to go.

...

She wound up taking me to the bedroom. After that it was insults. When did I arrange this meeting and all this stuff? And I said, she phoned me at work and I told her what is going on with us, and she said, did I want to meet her and just talk about it, and I said, I would. Then she was fussing and screaming and said, how can you do that after this? And I said, I won't do it, just say you don't want me to go and that'll do more good than anything. She said, you want to go anyway don't you? I said, if you don't care, don't give a shit, I'm going to go because I need some kind of companionship. So I went, of course, but I figured there was some hope even after then. (Hank, September 1991)

Hank's account of 'the incident' leading to his arrest is a vivid description of male-driven reciprocal spousal, or rather family, violence. From Hank's perspective, his wife 'staged' his repeated insistence that she either condone his plan to continue an affair with another woman or agree to a reconciliation, 'staged' his pursuit of her through three levels of their spacious house when she refused to agree to either, 'staged' her attempt to protect herself and their daughter from what she believed was an imminent attack, and 'staged' their daughter's desperate attempts to protect her mother:

Our friends [dinner guests] left about nine o'clock, and I said, Vicki, there is something I want to talk to you about, would you sit down for a minute. So we sat down in the kitchen, and I started to tell her what my plan was and, of course, between every sentence was – if you think it's over. I kept begging and pleading because I said I couldn't live with this anymore. About every two minutes, we were interrupted by one of the kids, 'cause Melissa was home from college. So I said, we could always go to my room if you want to finish the conversation. Of course, I said that rather smart-alecky, you know [implying sex] ... After I let the dog out for a walk and everything. When I went upstairs, Melissa was in bed in her room and Vicki was in Debbie's room. So I just rapped on Debbie's door and said, I'm up here now if you are ready, and she said, no, go to bed. I screamed, if you can't spare two fuckin minutes after twenty years, some sort of insult.

...

Eventually she got up and came in my room, and so I told her what my plan was. And she gets in with, well that's what you want to do, in a tone that meant, well, I'm the guy who wants to get out of here, but I really didn't, I never ever did. I said, Vicki, if you want me to tell you what I want, I will tell you what I want, I want to stay, I want to continue working, I want us as a family to get some counselling, I want you to forgive what you think I have done. She didn't know half of it. It is not that I'm a womanizer and I never was, but she had found a hotel receipt in my pocket. Anyway, she said something to me about this friend of hers from work and I said, I've heard enough about that slut, that old lesbian bitch. I threw the blankets back and at that moment she jumps up, runs out of the room downstairs to the first level.

...

So I got up and followed her without a pajama top on. I followed her, and with this commotion Melissa came down. And when I went down, my wife went down another level and she screamed back to Melissa, call the police. So I just yanked the phone out of her hand. At this time my wife came up to the kitchen level and I said, Melissa, go to bed, you interrupted our conversation, this has nothing to do with you. I didn't think I was bullying.

...

At this time, Melissa walked away from me and then came back and pushed me. And I kicked the phone and Vicki went to where the knives were and grabbed one, like that, and I punched her in the face. One punch. [Hank maintained that the most he had ever done before was push Vicki against a wall once.] At that point, she dropped the knife and fell on the floor ... She would have cut my throat and I truly believe that – of course, I am the guy who committed the hostile act and everything. At this time, Melissa charged back at me and I turned to contend with her. Right at that moment I was just weak, limp from what had happened.

...

While I'm containing Melissa, my wife came at me and Debbie came down. She came down the other staircase. My wife came at me from behind and started beating on me, and I turned to deal with her because at this time Melissa wasn't really a threat. I grabbed Melissa by the wrist and she flung her arm out of my hand. When I turned to deal with my wife, Melissa starts beating on me and I turn and hit her.

...

At this time I had mellowed out, but I couldn't get stopped. I grabbed Melissa with tears in my eyes and said, sit down Melissa, I want to apologize, and everything. My wife had ran down to the lower level and that is the exit. And I thought she is going to try and leave again. I went to plead with her. I'm not going to do anymore, it's over with.

...

Melissa came down and attacked again because I am holding my wife. I turned to deal with Melissa a second time and my wife starts hitting me with her fists, on the back, on the side, the ear. So I got her by the throat, and I was holding her against the basement door trying to deal with Melissa with my right hand. Melissa hit me on the nose and I was already in tears but I could feel it. The only thing I could see to do was grab them and pull them in together. When I did, they both fell down on top of one another. I asked them if they would stop and just let me talk to them. Actually they struggled until they got up.

...

And about this time, Debbie has come down and she is going out to call the police. I was just sitting there thinking, what do I do now? They left and came back, and my wife came upstairs and got her purse and they were looking for Debbie. Debbie had come in and gone around the house with the little dog. They were hunting through the house for Debbie and Debbie was out sitting in the car.

...

So I just went to bed, and eventually the police came and arrested me ... I was arrested and put in jail. That took two days because you have to appear in court, and they took me back to jail and the justice of the peace came the next day. (Hank, September 1991)

After his arrest, Hank was allowed back in the house once, accompanied by a policeman, to collect his clothes. The policeman would not let him take other items, and advised Vicki that these were 'family property' and should be included in a legal division of assets. Hank maintained that Vicki subsequently sabotaged attempts to sell the house so as to divide the assets. He denied that it was he who harassed Vicki on the phone, and he denied that it was he who broke into the house prior to the police advising Vicki to get a guard dog. Hank maintained that men like him are unfairly being made to 'pay' for things that are not their fault. He maintained that he and Vicki would have resolved things had the police and court not intervened:

> [T]he plan has kicked right in and everyone is on her side and nobody cares about me ... I think some of us guys are paying for deeds our grand-fathers done. To me I am not at fault for the assault and that sort of thing. But I am and I wished I had never done it. But I would like to pay off that debt. A murderer gets out of jail after a period of time, and they have paid their debt.
>
> ...
>
> It is just what I see as rights and what has been done to me because of these laws. I am very sure that had that assault occurred and I was never arrested, that my wife and I could have resolved our differences; maybe never live together again, but we could have resolved it. (Hank, September 1991)

Unlike the other two men, Hank experienced himself more as a victim than as a perpetrator, and, unlike the other two men, Hank conveyed no vision of himself as a survivor. Hank remained convinced that he and Vicki had no real problem, and therefore that he had no real problem; or, rather, that substance abuse, jealousy, and anger were minor problems. He maintained that Vicki 'engineered' his violence, and that her friend, their daughters, the police, the courts, and society in general unfairly supported her. This claim was offset by Hank's graphic portrayal of himself as Vicki's assailant. Hank is an example of someone who cannot hear his own story. Hank could only hear his justifications. Hank's story is a story rife with apparent bad faith. It is a story of an abuser who will not or who cannot see his abusiveness.

Victimization, Perpetration, and Survival

In all seven narratives, and in account after account of abuse provided by Township residents, abuse does not occur as an isolated private incident. It occurs as part of a field of painful experiences that reach across generations and throughout extended family networks. Each story is peopled with hosts of characters, hosts of abused and abusive women, men, and children, hosts of selves in abuse. Some narrators and supporting characters voluntarily entered violent and abusive life worlds; most were born into abuse. Some narrators and supporting characters appear to escape, some struggle to escape, some repeatedly

escape and return. Others appear to embrace perpetration or victimization. Regardless, abuse is manifested in power and control tactics.
Especially in male accounts, abuse has an instrumental feature. Perpetrators inflict abuse when their honour or worth is threatened, when
they are not listened to, when they are not taken seriously. Victims
resist or retaliate with the aim of coping with, or managing, their partner's, or their parents', behaviour.

Just as powerfully, however, abuse appears rooted in emotionality, in
the tortured dynamics of love and its antithesis, hate. All seven narratives are marked by an intermingling of these themes. Mothers,
fathers, grandmothers, grandfathers, aunts, siblings, cousins, and narrators excused their own or each other's perpetration, or denied that
abuse occurred or that it was likely to recur – out of love. Most who
engaged in these denials and excuses were themselves victims of
abuse, and most appeared to hate themselves for the behaviours they
perpetrated and tolerated. Actors' defences, excuses, denials, and justifications appear grounded in an all-encompassing love/hate that
undermines possibilities of fully perceiving the 'authentic,' deeply self-
destructive reality of abuse, as participants themselves experience and
name it, and as others perceive it.

In only three of the seven accounts does recovery or survival appear
as an achievement or active project – Anne's, Yvonne's, and Keith's.
These accounts share a number of commonalities. First, all three survivors or would-be survivors believed that knowledge of self and the
world is essential to breaking abusive patterns, especially knowledge
gained from one's own experiences, negative and positive. Second, all
three believed that they were unlikely to overcome or continue to overcome abuse on their own; all had established contact with a world not
mired in abuse, whether through professionals or self-help organizations. Third, all three believed that they could and that they must
assume full responsibility for their own actions and the consequences
of their actions. Finally, all had a vision of themselves as capable of
love, and as loved – all experienced love from at least one parent while
growing up, and all loved both their partners and their children.

For Anne, abuse was an episode, a strangely exciting visitation with,
rather than surrender to, abuse. Emotionally, intuitively, cognitively
Anne 'knew' that abuse is not normal. Her parents, her child, and the
concerted voices of Regional shelter workers reinforced Anne's inner
voice that was asserting this. Anne consequently had no difficulty recognizing and naming the structures of bad faith she participated in.

Anne recognized that she could not allow herself to surrender. Her love for her child compelled her to make the necessary break and establish, or re-establish, a life world outside abuse. This world outside abuse was a world Anne already 'knew.'

For Yvonne the break with abuse appeared far more difficult. Emotionally, intuitively, and cognitively, it was abuse that was familiar, normal. Yvonne reached towards a new normality, a non-pathological normality, but she did not really 'know' if a world outside abuse was attainable. Yvonne's experience of herself as authentically loved by her mother fuelled the self-confidence necessary to struggle towards recovery, survival, wholeness. On the other hand, it was love for her abusive father that originally bound her to abuse. Yvonne 'knew' that these contradictory processes lay behind her own propensities to be abusive. Yvonne hoped to be able to overcome them, and she worked to overcome them, but she did not yet 'know' that this was possible.

As did Anne and Yvonne, Keith worked to build positive possibilities for himself and his family. However, in Keith's account, the violent self and the addicted self were intricately connected. Keith's recurrent relapses into addiction coincided with recurrent delusions that he could manage substances, that he could use rather than abuse alcohol, cocaine, and cannabis. At the time of the last interview, these structures of bad faith had once again collapsed. Keith's commitment to re-achieve sobriety and non-abuse was rooted in his love for his wife and children. However, his ability to love and respect himself, and his ability to succeed, appeared more tenuous than Yvonne's. Keith's relapses fuelled self-hatred rather than self-love. His inability to consistently heed an inner voice urging responsibility fostered feelings of defeat, feelings of worthlessness. Regardless, Keith continued to long for a world outside abuse. As did Yvonne, he expressed both determination and uncertainty over his ability to attain this.

The four accounts in which recovery or survival appears most elusive are very different – Kim's, Sam's, Hank's, and Tracy's. In these accounts, the narrator appears to regard him- or herself either as a provoked or manipulated perpetrator, or as a victim. Kim and Sam presented themselves primarily as perpetrators, perpetrators primed to attack when slighted, harassed, insulted, assaulted, or intoxicated. Tracy and Hank presented themselves primarily as victims, victims who were sometimes violent because others drove them to violence. Of the four, only Tracy talked very much about love. Her talk centred, not on being loved or on loving, but on her intense need to be protected, to be petted, to be indulged. Sam talked about his 'lost' love; however, he seemed more concerned with his need to be taken seriously than his need to be loved. Kim and Hank hardly talked about love at all. They were more concerned about achieving or recouping power.

Gender and Abuse

Taken together, the seven accounts confirm that abuse is highly gendered. As in the survey, accounts of violence in dating and marital relationships, and accounts of family-of-origin and extended *family violence*, were overwhelmingly accounts of male-perpetration. Fathers, grandfathers, brothers, male cousins, boyfriends, and husbands inflicted severe physical and sexual violence. Males who described their own violence projected gendered images of themselves as needing to appear tough, as needing to appear serious, as needing to instil fear. To Keith, Sam, and Hank, however, violence appeared more than a means of achieving an immediate end. It was a generalized response to a deep-seated desire to be taken seriously, as well as a tool for revenge and defence. Keith and Sam were both seeking to move beyond this. Nevertheless, both acknowledged that abusive activities provided them with a sense of power, as they had recurrently since adolescence, or even childhood.

With the exception of Kim, who had self-consciously adopted 'the male attitude,' the women expressed very different needs, very different self-images. The women's accounts centred more on how they managed their relationships, than on how others saw them. Consequently, the women experienced extreme distress. They were distressed at the violence and abuse they engaged in, and they were distressed at the violence and abuse inflicted upon them. For women, violence and abuse connote failure, powerlessness, and defeat. With the exception of Anne, this had been a recurrent experience since childhood.

Conclusion

Denzin's theory of emotionality identifies the world of abuse as unequivocally deviant or pathological; he identifies a world of abuse as out of control, 'sick,' and maintains that this sickness is produced and reproduced through structures of bad faith. Virtually all who provided testimony to the lived reality of abuse described an all-encompassing emotional sickness that threatens to entrap, to engulf, all participants. They did not confirm, however, that this sickness is maintained by bad faith or self-deception. Some narrators and supporting characters appeared too young, some appeared too hurt, some appeared too confused, and some appeared too angry to recognize or to resist the self-annihilating and other-annihilating practices that produce and reproduce abusive worlds, selves, and families. Only a select few appear capable of recognizing their past bad faith, and of choosing what most of us consider responsible action.

Giddens's theory of agency identifies actors as subjects who knowingly choose to participate in their realities. Thus victims and perpetrators choose to behave abusively and to cope with abuse, and they choose to leave abuse behind or to remain in abuse. Virtually all who provided testimony to the lived reality of abuse provisionally confirmed that they had made these kinds of choices. All confirmed that as adults they felt they had chosen abusive relationships, and that they had chosen or were in the process of choosing to inflict, to cope with, and/or try to cease participating in abuse.

While all seven interviewees appeared to believe that their actions were influenced by both formally learned and intuitive knowledge of themselves and the world, this knowledge was clouded by and filtered through emotions. My readings of the narratives suggests that one of the most important forms of intuitive knowledge is knowledge that one is loved, and therefore that one is both lovable and capable of loving. This knowledge appears to foster hope, or belief, in the possibility of the self as both worthy and capable of surviving abuse. Conversely, knowledge or belief that one is not loved, and fear, dread, certainty, denial, and terror that one is neither lovable nor capable of loving, undermines efforts to achieve survival. In the seven narratives, love and agency emerge as interdependent aspects of experiential worlds in which abuse is sustainable, and in which abuse is survivable.

Love, agency, abuse, and its survival appear as eminently contingent accomplishments, produced and reproduced by subjects who choose and feel in the midst of realities whose meanings have been filtered through the lives of hosts of interacting selves, each embodying the forces, contradictions, and ideologies of an historical moment given and handed down to each and all of us by countless dead generations (Denzin, 1984: 487).[24] These are some of the realities that we address when we name abuse a social problem. These are some of the realities we collectively and individually struggle to understand, to act responsibly against, and to survive.

8

A Researcher's Construction of 'The Problem': Conclusion

This study addresses varying constructions of a social problem defined as *domestic abuse* by activists engaged in the development of a shelter for women in a small-town Ontario community during 1991–2. Following Herbert Blumer (1971) and Joel Best (1993), I have examined two theoretically distinct processes, the politics of abuse and the experiential reality of abuse. I have addressed the politics of abuse through an analysis of the practices of claims-makers competing for 'ownership' of the problem from 'mobilization of action' to 'implementation of an official plan of action'; and I have addressed the experiential reality of abuse through an analysis of accounts, understandings, and social correlates of abuse among residents reporting personal experiences of victimization, perpetration, and survival. My aim has been to provide a dialectical portrait of abuse, a portrait that recognizes ongoing reciprocity between lived realities defined as social problems (Blumer, 1971) and social actors' historically situated struggles to come to terms with these realities (Mills, 1959).

In this Conclusion, I make an argument about the nature of abuse and about the nature of social problems processes. I address three issues: first, the apparent similarities in the dynamics of abuse as lived experience and the dynamics of the social problem process; second, the relevance of this case study to the sociology of social problems; and third, the relevance of social problems sociology to social policy.

Abuse as Lived Experience

In the abuse literature, in the accounts of Township activists and professionals, and in the opinions and experiences of surveyed residents, power and control issues lie at the heart of abuse as lived experience. Abusers reportedly inflict abuse out of a desire or need to maintain, assert, or regain power or dominance. Bids for control and power coincide with distortions and denials, most especially denials of responsibility for the abusive situation. Behind this apparent desire or need for control lies an apparent dread or fear of powerlessness. These processes are theoretically rooted in two empirically supportable sets of social processes, structural and experiential. The first set is emphasized in *violence against women* discourse, as the root cause of abuse; the second set is emphasized in *family violence* discourse, as proximate factors or causes of this problem.

Violence against women proponents and pro-feminist helping professionals identify structural processes grounded in history and ideology as the ultimate cause of male abuse of women and children. As countless commentators have documented, across cultures and across time, males have asserted legal and social power over wives and children. In recent history, that is, for the past hundred years, male control has been circumscribed, at least in the industrialized West. Women have achieved equal rights to political participation, education, property, and protection. Nevertheless, socialization practices and institutional arrangements continue to foster male dominance. Many males still expect that women, children, and situations will be under their control, and males still tend to hold the economic, social, and physical resources that make this likely. Men continue to kill, rape, beat, and otherwise abuse wives, lovers, and children, and men continue to exert dominance in social institutions and communities. *Violence against women* proponents and pro-feminist helping professionals typically identify these practices and outcomes as intentional or willed. Regardless, male violence functions to maintain male power and privilege, in the family and in society.

This study took place in an allegedly 'high-risk' community mobilized to address the problem of abuse in response to media coverage of a rash of domestic homicides in which men brutally killed or attempted to kill wives and lovers – with axes, knives, and guns. In this community, one in three randomly surveyed residents reported that they had experienced child abuse or that they had witnessed parental spouse abuse, and close to one in five reported serious or life-threatening violence at some time in a current or previous dating or spousal relationship. In the survey and in personal interviews, across genders and across generations, the vast majority of identified perpe-

trators were male, and in the estimation of victims, sexist.[1] These findings support feminist *violence against women* constructions of abuse as
ideologically fostered instrumental behaviour through which individual males assert and maintain power and control over *their* wives and
children.

Family violence sociologists and traditional or non-feminist helping
professionals identify personal experiences of victimization as proximate causes of abuse. Adult perpetration and tolerance of perpetration
are theoretically rooted in traumatic physical, sexual, and emotional
experiences of child abuse, child neglect, and substance abuse, and in
abuses and deprivations experienced in previous adult relationships.
Perpetrators purportedly engage in increasingly irrational and out-of-
control bids to control or dominate wives and children who fail to provide satisfaction, recognition, respect, or compliance. Victims engage
in symmetrical bids to assert and maintain control, or in complementary bids to avoid, forestall, or escape abuse, or to extract revenge.
These practices theoretically reflect needs or aims to regain something
lost or never achieved as a child, namely a self capable of sharing connectedness with or love for others, and therefore for the self. Regardless, they produce escalating schisms within the self and within the
family or relationship, grounded in denials of responsibility, projections of blame, and inappropriate acceptance of or collusion in blame.
These schisms are amplified by substance abuse and by futile attempts
to cope with or accommodate substance abuse. *Family violence* sociologists and traditional or non-feminist helping professionals maintain
that these dysfunctional relationship processes have equally destructive effects on males and females, and that males and females alike
assume both victim and perpetrator roles.

In this study, many 'high risk' survey respondents reported success
in avoiding abuse in dating and spousal relationships; others reported
that they had ended an earlier abusive relationship and established
violence-free, and abuse-free, lives. Nevertheless, there was a strong,
statistically significant relationship between childhood or family-of-
origin abuse and current relationship violence. There was an even
stronger relationship between current relationship violence and substance abuse.[2] In account after account, in the survey and in personal
interviews, this trilogy of childhood abuse, substance abuse, and spousal or partner violence permeated social and extended-family networks, which observers and participants alike described as confused,
pained, entrapping, deviant, 'sick.' Most identified abusers were male,

but few, whether female or male, held men solely responsible. More-over, most, whether female or male, regarded violence as at least some-times 'justifiable,' especially for women.[3] Indeed, in the survey and in personal interviews, women as well as men identified themselves as sole or primary perpetrators of both minor and severe assaults, and men as well as women described themselves as victims. These findings support therapeutic or *family violence* constructions of abuse as experi-entially fostered expressive behaviours that bind abusers and victims across genders in an increasingly out-of-control field of negative emo-tionality and violence.

Regardless of whether our analysis focuses on socially institutional-ized patterns of male-perpetrated *violence against women* and children, or on the pathological interpersonal contexts in which perpetration and victimization occur, power and control emerges as an overriding theme.[4] Male perpetrators inflict abuse to regain something that all feminists hope and that many men fear will soon be lost in history, and perpetrators across genders inflict abuse to regain something tradi-tional helping professionals and *family violence* sociologists believe was lost or never achieved in childhood. In both cases, abuse reflects and expresses a need for power, and a fear of powerlessness. In both cases, bad faith appears as a corollary of power and control practices. In both cases, abuse produces a field of experience that undermines possibili-ties of authentic connectedness, respectful communication, and mutual accommodation.

Social Problems Processes

In the research community, the social problems process was grounded in a power and control dynamic similar to that which appears to drive abusive relationships. Through various phases of shelter development, power plays and control bids escalated as contenders struggled to assert and maintain unequivocal ownership over definitions, policies, and practices. These processes polarized, radicalized, and vilified par-ticipants into mutually hostile us-against-them camps. During shelter development, core activists and their supporters maintained that the 'male hierarchy' was responsible for the male-against-female, feminist-against-non-feminist polarizations that led to the divorce of the Town-ship shelter from the resource centre that sponsored it. The opposition blamed these developments on a radical feminist takeover of the Domestic Abuse Committee and shelter board. These reciprocal allegations mask the extent to which loyalties cut across gender and ideological boundaries. As interviews with participating activists and professionals demonstrate, escalating polarizations drew on feminist and community development ideologies, but they were not grounded in substantively different visions, goals, or definitions. Rather, emergent and escalating polarizations were grounded in perceived needs for and rights to power and prestige, fear or dread of powerlessness, and self-righteous justifications of action. These needs, fears, and rationalizations were expressed both by female pro-feminist activists and by the males who publicly opposed them.

The issue that spawned the polarizations was essentially a bad faith issue that took on moral or ideological tones. This was the rather prosaic issue of where to locate the new shelter. The opposition interpreted the Domestic Abuse Committee's refusal to seriously consider their proposed shelter site donation as evidence that the committee had been taken over by radical feminists intent on monopolizing control over the shelter and other abuse interventions; and the Domestic Abuse Committee interpreted the opposition's refusal to defer to the decision of their site selection committee as evidence that 'the male hierarchy' was intent both on co-opting the shelter and on stigmatizing abused women.

These mutually derogatory constructions undermined possibilities of respectful communication or mutual accommodation, evidenced in core activists' claims that they had 'no choice' other than to reject the opposition's proposed 'gift.' Those making this claim drew on *violence against women* conceptualizations, making the location of the shelter a strategy for combating stereotypes of abused women as poor and troubled. This strategy allowed activists to dismiss arguments about the importance of access to services.[5] It allowed them to 'not hear' dissension within their own midst about the advisability of at least considering the gift. Most importantly, it allowed them to not honour their own publicly voiced commitments to resident participation, including their repeated calls for males to join in efforts to develop a community-wide response to *domestic abuse*. Conversely, the opposition drew on community development principles, and implicitly on *family violence* conceptualizations, to justify their unrelenting attempts to discredit the women without whom there would have been no shelter. The men, infuriated at not being taken 'seriously,' self-righteously focused on the alleged need to expose and resist a radicalism to which no one subscribed. In the process, they forgot their commitment to public good.

These power struggles and associated bad faith continued into the implementation phase when controlling practices became an explicit focus of concern. As reportedly occurs in many shelters, major points of contention were mundane daily practices imposed on staff and clients by administrators and board members, epitomized in the Township shelter by discord over whether shelter residents and their children would be fed block or sliced cheese, and by tensions over stained teacups. At a general level, controversies centred on housekeeping standards and nutritional guidelines, the imposition of rigid mealtimes, bedtimes, and curfews, mandatory client participation in educational programs, the transformation of staff meetings into training seminars, and the exclusion of junior staff from virtually all decision-making. The shelter director and her supporters on the shelter board justified these practices as necessary because of the social characteristics of clients, many of whom manifested substance problems, emotional instability, and violent behaviours, especially against children, and because of the inexperience, lack of training, and unresolved abuse issues of 'unprofessional' junior staff.

During shelter development, core activists managed to convince themselves and their supporters that locating the shelter on the periphery of a notoriously troubled area was inherently stigmatizing, inherently anti-feminist, but they failed to recognize the stigmatizing implications of hiring a 'problem population' expert to direct the shelter. Then they convinced this director to hire local abuse survivors and housewives to staff the shelter, because these women needed 'opportunities.' During implementation, they convinced themselves that the problems and conflicts manifested in the shelter were the result of the characteristics of junior staff and clients, and not of shelter practices that left these women feeling demeaned and disempowered. In the end, the winning 'strongly feminist' professionalist contingent convinced themselves that internal dissent was tantamount to unprofessional disloyalty. This alleged disloyalty was to the Township shelter, to the shelter movement, to feminism itself. Stigmatized junior staff and their supporters on the shelter board and in the community, feminists and non-feminists alike, maintained that all concerned owed loyalty solely to abused women.

During shelter development and during implementation, control was achieved and maintained through exclusions, marginalizations, falsifications, and denigrations. In both phases, critics were presented with only two choices: they could withdraw and form a disloyal opposition; or they could submit. This either/or construction of participation produced personal outrage, resistance, defensiveness, and rancour – especially since monopolizations of power contradicted the community development and feminist principles fostered by core activists throughout the shelter process. As in abusive relationships and families, emotionally charged 'interacting at' replaced 'interacting with' (Denzin, 1984). These practices appeared as unintended emergents of the social problems process. At the same time, they mirror and replicate the acrimonious and polarizing rhetorical exchanges between *violence against women* and *family violence* claims-makers that continue to take place in academic and professional books and journals.

Social Problems Sociology

In the social problems literature, some social problems analysts focus exclusively on struggles for ownership or control over definitional processes; others address the dualism of definitional processes and social conditions. Regardless, social problems analysts recognize that power plays an important role in the public construction of social problems, and that socially constructed truths are contended. Finally, most or all recognize that it is difficult to disentangle what is from what is claimed to be when truth-claims reverberate back on realities.

The social problems literature has produced claims about the nature of social problems processes that have reverberated back on that reality. Since Blumer's 1971 article, 'Social Problems as Collective Behavior,' numerous social problems analysts have addressed the ways 'putative' or 'objective' conditions acquire recognition as social problems, achieve legitimization, undergo mobilization of action, and become institutionalized or co-opted through the drawing up and implementation of official and competing plans of action. Long before this study was initiated, these analyses have informed social problems activities, as evidenced in Schuyler's 1976 plan of action for pro-feminist social workers confronting the problem of woman abuse.

In the professional literature, in feminist literature, and in the research community, social problems terms such as 'ownership' and 'co-optation' are in common usage. In all of these contexts, actors appear to believe that they can and must assert and maintain ownership over definitions; they appear to believe that they can and must resist co-optation. However, actors appear to be unaware of the seemingly ubiquitous problem of unintended consequences.

Blumer (1971) notes that actors typically bend official plans, substituting their own policies or agendas for those underlying the plan, and he identifies the unforeseen and unintended restructurings that arise from these practices as an important and largely neglected area of social problems research. That this area of research remains neglected helps account for actors' erroneous beliefs that winning control of definitions and resisting co-optation coincides with successful implementation When this fails to occur, actors are stunned, dismayed, betrayed. As in the case of abuse survivors struggling to overcome processes of personal victimization, activists think that they know what they are doing and why they are doing it, but they do not know why they fail to achieve their goals.[6]

In the Township, unintended outcomes were associated with three theoretically related processes. The first was the emergence of control as an overriding orientation, discussed above. The transformation of the Township's broadly supported shelter initiative into what abuse survivor and shelter worker Lisa named 'a living hell' proceeded through the actions of 'power-hungry people that wanted to control and manipulate their place of power' (see 'Lisa' in appendix 8). This hunger for power, and controlling and manipulative behaviours, were emergents of the process. They are what appears to happen when actors allow control to become an end in itself.

Second, this emergence of control as an end in itself coincided with bad faith, the largely unintentional and unconscious denials or suppressions of the reality of the situation as participants themselves 'knew' it, and as others saw it. In interviews with activists, professionals, and survivors, it was evident that everyone involved with the shelter 'knew' that abused women contend with a host of 'personal issues,' namely, substance issues, family-of-origin issues, anger or violence issues, and poverty issues. That shelter board members regarded these concurrent social problems as important is most keenly evidenced in their decision to hire an acclaimed 'problem population' expert to direct the shelter. It seems that activists seized upon the allegedly stigmatizing location of the proposed site donation, not because they were wearing 'rose-coloured glasses' and not because of clearly articulated ideological commitments, but because doing so justified, indeed necessitated, their bids to maintain unilateral control over the site selection process, and consequently the shelter.

Third, power and control issues and bad faith coincided with actors' propensities to reify myths or social representations, to treat these as real. *Violence against women* and *family violence* perspectives are varying lenses; they are also competing myths. As lenses, they bring varying aspects of the problem into focus. As myths, they purport to capture the whole or the essence of abuse, and to guide us to the correct or complete solution (Therborn, 1980; Watzlawick, 1984b; Hirsh, 1994). When actors posit a singularly privileged standpoint or perspective, they fall prey to reifications, whether said standpoint is common sense, sociological, feminist, or professionalist. But when they recognize or privilege partial, imperfect truths – truths circumscribed by the irre-solvable limitations of historically situated human consciousness – they foster something very different, something aimed less at winning and more at accommodation and reconciliation.[7]

The majority of Township activists subscribed to the latter position, at least initially. But as Kathryn notes in her response to the book, those at the core of activism became 'caught up in the emotion of the issue' and 'forgot' (see 'Kathryn' in appendix 8). Forgetting, core actors 'lost perspective'; they fell prey to ideologically constituted conceptualiza-tions or approaches that they themselves distrusted – first, radical fem-inism, and then an elitist version of professionalism. Once adopted, these conceptualizations justified and necessitated escalating bids to assert, resist, and maintain control. This action fostered a series of deepening schisms, marginalizations, and exclusions that no partici-pating actor wanted or intended.[8]

In the Township, unintended outcomes were associated with zero-sum bids for power and control, and the emotionally laden and ideologically fostered bad faith practices that justified these control bids. This study brings these interrelated processes into social prob-lems discourse.

Social Policy

Social policy does not create social problems processes, but it plays a role in molding public responses. Generally, policy-makers choose among contending plans of action put forward by a mobilized and ideologically divided public. Though their choices have come increas-ingly under challenge, in Canada, policy-makers have directed con-siderable resources towards *violence against women* interventions and research which explicitly or implicitly privilege a feminist or pro-feminist construction of abuse. The joint provincial and federal initia-tive that expanded the shelter network in the early 1990s is one example, another is the 1993 Statistics Canada Violence Against Women Survey; and a third example is the ongoing provincially sponsored expansion of domestic violence courts and mandated batterer programs in Ontario.[9]

Family violence definitions and remedies inevitably enter into *violence against women* definitions and remedies, as evidenced in the Township. Conversely, *violence against women* definitions and remedies enter into *family violence* initiatives (see Beaudry, 1982; Schechter, 1988). Many social problems analysts and activists attribute this hybridization to co-optation, suggesting that it is something that can or should be resisted. This implies that there is an unequivocal 'right' side; that, in the case of abuse, we rightfully focus on personal issues or we rightfully focus on attitudes and structures. Explicitly or implicitly, this 'either/or' conceptualization promotes and justifies efforts to assert all-out control or ownership; it promotes reifications and bad faith. In contrast, a 'both/and' approach recognizes that it is troubled persons who participate in and who seek and receive support from education and counselling services; that personal troubles are rooted in prevailing sexist, racist, and classist social structures; and that solutions to both components of 'the problem' are elusive. This approach promotes and fosters efforts to negotiate an invariably difficult balance, one that draws on the strengths of our competing and unavoidably flawed lenses. This balance is inevitably temporary and imperfect (Caringella-MacDonald and Humphries, 1991; Loseke and Gelles, 1993; Yllo, 1993: Hirsh, 1994).[10]

These issues are of particular salience given the ethereal nature of social problems mobilizations. As Mauss (1975) points out, social problems emerge into public awareness, receive public attention, and then subside or die out, to be replaced or supplanted by new or other problems. In some cases, the public assumes that the issue is being addressed in the best way possible; in others, it despairs of the possibility of achieving a viable solution or remedy. Regardless, in the majority of cases, the problem, the condition, remains largely 'untouched.' As many theorists have pointed out, social conditions tend to remain largely the same because social problems mobilizations fail to effect lasting structural changes. This consistent failure is related to the power and momentum of prevailing structures and ideologies (Foucault, 1980; Therborn, 1980). It is also related to the 'fact' that social reality is far too complex to control through definitional or technical means. Attempts to assert and maintain all-out control are consequently inherently destructive.[11]

Policy-makers and social activists who find these arguments compelling may wish to incorporate insights from social problems sociology into their action plans. This entails a shift to second-order thinking, to thinking that focuses less on the nature of a given problem and arguments for or against proposed solutions, and more on the social problems process itself. This shift facilitates recognition of the 'fact' that contending claims reflect our varying and unavoidably biased interpretations of the social world, and that we advance these claims for a myriad of personal, professional, and political reasons, including emotionally charged and ideologically fostered desires or 'needs' for social respect, social prestige, and social power.[12] Recognizing this, and the risk and probability of bad faith, policy-makers and activists may wish to remind themselves and each other of the apparent certainty of unintended outcomes when actors allow issues of control or ownership to become their overriding concern.

Concluding Statement

This study was undertaken from the sociology of social problems perspective Joel Best named contextual constructionism, an approach that reasserts the legitimacy of the task C. Wright Mills identified as the central concern of sociology, the task of establishing theoretical and empirical links between personal troubles and social issues.[13] My attempt to do so has resulted in a redefinition of the problem named *domestic abuse* in the research community, and *violence against women* or *family violence* in professional and academic discourse. I redefine the problem as control and the emotionally laden and ideologically fostered bad faith practices that bolster control. This, of course, is a claim, not a truth; or, rather, as are all truths, it is partial, imperfect, theory-laden, and contingent. This claim coincides with a second claim, the claim that efforts to implement effective social problems interventions fall short of collective goals for the same reasons that efforts to overcome abuse fall short: because they are rooted in bad faith attempts to control, rather than responsibly confront, the reality of the situation, and our own actions in producing and maintaining this situation. Finally, this investigation results in a proposed solution. The solution is social awareness of the inherently dysfunctional nature of zero-sum power and control processes, and of the need to repudiate these, and their corollary, bad faith, at personal and collective levels.

It is with these considerations in mind that I address the final issue.

Social problems processes seem inevitably to entail competition for ownership or control. If unintended outcomes are a result of this inevitable competition, social problems processes appear doomed from the onset. However, positive outcomes are conceivable. They are conceivable because human beings can and do put a stop to abusive and controlling practices, as evidenced in the accounts of participating survivors, and as evidenced in the testimony of Regional shelter workers who learned the importance of not 'taking on the role of the abuser in the name of saving the woman.' I suspect that, as our understandings of survivorship practices evolve, so will our insights into ways to overcome the dysfunctional practices evidenced again and again in our collective attempts to establish and implement viable responses to abuse and other social problems. As a feminist and as a sociologist, I endorse reaching towards this Enlightenment goal. Consequently, I endorse the abandonment of 'either/or' and the adoption of 'both/and' approaches to research and social action. This endorsement is predicated on the assumption that various lenses provide sometimes overlapping but always incomplete and unavoidably distorted views of the social world, that no lens is adequate, and that none provides a complete or correct view. Most importantly, none guides us towards a complete solution. I already thought that I knew this when I initiated this study. I think I know it even better now.

Appendix 1

General Ethical Considerations

This study was subject to review by the Human Subjects Review Committee of the University of Toronto. Letters of Introduction, Consent Forms, Interview Schedules, and the Questionnaire were designed to comply with guidelines outlined in a Code of Ethics instituted by the American Sociological Association in August 1989, and were amended to meet specific concerns of the Ethics Review Committee.[1]

There were three major ethical considerations. First, an investigation of violence or abuse between partners entails intrusion into a domain whose privacy is considered sacred by many or even most Canadians. Gaining the cooperation and confidence of residents requires sensitivity and tact, especially when both partners of a couple participate. Participants were consequently assured that anonymity and confidentiality would be maintained, not only with the general public, but also with partners. They were assured that partners would not be contacted without their consent, that they could decline to answer any question, and that they could withdraw from the study at any time. For reasons of safety, no request was made to approach partners of survey participants who reported ongoing or previous patterns of 'severe' violence in their current relationship.

The second ethical consideration relates to the legal limits of confidentiality and anonymity. It is the legal responsibility of all Canadians to report knowledge of ongoing child abuse to the Children's Aid Society. Moreover, the courts can subpoena research data. Respondents were explicitly informed of these contingencies.

A third ethical consideration relates to the politics of research. I recognized that my essentially mainstream approach to research might offend the political sensibilities of some study participants, notably pro-feminist counsellors and women's shelter workers. In conducting interviews with self-identified feminists, I made it a point to state that I was a feminist, but that I had not yet come to closure about the nature and causes of abuse. I told respondents across social categories and affiliations that I depended on residents from across the community to inform me about the problem – lay and professional, male and female. No study participant objected to my attempt to maintain a degree of detachment.

Appendix 2

Data Collection Methods

Qualitative Data

Qualitative data were gathered through participant observation in activists'
organizations and at social events, and through in-depth interviews with activists, professionals, and concerned residents – including numerous abuse
victims, perpetrators, and survivors. In all contexts, formal and informal, I
identified myself as a researcher engaged in a community-based study of
domestic abuse and domestic abuse intervention. In formal contexts, I requested
and received permission either to tape-record proceedings or to take notes.

When interviewing, I focused questioning on how the interviewee had
become involved with abuse, and on the ways personal, family, agency,
and professional practices affected understandings. When interviewing self-
identified abuse victims, perpetrators, and survivors, I focused questioning on
abuses experienced as an adult and as a child, and on how respondents coped
with and made sense of these experiences. In all instances, I encouraged
respondents to take the lead, to describe events and attitudes as part of an
open conversation on the nature of abuse, its causes, and its solution. In all
instances, I shared opinions, knowledge, and experiences (Douglas, 1985). My
principal position was that I had read a great deal about abuse, but had not yet
come to closure on a number of contentious issues, and that I relied on respondents from across the community to inform me about the problem as they
experienced and understood it.

Quantitative Data

Quantitative data were gathered through a semi-structured questionnaire on
violence and abuse administered by telephone to a randomly recruited sample

of residents and spouses in July and August 1992. In the first round, 97 individuals from 150 contacted households completed full questionnaires (a 65 per cent response rate). Thirty-two qualifying and willing married and cohabiting partners participated in the couples follow-up. Attitudinal questions focused on how respondents preferred to define the problem, on whom they held responsible, on whether they thought violence or abuse was ever justified, on what they thought motivates abusers, and on what they thought were the major or most important causes of abuse. Personal questions focused on abuses witnessed or experienced in childhood, family and personal histories of substance abuse, abusive practices in current and previous dating and spousal relationships, and help-seeking activities. Respondents were also asked to evaluate a number of existing and proposed abuse interventions.

In the questionnaire, I defined abuse as 'any physical, psychological or sexual act which people experience as abuse.' Abuse variables are listed in table 3.

Appendix 3

Letter of Introduction (Hand-delivered to All Interview Respondents)

(Printed on University of Toronto letterhead)

Dear Residents and Professionals:

My name is Ruth Mann. I am a Ph.D. candidate at the University of Toronto, working under the supervision of Dr. Norman Bell in the Department of Sociology. We are conducting a study on the ways residents and community agents in the Township experience and interpret the problem of violence or abuse between adult partners who are married, cohabiting or dating. We are examining the ways intervention services are being organized, and the ways residents across the community evaluate these services.

Research procedures follow strict ethical guidelines. Every precaution is being taken to insure that those who participate in the study remain anonymous, and that information provided in interviews and questionnaires remains strictly confidential. This is accomplished by established coding and storage procedures designed to prevent identification of individual respondents. Names will not be used in publications or discussions.

You are free to refuse to answer any question, and to withdraw from the study at any time.

Please note, while the object of the study is not to address child abuse practices, participants should know that the researcher would be legally compelled to report any information that comes to her attention about physical child abuse, to the Children's Aid.

Your participation in the study is greatly appreciated.

Respectfully submitted,

Ruth Mann
Ph.D. Candidate
Department of Sociology
Township Phone: 000-0000

Please feel free to call at any time. We value your comments, suggestions, and observations.

Appendix 4.1

Consent Form for Interviewees – Activists and Professionals

(Printed on University of Toronto letterhead)

I agree to participate in the study being conducted by Ruth Mann, a Ph.D. candidate in the Department of Sociology at the University of Toronto. She has informed me that this is an exploratory study designed to obtain information on how community agents and residents perceive the problem of domestic violence or abuse, and on how community resources are being organized to deal with it.

I understand that:
- Participation in the study will involve one or more interviews whose number and duration will be mutually agreed upon by the researcher and myself.
- Interview sessions will be tape recorded.
- Unless expressly waived through written consent, or in the unlikely event of a court subpoena, all my responses will be held in strictest confidence and all individuals, agencies or institutions mentioned, including myself and the Agency with which I am affiliated, will remain anonymous. Pseudonyms will be assigned for publications and presentations.
- I do not have to respond to every question or provide information I do not want to provide.
- I can terminate my participation at any time.
- Information gathered in the study will be used solely for professional and educational purposes.
- The researcher may contact me within the next two years to request my participation in follow-up interviews. However, I understand that codes

identifying participants will be kept in a locked safe at the University of Toronto so as to safeguard the anonymity of myself, my agency, and all individuals directly or indirectly referred to in the interview(s). I understand that after two years all code lists will be destroyed.

Date _____   Signature_____

Appendix 4.2

Consent Form for Interviewees – Residents

(Printed on University of Toronto letterhead)

I agree to participate in the study being conducted by Ruth Mann, a Ph.D. candidate in the Department of Sociology at the University of Toronto. She has informed me that this is an exploratory study designed to obtain information on how community agents and residents perceive the problem of domestic violence or abuse, and on how community resources are being organized to deal with it.

I understand that:
- Participation in the study will involve one or more interviews whose number and duration will be mutually agreed upon by the researcher and myself.
- Interview sessions will be tape recorded.
- All my responses will be held in strictest confidence and all individuals, agencies or institutions mentioned will remain anonymous.
- I do not have to respond to every question or provide information I do not want to provide.
- I can terminate my participation at any time.
- Information gathered in the study will be used solely for professional and educational purposes.
- Neither my identity, my place of residence, my place of employment, nor that of any member of my family will be identifiable in any publication or presentation, rather, pseudonyms will be used; except in the unlikely event of a court subpoena, no individual will be named in any context.
- The researcher may contact me at a later time to request my participation in

a follow-up interview. However, I understand that codes identifying partici-pants will be kept in a locked safe at the University of Toronto, so as to safe-guard the anonymity of myself and anyone other than myself referred to in the interview(s). I understand that after two years all code lists will be destroyed.

Date _____   Signature_____

___ I grant permission to the researcher to request an interview with my partner or ex-partner.

___ I **DO NOT** grant permission to the researcher to request an interview with my partner or ex-partner.

Please note, while the object of the study is not to address child abuse prac-tices, participants should know that the researcher would be legally compelled to report any information that comes to her attention about physical child abuse, to the Children's Aid Society.

Appendix 5

Letter of Introduction (Mailed to Prospective Survey Respondents)

(Printed on University of Toronto letterhead)

Dear Resident:

My name is Ruth Mann. I am a researcher at the University of Toronto, Department of Sociology. Yours is one of more than a hundred randomly selected households from across the Township selected for possible participation in my study. The study addresses violence and abuse between people who are married, living together, and dating.

I will be calling soon to ask you a set of questions about what you think about violence and abuse in relationships. I will ask you about experiences which may have influenced your attitudes. Finally, I will ask what you think of intervention services, including police, women's shelters, and counselling programs.

You do not need to have had experience with violence or abuse to participate. You only need to have an opinion. Further, the opinions of men and women are equally valued.

The study follows strict ethical guidelines set out by the Office of Research Administration at the University of Toronto. To prevent anyone from being identified names, telephone numbers, and addresses of participants are destroyed immediately after questionnaires are completed. Every precaution is taken to ensure confidentiality and anonymity to all who participate.

If you participate you can refuse to answer any question you do not want to answer, and you are under no obligation to complete the entire question-naire.

If you do not wish to be contacted, please leave your number and instructions that you do not wish to be contacted on the answering machine connected to the number listed below.

Thank you. I look forward to talking to you in the near future.

Ruth Mann
Ph.D. Candidate
Department of Sociology
Township Phone: 000-0000

Appendix 6

Phone Introduction: Survey on Violence and Abuse

Hello, I am Ruth Mann, the Researcher at the University of Toronto who sent you a letter last week. Did you receive my letter?

As I stated in the letter, I am doing doctorate research on violence and abuse between people who are married, living together, and dating. Your household is one of one hundred households randomly selected for participation in this study.

To participate you must be at least eighteen years of age. You do not need to have personal experience with violence or abuse. Do you qualify for the study?

I want to state again that the study follows strict ethical guidelines set out by the Office of Research Administration of the University of Toronto. You will remain anonymous. Lists of everyone who participates will be destroyed. Of course, you can refuse to answer any question you do not want to answer, and you are under no obligation to complete the entire questionnaire. I will not call you back should you discontinue participation unless you instruct me to, and I will not call your partner to ask him (her) to participate unless you expressly permit this.

Finally, I must remind you that researchers are legally required to report information about ongoing physical child abuse to the Children's Aid.

The questionnaire takes approximately thirty minutes to complete. Is now a good time for you? (Yes/No)

Would you prefer that I call back at a later time? (Yes/No)

Call back at: _____.

Appendix 7

Request to Contact Partners for Couple Follow-up: Survey on Violence and Abuse

IF PART OF A CURRENTLY MARRIED OR COHABITING COUPLE

I would like to ask your partner (husband/wife) to participate in the study. I will only ask him/her to participate if you feel comfortable with this. Of course, I will not tell him/her how you answered any of the questions.[2]

DO YOU MIND IF I ASK YOUR PARTNER TO PARTICIPATE? (YES/NO)

IS YOUR PARTNER AVAILABLE NOW? (YES/NO)

WHEN DO YOU SUGGEST I TRY TO REACH YOUR PARTNER (HUSBAND/WIFE)?

TIME: _____.

Appendix 8

Respondents' Responses to the Manuscript (April 1997)

Kathryn

Kathryn was a pro-feminist community development worker, shelter activist, and Township Women's Shelter board member.

Dear Ruth:

It was with trepidation that I picked up 'the Manuscript.' I wondered if on those pages I would find that I had done something wrong, or that there might have been something I could have done differently, or better. Building the Township shelter seemed to tear our community apart, pitting groups against one another ... I wondered if your work could shed light on why things got so terribly out of hand.

There were several things that I found helpful. First, there is your very important reference to how people view abuse – either as 'violence against women' or 'family violence.' Your discussion of how people frame the issue calls attention to the fact that when a community works on a social issue there will be a variety of belief systems at play. I think that most people working on the Township shelter on some level knew this, but it would seem we forgot to be flexible and tolerant of others' views. I know that I lost all perspective on the matter, and felt that there was only one way to view abuse. I think collectively we forgot that important adage – 'that it's OK to agree to disagree.'

I found your account of the shelter opening especially illuminating. You captured the mood of the opening; our elation and celebration, but you also captured the underlying tension that remained between the two camps. In particular you drew attention to the way town officials and men were treated. I literally gasped reading the passage where our one lone male board member commandeered the microphone to thank town officials. I find it hard to believe that we had not acted more diplomatically – I sincerely wish we had.

But for me the most important aspect of your work was the way in which you try to make sense of the process of social action. It wasn't long after I began working on the shelter that I sensed something was amiss. It was difficult to articulate what was happening, but I remember telling people, 'It is as if the process of working on the shelter takes on a life of its own.' With all the bright, well-meaning, committed individuals, why did we have so many problems? Why were people so divided? It wasn't as if we weren't warned; many people who had gone through similar work told us, 'Watch out, things get crazy' – but like first-time parents I think we believed we had a handle on everything, there would be so surprises for us.

If I could offer any advice to others, it would be to truly understand that the process does have a life of its own – that it will test people and challenge people in ways they could not imagine. You put it so eloquently in the last few lines of your book – 'various lenses provide sometimes overlapping but always incomplete and unavoidably distorted views of the social world [and] no lens is adequate, none provide us with a complete or correct view.' It is not that those of us working on the Township shelter couldn't comprehend this. I think many of us did understand your point about the process of social action, but – caught up in the emotion of the issue, and the exhausting work – many of us forgot.

Kathryn

Lisa

Lisa was an abuse survivor, domestic violence activist, and Township Women's Shelter worker.

Well done Ruth,

A very knowledgeable work, the events and observations were very accurate. Overall a piece of work well worth sharing.

I must tell you how I felt as though I was time travelling into a life that I had once lived so long ago. Bob is now light years sober, and we certainly have come a long way. Alcohol was a contributing factor but I think the problems we shared were certainly a variety of things and not all alcohol related. Domestic abuse has so many veins and cannot be placed in just one area. You have to dig deep and pull out the real stuff.

The community can play an important role in supporting the family on a road to recovery. Subsidized housing is one way and very helpful if it is needed, but there are so many other ways the community can contribute like support groups, family counselling, available information, etc.

As far as the shelter, well I can only say that what started off with good intentions to be something so needed in the community turned out to be a living hell. It's not the shelter or the purpose that burnt people out, it was the power-hungry people that wanted to control and manipulate their place of power to fill their own agenda that ruined it. Feminism had nothing to do with the conflicts of the shelter. Although I experienced the down side of the shelter the good thing I took was that if a community wants something bad enough and works together they can get it. First we all need to be humanist to accomplish one task that will benefit us all.

Community work is very tiring and sometimes seems useless but if one family benefits, it's all worth it in the long run.

Thanks for sharing the book.

Lisa

Charles

Charles was a community development expert, domestic violence activist, and executive coordinator of the Township Resource Centre.

My general reaction on reading the manuscript is that, so far as I can recall, the author fairly 'called them as she saw them,' in reference to events concerning the issue of violence against women in the Township.

As one who was a partisan in terms of trying to do something to prevent violence against women in the community, it's impossible for me to be objective about the events that she describes.

During the time before I was pulled into the 'shelter fray' I had a unique opportunity to apply my own training and experience in community development work to prevention in the area of woman abuse. I was proud of my work in our housing co-op ... The experience proved again to me that the process of community development can be a powerful and positive force for social change.

It's not appropriate for me to comment on the events that led to the creation of the shelter because I can't separate my own biases from the events described in the manuscript. I do hope that our experiences in the Township can help build a body of research in this area, and perhaps some other communities can learn from our successes and failures.

Charles

Tables: Summaries of Demographic and Survey Data

TABLE 1.a
Official statistics (1991 census): Incomes

| | Household incomes | | | Designated low incomes | | Receiving income from government sources (%) |
	Average household income (dollars)	Below $20,000 (%)	Over $50,000 (%)	Indiv. (%)	Family (%)	
Nation	51,342	8.0	36.5	13.2	36.5	11.4
Province	57,227	5.6	43.5	10.9	31.4	9.7
Region & outside						
Township	49,470	5.1	44.7	7.7	28.1	11.0
RA-ville	84,133	2.8	63.5	4.2	27.7	4.7
RB-ville	69,455	2.0	61.7	3.3	14.9	5.7
RC-ville	74,745	2.6	67.0	6.2	28.2	4.6
RD-ville	71,137	3.4	63.2	7.0	29.6	5.2
OA-ville	40,603	6.1	30.1	9.6	27.6	16.2
OB-ville	60,662	4.1	57.7	5.4	19.5	6.3
OC-ville	52,339	3.9	50.2	5.6	20.1	7.7
OD-ville	41,545	5.6	30.4	10.7	26.6	15.2

TABLE 1.b
Official statistics (1991 census): Education and employment

	Education		Labour force participation rate			Occupations	
	Through H.S. (%)	Post-H.S. (%)	Males (%)	Females (%)	All (%)	Middle-class[a] (%)	Working-class (%)
Nation	53.0	47.1	76.7	59.9	69.6	29.9	70.1
Province	51.9	48.2	77.4	62.1	67.9	31.9	68.1
Region & outside							
Township	60.1	39.3	76.7	59.6	67.3	26.9	73.1
RA-ville	46.4	53.6	81.9	65.5	73.9	38.5	61.5
RB-ville	51.9	48.0	84.3	65.9	75.1	34.0	66.0
RC-ville	42.0	58.0	85.7	69.9	72.1	41.1	58.9
RD-ville	41.7	58.3	82.4	68.1	75.1	40.5	59.5
OA-ville	59.1	41.0	71.2	54.4	62.2	29.7	70.3
OB-ville	56.9	43.2	86.6	69.6	78.2	25.7	74.3
OC-ville	56.0	43.9	85.1	66.9	75.7	26.3	73.7
OD-villeA	55.9	44.0	73.7	55.7	64.0	31.5	68.5

[a] Middle-class occupations include managerial and professional occupations, including self-employed entrepreneurs; working-class occupations include labour, manufacturing, transport, clerical, and service occupations.

TABLE 1.c
Official statistics (1991 census): Migrations, family structures, religion, and crime

	Population increase (1986–91) (%)	Family structure			Religious affiliation		Violent crime rate[a]
		Sing. P. (%)	Mar. (%)	Coh. (%)	Protest. (%)	Secular (%)	
Nation	7.9	9.9	58.8	7.5	35.8	12.4	1099
Province	10.8	9.7	62.6	5.2	43.9	12.4	1097
Region	44.0	7.4	78.5	3.8	35.6	13.1	540 (622)
Township	32.3	8.2	67.2	8.4	57.9	19.5	(988)
RA-ville	13.6	5.7	78.6	4.6	49.8	14.7	(569)
RB-ville	21.3	6.0	73.6	4.9	59.9	10.4	–
RC-ville	40.9	8.3	73.1	5.3	51.4	15.7	(569)
RD-ville	71.4	7.9	73.7	4.1	33.1	14.0	(569)
Outside region							
OA-ville	15.5	10.0	52.3	5.7	64.6	11.8	1994
OB-ville	34.1	6.8	76.3	5.4	48.1	12.5	577
OC-ville	24.0	8.4	65.6	5.9	63.5	14.9	1421
OD-ville	7.4	10.7	53.0	6.1	61.5	14.5	1909

[a]Data on crime rates within the Region were provided by the Regional Police and are shown in brackets. Two districts are applicable: the Township; and a second district comprising RA, RC, and RD. The rate is per 100,000 population.

TABLE 2
Representativeness of survey respondents (survey, random, and couples samples)

Social demographic marker	Township (1991 census)	Full survey (July 1992)	Random (July 1992)	Couples (July / Aug. 1992)
Population age 15 to 18 or higher	27,000	n = 97	n = 83	32 + 32 = 64
Female / male	51% / 49%	69% / 31%	68% / 32%	50% / 50%
Age				
18–25 / 26–35	15% / 28%	11% / 32%	10% / 36%	3% / 45%
36–45 / 46–55	20% / 12%	17% / 15%	18% / 16%	23% / 19%
56–65 / 66+	10% / 15%	9% / 15%	10% / 11%	4% / 4%
Marital status / family structure				
Married / H/W married	62% / 66%	64% / 64%	75% / 75%	81% / 81%
Cohabiting / H/W cohabiting	8% / 11%	16% / 16%	19% / 19%	19% / 19%
Separated or divorced	10%	8%	0%	0%
Single parent	8%	5%	2%	0%
Never married / live alone	23% / 16%	10% / 15%	6% / 6%	0% / 0%
Education				
Less than grade 9	10%	13%	12%	11%
Grade 9–11	34%	20%	23%	16%
High school diploma	17%	35%	33%	36%
College / trade school	7%	16%	15%	19%
Some university	20%	5%	6%	8%
University degree	6%	11%	12%	11%

TABLE 2–*Concluded*
Representativeness of survey respondents (survey, random, and couples samples)

Social demographic marker	Township (1991 census)	Full survey (July 1992)	Random (July 1992)	Couples (July / Aug. 1992)
Occupation				
Managerial & professional	20%	20%	22%	21%
Soc., therapy, com. wk.	7%	4%	4%	4%
Clerical, sales, service	38%	43%	35%	30%
Manufacture & repair	11%	11%	10%	25%
Construction & transport	14%	19%	14%	19%
Not in paid employment	32%	20%	16%	10%
Household income				
Less than $10,000	5%	8%	2%	0%
$10,000–$19,000	12%	18%	19%	3%
$20,000–$29,999	11%	12%	12%	3%
$30,000–$39,999	14%	8%	6%	7%
$40,000–$49,999	13%	3%	6%	10%
$50,000 and up	45%	51%	55%	78%
Average household	$49,470	$51,900	$53,000	$68,700
Length of residence				
5 yrs. or less / 5 to 10 yrs.	32% / –	37% / 17%	42% / 17%	45% / 23%
10+ years	–	45%	41%	29%

Notes: (1) Percentages do not always add up to 100 per cent. (2) *Survey, random,* and *couples* samples overlap. The *survey* sample includes all respondents who participated in the first phase of the survey, including those who were not currently 'partnered.' The *random* sample includes all married, cohabiting and dating first-respondents. The *couples* sample includes 32 married and cohabiting *random* respondents and their partners.

TABLE 3
Abuse measures

Acronyms	Definitions & operationalizations
FCHA	FAMILY CHILD HISTORY OF ABUSE: Measures derived from an open-ended question: 'Did you ever experience abuse as a child, or did you ever witness the abuse of anyone in your family?' Measure includes:
CA	CHILD ABUSE: Physical, sexual, or emotional abuse experienced as a child;
WMA	WOMAN ABUSE, MAN ABUSE or PARENTAL SPOUSE ABUSE: Unidirectional or reciprocal wife or spouse abuse;
CA/WMA	CHILD ABUSE/WOMAN-MAN ABUSE: 'Double whammy' of child abuse and parental spouse abuse, included in measures of CA and WMA;[a]
CSA	CHILD SEXUAL ABUSE: Child sexual abuse, included in measures of CA.
CGSA	CURRENT GENERATION SUBSTANCE ABUSE: Respondent-identified patterns of substance abuse by her- or himself and/or current partner, including ongoing, recovering, and recovered patterns.
PGSA	PREVIOUS GENERATION SUBSTANCE ABUSE: Respondent-identified substance problems in family or origin.
RR	RELATIONSHIP RATING: Respondent evaluation of the nature and quality of current relationship, based on two closed-ended questions.
A/D?	ABUSIVE/DISTRESSED/EQUIVOCAL: Assigned to relationships described as currently or previously abusive and/or as distant, disturbed, conflicted, or equivocal.
N/LF	NOT ABUSIVE, LOVING OR FRIENDLY: Assigned to relationships described as non-abusive and as unequivocally loving and/or friendly.
CTS by level	CONFLICT TACTICS SCALE (Gelles & Straus, 1988): Abusive and violent acts expressed and sustained over the previous twelve months, including:
CTS PSY6+	CTS PSYCHOLOGICAL OR EMOTIONAL ABUSE: Cases in which one or both partners engaged in swearing, sulking, spite, and/or stomping out at chronic rates, defined as 6+ to 20+;
CTS I	CTS OBJECT AGGRESSION: Cases in which one or both partners threw or smashed objects;
CTS II	CTS THREATS: Cases in which one or both partners threatened to assault;
CTS III	CTS MINOR VIOLENCE: Cases in which one or both partners threw things at the other partner, pushed, grabbed, shoved, or slapped;

TABLE 3–*Concluded*
Abuse measures

Acronyms	Definitions & operationalizations
CTS IV	CTS SEVERE VIOLENCE: Cases in which one or both partners kicked, choked, hit with a fist or object, beat up, and/or assaulted with a weapon;
CTS II+	CTS CRIMINAL CODE VIOLENCE: Cases in which one or both partners engaged in acts defined as Criminal Code violence in Canada; includes all reports of threats and assault.
CRV	CURRENT RELATIONSHIP VIOLENCE: All reported chronic (3+ over a 12-month period) or severe violence ever in current relationship. Derived from CTS measures, responses to open-ended questions, and general comments.
PRV	PREVIOUS RELATIONSHIPS VIOLENCE: All reported chronic or severe violence in previous dating, cohabiting, or marital relationships.
ARV	ADULT RELATIONSHIP VIOLENCE, CHRONIC OR SEVERE: All reported chronic or severe violence in any and all (current and previous) dating, cohabiting, or marital relationships.

[a]Straus et al. (1980) coined the term 'double whammy' in response to the exceptionally high rates of violence in adult relationships among respondents reporting both child abuse and parental spouse abuse.

TABLE 4
Random and couples data summaries

Demographic characteristics

	Sex	Age			Education	Occupation			Income		Residence		Marital Status		
	F / M	Yg	Mid	Older	HS / Post	WC	MC	Hm	<50	>50 (× $1,000)	<10	>10 (years)	Mar.	Coh.	Dat.
83/83 Random	68 32	46	34	21	67 33	59	25	16	39	49	59	41	75	19	6
64/32 Couples	50 50	48	42	9	62 38	66	23	11	25	69	69	31	81	19	

Childhood abuses and substance abuse

	Childhood abuse					Substance abuse				
	FCHA Self	CA Self	WMA Self	CA/WMA	CSA	PGSA Self	PGSA Partner	CGSA Self	CGSA Partner	CGSA Self/Part
83/83 Random	34	25	19	11	7	24	24	10	13	20
64/32 Couples	34	23	19	8	3	31	–	19	–	30

Adult relationship abuse

	CTSPSY @ 6+	CTS I	CTS II+	CTS III	CTS IV	CRV III/IV	PRV III/IV	ARV III/IV	RR A/D?
83/83 Random	35	24	17	11	4	10	10	17	25
64/32 Couples	31	30	17	9	0	6	3	9	31

TABLE 4—*Continued*
Random and couples data summaries

Preferred definitions and attributions

	Extent: above average	Define: domestic abuse	Define: woman abuse	Define: other	Male primarily respon.	Female[a] (child) hurt	Justification for male provoked/ self-defence	Justification for female provoked/ self-defence
83/83 Random	48	67	24	18	29	47 / 27	10 / 49	15 / 65
64/32 Couples	40	70	17	13	27	48 / 19	6 / 46	9 / 61

Perceived causes and motives

	Cause alc/sub abuse	Cause hist. fm. v.	Cause econ. stress	Cause infidelity	Cause sexism	Cause nature	Motive power/ control	Motive hurt/ punish	Motive gen. frust.	Motive loss of control
Random: major	66	53	40	19	8	4	37	17	17	11
major-important	90	75	64	37	27	8	64	45	48	28
Couples: major	59	53	33	14	14	2	28	17	27	8
major-important	84	78	61	42	34	9	59	45	56	25

TABLE 4—*Concluded*
Random and couples data summaries

	Evaluations of intervention / prevention measures									
	Women shelters	AA (subs.)	RSAP (sex)	TFS (fam.)	RWAP (wife)	Police	Courts	Change attitude	Empower women	Spend money
Random: very helpful	66	54	58	48	43	29	7	65	46	66
very helpful–helpful	87	82	82	72	71	40	22	84	70	
Couples: very helpful	64	55	55	45	36	30	6	67	38	72
very helpful–helpful	89	80	81	72	61	42	14	86	64	

	Preferences for intervention board & staff				
	Abuse professionals	Abuse survivors	Concerned residents	Community leaders	Feminist activists
Random: prefer	65	55	13	7	2
good	21	20	25	23	13
accept	13	18	40	27	31
reject	1	6	22	43	49
Couples: prefer	53	56	14	6	3
good	27	28	25	22	8
accept	17	13	39	23	34
reject	3	3	22	48	53

Note: All entries in the table are percentages of the sample (random or couples). Data on ratings of services and on service board and staff do not always add up to 100 per cent; 'don't know' responses are included in calculations but are not displayed.
[a]The question posited 'most harm to females;' 'most harm to males;' 'varies;' 'equal,' and 'don't know/other.' A large minority maintained that children are most hurt, and that 'most harm to children' should have been on the list.

TABLE 5
Identification of abusers by gender: random sample (dating, cohabiting, and married respondents)

	N	%	Abuser Male		Abuser Female		Abuser Both		Abuser Unspecif.	
			N	%	N	%	N	%	N	%
FCHA: all abuse	52	31	32	62	4	8	11	21	5	10
CA (not incl. CA/WMA)	22	13	13	59	2	9	2	9	5	23
CA/WMA	17	10	14	82	1	6	2	12		
WMA (not incl. CA/WMA)	13	8	5	38	1	8	7	54		
FCHA: phy/sex abuse	38	23	29	76	4	11	3	8	2	5
Phy/sex CA (incl. CA/WMA)	28	17	21	75	3	11	2	7	2	7
Phy WMA (incl. CA/WMA)	22	13	18	82	2	9	2	9		
Substance abuse										
PGSA	39	23	27	69	2	5	10	26		
CGSA	17	20	14	82	1	6	2	12		
CTS violence										
CTS I (throwing/smashing)	12	14	4	33	3	25	5	42		
CTS II (threats of assault)	6	7	0	0	6	100	0	0		
CTS III (minor assaults)	6	7	0	0	5	83	1	17		
CTS IV (severe assaults)	3	4	0	0	0	0	3	100		
CTS II+ (all threats / assaults)	14	17	0	0	10	71	4	29		
'Serious' violence										
CRV III/IV (chronic/severe)	8	10	1	13	2	25	5	63		
PRV III/IV (chronic/severe)	8	10	6	75	1	13	1	13		
ARV III/IV (chronic/severe)	14	17	5	36	3	21	6	43		

Notes: (1) N = 166 for FCHA and PGSA. (2) N = 83 for CTS, CRV, PRV, ARV, and CGSA. (3) *Random* and *couples* respondents reported virtually identical perpetrator patterns.

TABLE 6
Demographic correlates of abuse (random sample)

	Household income	Education	Occupation	Marital status	Residency	Age	Gender[a] of respondents
FCHA (self)	p < .1346 < 50 / > 50 (× $1,000) 1.8 ×	p < .1962 H.S./Post 1.5 ×	p < .1363 Hm/Md-Wk 1.9 ×	p < .0971 Coh./Mar. 1.9 ×	p < .6268 Estab./New 1.2 ×	p < .5007 Yg-Mid/Old 1.5 ×	p < .0738 Fem./Male 2.2 × ◄
PGSA (self)	p < .3967 < 50 / > 50 (× $1,000) 1.6 ×	p < .2718 H.S./Post 1.6 ×	p < .2955 Hm/Md-Wk 2.0 ×	p < .1233 Coh./Mar. 2.2 ×	p < .3770 New/Extab. 1.6 ×	p < .6113 Yg-Mid/Old 1.4 ×	p < .9974 Fem./Male 1.0 × ◄
CGSA (self)	p < 1.0000 < 50 / > 50 (× $1,000) 1.0 ×	p < .3815 H.S./Post 3.3 ×	p < .2293 Hm/Wk-Md 2.9 ×	p < .7104 Coh./Mar. 1.3 ×	p < .5567 New/Extab. 2.3 ×	p < .0285 Mid-Yg-Old 4.1 ×	p < .0214 Male/Fem. 6.3 × ◄
ARV III/IV	p < .2667 <50 / >50 (× $1,000) 2.0 ×	p < .9729 Post/H.S. 1.0 ×	p < .9520 Md/Wk/Hm 1.0 ×	p < .5963 Coh./Mar. 1.7 ×	p < .2928 Estab./New 2.0 ×	p < .6302 Yg-Mid/Old 2.0 ×	p < .5095 Fem./Male 1.7 × ◄

Household income and abuse (N = 73)[b]

Reported abuse	n	Low / medium / high			Lower / higher	
		< $20,000	$20 – $50,000	> $50,000	< $50,000	> $50,000
FCHA	24/73	40%[c]	47%	24%	44%	24%
Significance			p < .1987		p < .1346	
WMA	14/73	33%	29%	10%	31%	10%
Significance			p < .0660		p < .0439	
FCHA	24/73	40%[c]	47%	24%	44%	24%
Significance			p < .1987		p < .1346	

TABLE 6—Concluded
Demographic correlates of abuse (random sample)

Reported abuse	n	Household income and abuse (N = 73)[b]				
		Low / medium / high			Lower / higher	
		< $20,000	$20 – $50,000	> $50,000	< $50,000	> $50,000
WMA	14/73	33%	29%	10%	31%	10%
Significance			p < .0660		p < .0439	
CA	17/73	20%	29%	22%	25%	22%
Significance			p < .7832		p < .9787	
CA/WMA	7/73	13%	12%	7%	13%	7%
Significance			p < .7485		p < .7296	
CSA	5/73	7%	12%	5%	9%	5%
Significance			p < .6395		p < .7735	
PGSA	16/73	27%	29%	17%	28%	17%
Significance			p < .5174		p < .3967	
CGSA	16/73	33%	24%	17%	28%	17%
Significance			p < .4210		p < .3967	
CLIENTS	11/73	20%	12%	15%	16%	15%
Significance			p < .8041		p < 1.0000	
RR = A/D?	18/73	27%	24%	24%	25%	24%
Significance			p < .9774		p < 1.0000	
CTS II+	14/73	27%	18%	17%	22%	17%
Significance			p < .7098		p < .8278	
CRV III/IV	8/73	20%	12%	7%	16%	7%
Significance			p < .4015		p < .4533	
ARV III/IV	13/73	27%	14%	12%	25%	12%
Significance			p < .3558		p < .2667	

Notes: (1) *Random* sample consists of 83 married, cohabiting, or dating respondents. Pearson correlation statistical significance is after Yates Correction, where applicable. Values at $p < .0000$ to $p < .0500$ are conventionally regarded as significant.
[a]Relationships between demographics and reported abuses were similar across *random* and *couples* samples. The exception was gender. In the *random* sample, females reported noticeably higher rates of childhood and family-of-origin abuse; in the *couples* sample, males and females reported similar rates.
[b]Income data are incomplete. The Statistics Canada *Violence against Women Survey* (1993) similarly reported that 12 per cent of respondents declined to provide information on incomes. See Wilson et al., 1995.
[c]The percentages in categories for income in the portion of the table headed 'Household Income and Abuse' indicate the percentage of respondents in each income category who reported abuse experiences, and do not add up to 100 per cent.

TABLE 7
Experiential correlates of abuse (random sample)

	n	PGSA n = 20	Clients n = 16	A/D? n = 21	CGSA n = 17	CTS II+ n = 14	CRV n = 8	ARV n = 14
				Childhood risks by adult abuse (N = 83)				
FCHA	28/83	75% $p < .0000$	75% $p < .0003$	57% $p < .0184$	59% $p < .0303$	57% $p < .0851$	75% $p < .0276$	86% $p < .0000$
CA	21/83	50% $p < .0088$	63% $p < .0005$	53% $p < .0026$	33% $p < .1689$	43% $p < .1868$	75% $p < .0029$	71% $p < .0001$
WMA	16/83	60% $p < .0003$	38% $p < .0884$	24% $p < .7724$	44% $p < .0263$	38% $p < .0374$	19% $p < .3665$	44% $p < .0047$
CA/WMA	9/83	35% $p < .0004$	25% $p < .1142$	19% $p < .3207$	24% $p < .1473$	29% $p < .0617$	38% $p < .0508$	38% $p < .0049$
CSA	6/83	10% $p < .9571$	31% $p < .0003$	24% $p < .0036$	12% $p < .7759$	21% $p < .0921$	38% $p < .0058$	29% $p < .0049$
PGSA	20/83	na redundant	44% $p < .0853$	29% $p < .7952$	41% $p < .1264$	21% $p < 1.0000$	25% $p < 1.0000$	43% $p < .1450$

TABLE 7–*Concluded*
Experiential correlates of abuse (random sample)

	n	Clients n = 16	A/D? n = 21	CGSA n = 17	CTS II+ n = 14	CRV n = 8	ARV n = 14
				Relationships among adult abuses			
CTS II+	14/83	44%	33%	41%	redundant	88%	64%
Criminal code		p < .0047	p < .0461	p < .0083		p < .0000	p < .0000
CRV II/IV	8/83	31%	29%	29%	50%	redundant	redundant
Chronic/severe		p < .0053	p < .0144	p < .0084			
PRV III/IV	9/83	44%	24%	35%	29%	33%	redundant
Chronic/severe		p < .0000	p < .0711	p < .0014	p < .0000	p < .0508	
ARV III/IV	14/83	56%	38%	53%	64%	redundant	redundant
Chronic/severe		p < .0000	p < .0076	p < .0000	p < .0000		
CGSA	17/83	31%	48%	redundant	50%	63%	64%
		p < .3991	p < .0011		p < .0083	p < .0084	p < .0003
A/D?	21/83	56%	redundant	59%	50%	75%	57%
Abusive/distressed		p < .0044		p < .0011	p < .0461	p < .0029	p < .0076

Note: Data on abuse intervention experience were derived from general comments and an open-ended question about seek-help activity.

TABLE 8
High risk respondents (random sample)

'Double whammy' – experienced child abuse & witnessed parental spouse abuse
(12% of females; 11% of males; 11% all)

	Reporting CSA	Reporting CGSA	Reporting CTS II+	Reporting CRV III/IV	Reporting ARV III/IV	Reporting RR = AD/?
Abuse clients 44% $p < .1142$	11% $p < 1.0000$	44% $p < .1473$	44% $p < .0617$	33% $p < .0508$	56% $p < .0049$	44% $p < .3207$

Effects of 'double whammy' reports on survey findings

n = 9	Clients	CSA	CGSA	CTS II+	CRV	ARV	A/D?
Double whammy CA/WMA	25% $p < .1142$	17% $p < 1.0000$	24% $p < .0473$	29% $p < .0617$	38% $p < .0508$	36% $p < .0049$	19% $p < .3207$

Child sexual abuse victims
(11% of females; 0% of males; 7% all)

	Reporting CA/WMA	Reporting CGSA	Reporting CTS II+	Reporting CRV III/IV	Reporting ARV III/IV	Reporting RR = AD/?
Abuse clients 83% $p < .0003$	17% $p < 1.0000$	33% $p < .7759$	50% $p < .0921$	50% $p < .0058$	67% $p < .0049$	83% $p < .0036$

TABLE 8—*Concluded*
High risk respondents (random sample)

Effects of child sex abuse reports on survey findings

n = 6	Clients	CA/WMA	CGSA	CTS II+	CRV	ARV	A/D?
Child sex abuse CSA	31% $p < .0003$	6% $p < 1.0000$	12% $p < .7759$	21% $p < .0921$	38% $p < .0058$	29% $p < .0049$	24% $p < .0036$

Abuse intervention clients[a]
(23% females; 11% males; 19% all)

Reporting CA/WMA	Reporting CSA	Reporting CGSA	Reporting CTS II+	Reporting CRV III/IV	Reporting ARV III/IV	Reporting RR = AD/?
25% $p < .1142$	31% $p < .0003$	31% $p < .3991$	44% $p < .0047$	31% $p < .0053$	56% $p < .0000$	56% $p < .0044$

Effects of abuse intervention clients' reports on survey findings

n = 16	CA/WMA	CSA	CGSA	CTS II+	CRV	ARV	A/D?
Abuse clients	44% $p < .1142$	83% $p < .0003$	29% $p < .3391$	40% $p < .0047$	63% $p < .0053$	64% $p < .0000$	43% $p < .0044$

[a]Includes those involved as clients with shelters, with counselling and medical services, with substance abuse programs, and with services and programs provided and administered by the police and courts.

TABLE 9
Intergenerational patterns of vulnerability and resiliency (sole-respondent random and dual-respondent couples comparisons)

FCHA across samples

FCHA	CGSA Self/part.		RR		CTS I Throw things		CTS II+ Crim. code		CRV III/IV		PRV III/IV		ARV III/IV	
	yes	no	A/D?	N/LF	yes	no	yes	no	yes	no	yes	no	yes	no
Random (n = 16)	59%	27%	57%	26%	60%	25%	57%	30%	75%	29%	100%	26%	86%	23%
Significance	$p < .0303$		$p < .0184$		$p < .0099$		$p < .0851$		$p < .0276$		$p < .0000$		$p < .0000$	
Couples (n = 12)	37%	33%	55%	25%	53%	27%	27%	36%	50%	35%	50%	34%	33%	34%
Significance	$p < 1.0000$		$p < .0396$		$p < .0872$		$p < .8445$		$p < 1.0000$		$p < 1.0000$		$p < 1.0000$	

WMA across samples

WMA (self-reports)	CGSA Self/part.		RR		CTS I Throw things		CTS II+ Crim. code		CRV III/IV		PRV III/IV		ARV III/IV	
	yes	no	A/D?	N/LF	yes	no	yes	no	yes	no	yes	no	yes	no
Random (n = 16)	42%	14%	24%	18%	25%	18%	43%	15%	38%	17%	56%	15%	50%	13%
Significance	$p < .0263$		$p < .7724$		$p < .6749$		$p < .0347$		$p < .0047$		$p < .0133$		$p < .0047$	
Couples (n = 12)	16%	20%	30%	14%	21%	18%	27%	17%	25%	18%	0%	19%	17%	19%
Significance	$p < .9651$		$p < .2266$		$p < 1.0000$		$p < .7104$		$p < 1.0000$		$p < 1.0000$		$p < 1.0000$	

TABLE 9—*Continued*
Intergenerational patterns of vulnerability and resiliency (sole-respondent random and dual-respondent couples comparisons)

CA across samples

CA (self-reports)	CGSA Self/part.		RR		CTS I Throw things		CTS II+ Crim. code		CRV III/IV		PRV III/IV		ARV III/IV	
	yes	no	A/D?	N/LF	yes	no	yes	no	yes	no	yes	no	yes	no
Random (n = 21)	41%	21%	52%	16%	55%	16%	43%	22%	75%	20%	78%	19%	71%	16%
Significance	p < .1689		p < .0026		p < .0013		p < .1868		p < .0029		p < .0006		p < .0001	
Couples (n = 15)	32%	20%	40%	16%	47%	13%	9%	26%	25%	23%	50%	23%	3%/3	22%
Significance	p < .4990		p < .0734		p < .0090		p < .3991 n.		p < 1.0000		p < .9577		p < .9244	

CGSA[a] across samples

CGSA (self/partner)	CGSA Self/part.		RR		CTS I Throw things		CTS II+ Crim. code		CRV III/IV		PRV III/IV		ARV III/IV	
	yes	no	A/D?	N/LF	yes	no	yes	no	yes	no	yes	no	yes	no
Random (n = 17)	r	r	48%	11%	35%	16%	50%	14%	63%	16%	67%	15%	64%	12%
Significance	*redundant*		p < .0011		p < .1264		p < .0083		p < .0084		p < .0014		p < .0000	
Couples (n = 12)	r	r	65%	14%	42%	24%	55%	26%	100%	25%	100%	27%	100%	22%
Significance	*redundant*		p < .0001		p < .2655		p < .1052		p < .0090		p < .1541		p < .0005	

TABLE 9—*Concluded*
Intergenerational patterns of vulnerability and resiliency (sole-respondent random and dual-respondent couples comparisons)

	CGSA Self/part.		RR		CTS I Throw things		CTS II+ Crim. code		CRV III/IV		PRV III/IV		ARV III/IV	
PRV (self-reports)	yes	no	A/D?	N/LF	yes	no	yes	no	yes	no	yes	no	yes	no
Random (n = 9)	35%	5%	24%	7%	25%	7%	29%	7%	38%	8%	*red*	*red*	*red*	*red*
Significance	*p < .0014*		*p < .0711*		*p < .0543*		*p < .0617*		*p < .0508*		*redundant*		*redundant*	
Couples (n = 2)	11%	0%	5%	2%	5%	2%	0%	4%	0%	3%	*red*	*red*	*red*	*red*
Significance	*p < .1541*		*p < 1.0000*		*p < 1.0000*		*p < 1.0000*		*p < 1.0000*		*redundant*		*redundant*	

Note: *Couples* correlational patterns derived from combined-partner data (data based on the combined responses of both partners) are very similar to patterns derived from displayed self-report data.
[a]These correlations are for all identified substance problems, current or past. An analysis that relies on current or ongoing substance problems yields similar results.

TABLE 10.a
Evaluations of feminists as intervention board and staff

Rated by reported experiences (80/83 partnered respondents)

	Clients (n = 13)		FCHA/CGSA (n = 34)		CRV (n = 8)		ARV (n = 13)		RR (n = 21)	
	yes	no	yes	no	yes	no	yes	no	A/D?	N/LF
Not acceptable/poor	33%	55%	42%	57%	27%	53%	33%	54%	47%	53%
Acceptable	47%	29%	36%	30%	43%	32%	42%	31%	26%	34%
Good/preferred	20%	15%	21%	13%	29%	15%	25%	15%	26%	13%
Significance	$p < .2929$		$p < .3748$		$p < .4190$		$p < .3840$		$p < .3829$	
Sign. reject/accept	$p < .2100$		$p < .2730$		$p < .3893$		$p < .3013$		$p < .9007$	

Rated by gender

	Not acceptable/poor		Acceptable		Good/preferred	
	Females	Males	Females	Males	Females	Males
Females	46%		33%		22%	
Males		64%		32%		4%

$p < .1046$ (reject/accept: $p < .1947$)

Rated by abuse clients, controlling for gender (12/55 females; 3/25 males)

	Not acceptable/poor				Acceptable				Good/preferred			
	Female		Male		Female		Male		Female		Male	
	clients	not	clients	not	clients	not	clients	not	clients	not	clients	not
Female clients	17%				58%				25%			
Female not		54%				26%				21%		
Male clients			100%				0%				0%	
Male not				59%				36%				5%

Females: $p < .0512$ (accept/reject: $p < .0527$) Males: $p < .3834$ (reject/accept: $p < .4571$)

TABLE 10.a—Concluded
Evaluations of feminists as intervention board and staff

Rated by high risk respondents (FCHA/CGSA), controlling for gender (25/55 females; 8/25 males)

Not acceptable/poor				Acceptable				Good/preferred			
Female risks	Female not	Male risks	Male not	Female risks	Female not	Male risks	Male not	Female risks	Female not	Male risks	Male not
28%	60%	88%	53%	44%	23%	13%	41%	28%	17%	0%	6%

Females: $p < .0592$ (accept/reject: $p < .0356$) Males: $p < .2365$ (reject/accept: $p < .2177$)

Rated by respondents reporting adult relationship violence, controlling for gender (10/55 females; 2/25 males)

Not acceptable/poor				Acceptable				Good/preferred			
Female ARV	Female not	Male ARV	Male not	Female ARV	Female not	Male ARV	Male not	Female ARV	Female not	Male ARV	Male not
20%	51%	100%	61%	50%	29%	0%	35%	30%	20%	0%	4%

Females: $p < .1987$ (reject/accept: $p < .1510$) Males: $p < .5426$ (reject/accept: $p < .7354$)

Rated by respondents reporting relationship abuse or distress, controlling for gender (14/55 females; 5/25 males)

Not acceptable/poor				Acceptable				Good/preferred			
Female A/D?	Female N/LF	Male A/D?	Male N/LF	Female A/D?	Female N/LF	Male A/D?	Male N/LF	Female A/D?	Female N/LF	Male A/D?	Male N/LF
29%	51%	100%	55%	36%	32%	0%	40%	36%	17%	0%	5%

Females: $p < .2356$ (accept/reject: $p < .2466$) Males: $p < .1724$ (reject/accept: $p < .1757$)

TABLE 10.b
Evaluations of community leaders as intervention board and staff

Rated by reported experiences (83/83 partnered respondents)

	Clients (n = 16)		FCHA/CGSA (n = 35)		CRV (n = 8)		ARV (n = 14)		RR (n = 21)	
	yes	no	yes	no	yes	no	yes	no	A/D?	N/LF
Not acceptable/poor	31%	46%	40%	46%	46%	50%	43%	43%	38%	45%
Acceptable	44%	22%	40%	46%	50%	43%	43%	44%	38%	45%
Good/preferred	25%	31%	26%	33%	25%	31%	14%	33%	19%	34%
Significance	$p < .2157$		$p < .3808$		$p < .9166$		$p < .2121$		$p < .1249$	
Sign. rej./accept	$p < .4189$		$p < .7601$		$p < .9820$		$p < 1.0000$		$p < .7566$	

Rated by gender

	Not acceptable/poor		Acceptable		Good/preferred	
	Females	Males	Females	Males	Females	Males
	36%	59%	30%	19%	34%	22%

$p < .1274$ (reject/accept: $p < .0732$)

Rated by abuse clients, controlling for gender (13/56 females; 3/27 males)

	Not acceptable/poor				Acceptable				Good/preferred			
	Female clients	Female not	Male clients	Male not	Female clients	Female not	Male clients	Male not	Female clients	Female not	Male clients	Male not
	23%	40%	67%	58%	46%	26%	33%	17%	31%	35%	0%	25%

Females: $p < .3331$ (accept/reject: $< .4503$) Males: $p < .5540$ (reject/accept: $p < 1.0000$)

TABLE 10.b—*Concluded*
Evaluations of community leaders as intervention board and staff

Rated by high risk respondents (FCHA/CGSA), controlling for gender (25/56 females; 9/27 males)

Not acceptable/poor				Acceptable				Good/preferred			
Female risks	Female not	Male risks	Male not	Female risks	Female not	Male risks	Male not	Female risks	Female not	Male risks	Male not
27%	43%	78%	50%	39%	23%	22%	16%	35%	33%	0%	33%

Females: $p < .3487$ (reject/accept: $p < .3180$) Males: $p < .1436$ (reject/accept: $p < .3324$)

Rated by respondents reporting adult relationship violence, controlling for gender (11/56 females; 3/27 males)

Not acceptable/poor				Acceptable				Good/preferred			
Female ARV	Female not	Male ARV	Male not	Female ARV	Female not	Male ARV	Male not	Female ARV	Female not	Male ARV	Male not
36%	36%	67%	58%	46%	27%	33%	17%	18%	38%	0%	25%

Females: $p < .3624$ (accept/reject: $p < 1.0000$) Males: $p < .5540$ (reject/accept: $p > 1.000$)

Rated by respondents reporting relationship abuse or distress, controlling for gender (15/56 females; 6/27 males)

Not acceptable/poor				Acceptable				Good/preferred			
Female A/D?	Female N/LF	Male A/D?	Male N/LF	Female A/D?	Female N/LF	Male A/D?	Male N/LF	Female A/D?	Female N/LF	Male A/D?	Male N/LF
20%	42%	83%	52%	53%	22%	17%	19%	27%	37%	0%	29%

Females: $p < .0707$ (accept/reject: $p < .2422$) Males: $p < .2889$ (reject/accept: $p < .3736$)

TABLE 10.c
Evaluations of abuse professionals as intervention board and staff

Rated by reported experiences (83/83 partnered respondents)

	Clients (n = 16)		FCHA/CGSA (n = 35)		CRV (n = 8)		ARV (n = 14)		RR (n = 21)	
	yes	no	yes	no	yes	no	yes	no	A/D?	N/LF
Not acceptable/poor	0%	2%	3%	0%	13%	0%	8%	0%	0%	2%
Acceptable	19%	12%	17%	105%	13%	13%	21%	12%	14%	13%
Good/preferred	81%	87%	80%	90%	75%	87%	71%	88%	86%	86%
Significance	$p < .6930$		$p < .3199$		$p < .0087$		$p < .0457$		$p < .8347$	
Sign. reject/accept	$p < 1.0000$		$p < .8732$		$p < .1688$		$p < .3734$		$p < 1.0000$	

Rated by gender

	Not acceptable/poor		Acceptable		Good/preferred	
	Males	Females	Males	Females	Males	Females
	0%	2%	22%	9%	78%	89%

$p < .2026$ (accept/reject: $p < 1.000$)

Rated by abuse clients, controlling for gender (13/56 females; 3/27 males)

	Not acceptable/poor				Acceptable				Good/preferred			
	Female clients	Female not	Male clients	Male not	Female clients	Female not	Male clients	Male not	Female clients	Female not	Male clients	Male not
	0%	2%	0%	0%	8%	9%	67%	17%	92%	88%	33%	83%

Females: $p < .8400$ (reject/accept: $p < 1.000$) Males: $p < .2196$ (reject/accept: $p < na$ 100%)

TABLE 10.c—*Concluded*
Evaluations of abuse professionals as intervention board and staff

Rated by high risk respondents (FCHA/CGSA), controlling for gender (26/56 females; 9/29 males)

	Female risks	Female not	Male risks	Male not
Not acceptable/poor	4%	0%	0%	0%
Acceptable	12%	7%	33%	17%
Good/preferred	85%	93%	67%	83%

Females: p < .4398 (accept/reject: p < .9424) Males: p < .6234 (accept/reject: p < na 100%)

Rated by respondents reporting adult relationship violence, controlling for gender (11/56 females; 3/27 males)

	Female ARV	Female not	Male ARV	Male not
Not acceptable/poor	9%	0%	0%	0%
Acceptable	18%	7%	33%	21%
Good/preferred	73%	93%	67%	79%

Females: p < .0544 (accept/reject: p < .4407) Males: p < 1.0000 (accept/reject: p < na 100%)

Rated by respondent reporting ralationship abuse or distress, controlling for gender (15/16 females; 6/27 males)

	Female A/D?	Female N/LF	Male A/D?	Male N/LF
Not acceptable/poor	0%	2%	0%	0%
Acceptable	7%	10%	33%	19%
Good/preferred	93%	88%	67%	81%

Females: p < .7707 (accept/reject: p < 1.000) Males: p < .8528 (accept/reject: p < na 100%)

TABLE 10.d
Evaluations of abuse survivors as intervention board and staff

Rated by reported experiences (82/83 partnered respondents)

	Clients (n = 13)		FCHA/CGSA (n = 34)		CRV (n = 8)		ARV (n = 13)		RR (n = 21)	
	yes	not	yes	no	yes	no	yes	no	A/D?	N/LF
Not acceptable/poor	0%	8%	0%	11%	0%	7%	0%	7%	0%	8%
Acceptable	6%	21%	14%	21%	0%	20%	7%	21%	5%	23%
Good/preferred	94%	71%	86%	68%	100%	73%	93%	72%	95%	69%
Significance	$p < .1610$		$p < .0787$		$p < .2394$		$p < .2416$		$p < .0502$	
Sign. reject/accept	$p < .5797$		$p < .1273$		$p < 1.0000$		$p < .6645$		$p < .4092$	

Rated by gender

	Not acceptable/poor		Acceptable		Good/preferred	
	Females	Males	Females	Males	Females	Males
	12%	15%	13%	30%	86%	56%

$p < .0068 (accept/reject: p < .0687)$

Rated by abuse clients, controlling for gender (13/56 females; 3/27 males)

	Not acceptable/poor				Acceptable				Good/preferred			
	Female clients	Female not	Male clients	Male not	Female clients	Female not	Male clients	Male not	Female clients	Female not	Male clients	Male not
	0%	2%	0%	17%	8%	14%	0%	33%	92%	83%	100%	50%

Females: $p < .6900$ (accept/reject: $p < 1.0000$) Males: $p < .2592$ (accept/reject: $p < 1,000$)

TABLE 10.d–Concluded
Evaluations of abuse survivors as intervention board and staff

Rated by high risk respondents (FCHA/CGSA), controlling for gender (26/56 females; 9/27 males)

Not acceptable/poor				Acceptable				Good/preferred			
Female risks	Female not	Male risks	Male not	Female risks	Female not	Male risks	Male not	Female risks	Female not	Male risks	Male not
0%	3%	0%	22%	12%	14%	22%	33%	89%	83%	78%	44%

Females: p < .6055 (accept/reject: p < 1.0000) Males: p < .1783 (accept/reject: p < .3382)

Rated by adult respondents reporting relationship violence, controlling for gender (11/56 females; 3/27 males)

Not acceptable/poor				Acceptable				Good/preferred			
Female ARV	Female not	Male ARV	Male not	Female ARV	Female not	Male ARV	Male not	Female ARV	Female not	Male ARV	Male not
0%	2%	0%	17%	9%	14%	0%	33%	91%	84%	100%	50%

Females: p < .8022 (accept/reject: p < 1.000) Males: p < .2592 (accept/reject: p < 1.000)

Rated by respondents reporting relationship abuse or distress, controlling for gender (15/56 females; 6/27 males)

Not acceptable/poor				Acceptable				Good/preferred			
Female A/D?	Female N/LF	Male A/D?	Male N/LF	Female A/D?	Female N/LF	Male A/D?	Male N/LF	Female A/D?	Female N/LF	Male A/D?	Male N/LF
0%	3%	0%	19%	7%	15%	0%	38%	93%	83%	100%	43%

Females: p < .5712 (accept/reject: p < 1.0000) Males: p < .0457 (accept/reject: p < .6132)

TABLE 11
Evaluations of women's shelters (random sample)

Shelter ratings by risks and experiences (79/83 partnered respondents)

	Clients (n = 16) yes	not	FCHA/CGSA (n = 35) yes	no	CRV (n = 8) yes	no	ARV (n = 14) yes	no	RR (n = 20) A/D?	N/LF
Not/somewhat helpful	25%	5%	9%	9%	13%	9%	14%	8%	20%	5%
Helpful	6%	25%	15%	27%	0%	24%	0%	26%	15%	24%
Very helpful	69%	70%	77%	64%	88%	68%	86%	66%	65%	71%
Significance	$p < .0177$		$p < .4296$		$p < .2927$		$p < .0880$		$p < .1130$	

Shelter ratings by gender

	Females (n = 53/79)	Males (n = 26/79)
Not/somewhat helpful	6%	15%
Helpful	21%	23%
Very helpful	74%	62%

Overall significance gender $p < .3216$

Shelter ratings, controlling for gender

	Clients all (n = 16) yes	not	Clients females (n = 13) yes	not	Clients males (n = 3) yes	not	ARV all (n = 14) yes	no	ARV females (n = 11) yes	no	ARV males (n = 3) yes	no
Not/somewhat helpful	25%	5%	15%	3%	66%	98%	14%	8%	9%	5%	33%	13%
Helpful	6%	25%	8%	25%	0%	26%	0%	26%	0%	26%	0%	26%
Very helpful	69%	70%	77%	73%	33%	65%	86%	66%	91%	69%	67%	61%
Significance	$p < .0177$		$p < .1153$		$p < .0299$		$p < .0880$		$p < .1545$		$p < .4704$	

TABLE 12
Evaluations of therapeutic interventions (random sample)

Evaluations of therapeutic interventions by reported abuse experiences

Family counselling services[a]

	FCHA/CGSA (n = 32)		Clients (n = 15)		CRV (n = 8)		ARV (n = 12)		RR (n = 20)	
	yes	no	yes	not	yes	no	yes	no	A/D?	N/LF
Not/somewhat helpful	22%	17%	40%	14%	38%	17%	33%	16%	20%	19%
Helpful	22%	31%	13%	31%	13%	29%	25%	27%	25%	24%
Very helpful	56%	52%	47%	56%	50%	55%	42%	57%	45%	57%
Significance	p < .6491		p < .0520		p < .3066		p < .3676		p < .5836	

Woman abuse counselling services[b]

	FCHA/CGSA (n = 34)		Clients (n = 15)		CRV (n = 8)		ARV (n = 14)		RR (n = 22)	
	yes	no	yes	not	yes	no	yes	no	A/D?	N/LF
Not/somewhat helpful	9%	32%	13%	23%	0%	24%	7%	25%	15%	24%
Helpful	35%	27%	33%	30%	50%	28%	43%	28%	40%	27%
Very helpful	56%	42%	53%	47%	50%	48%	50%	48%	45%	49%
Significance	p < .0550		p < .6987		p < .2221		p < .2904		p < .5121	

Child sex abuse counselling services[c]

	FCHA/CGSA (n = 32)		Clients (n = 15)		CRV (n = 8)		ARV (n = 12)		RR (n = 19)	
	yes	no	yes	not	yes	no	yes	no	A/D?	N/LF
Not/somewhat helpful	3%	12%	7%	9%	0%	9%	0%	10%	5%	9%
Helpful	19%	33%	13%	31%	13%	29%	17%	29%	26%	27%
Very helpful	78%	55%	80%	61%	88%	62%	83%	61%	68%	64%
Significance	p < .0961		p < .3646		p < .3437		p < .2889		p < .8565	

TABLE 12–Concluded
Evaluations of therapeutic interventions (random sample)

	Substance abuse counselling services[d]									
	FCHA/CGSA (n = 34)		Clients (n = 16)		CRV (n = 8)		ARV (n = 14)		RR (n = 20)	
	yes	no	yes	not	yes	no	yes	no	A/D?	N/LF
Not/somewhat helpful	15%	13%	13%	14%	38%	11%	21%	12%	29%	9%
Helpful	27%	31%	31%	29%	25%	30%	21%	31%	24%	31%
Very helpful	59%	56%	56%	57%	38%	59%	57%	57%	48%	60%
Significance	p < .9022		p < .9693		p < .1226		p < .5965		p < .0772	

Evaluations of therapeutic interventions by gender

	Family counselling						Woman abuse programs						Child sex abuse programs						Substance abuse programs					
	Not (%)		Help. (%)		Very (%)		Not (%)		Help. (%)		Very (%)		Not (%)		Help. (%)		Very (%)		Not (%)		Help. (%)		Very (%)	
	F	M	F	M	F	M	F	M	F	M	F	M	F	M	F	M	F	M	F	M	F	M	F	M
	23	9	23	36	54	55	20	25	37	17	43	58	8	9	25	32	67	59	13	15	32	23	55	62
Significance	Significance gender p < .2713						Significance gender p < .1956						Significance gender p < .7929						Significance gender p < .7093					

[a] Male abuse intervention clients were more likely both to reject family counselling and to rate it very helpful (p < .0881). Females who reported chronic or severe current relationship violence were considerably more likely both to reject family counselling and to rate it very helpful (p < .1561).

[b] 'High risk' respondents include those who reported childhood or family-of-origin abuse, or current generation substance abuse. A very high percentage reported both. 'High risk' females (FCHA/CGSA) were significantly more likely to rate woman abuse counselling helpful or very helpful (p < .0194), and 'high risk' males were considerably more likely to rate woman abuse programs helpful or very helpful (p < .1847). Women and men who reported chronic and severe adult relationship violence were noticeably more likely to rate woman abuse programs helpful or very helpful. Support was also very high among relationship-distressed (A/D?) females (p < .1478).

[c] 'High risk' respondents (FCHA/CGSA), abuse intervention clients, and respondents who reported chronic and severe adult relationship violence rated child sex abuse counselling more positively than respondents not reporting these experiences. Support was minimally higher among females.

[d] Across genders, respondents who reported chronic and severe relationship violence were highly unlikely to rate substance abuse programs helpful or very helpful.

TABLE 13
Evaluations of mainstream interventions (random sample)

Evaluations of mainstream interventions by reported abuse experiences

Police[a]

	FCHA/CGSA (n = 34)		Clients (n = 13)		CRV (n = 8)		ARV (n = 13)		RR (n = 21) A/D?	N/LF
	yes	no	yes	not	yes	no	yes	no		
Not/somewhat helpful	52	59	46	57	38	58	46	57	38	62
Helpful	9	15	23	10	13	12	8	13	19	9
Very helpful	39	27	31	33	50	30	46	30	43	28
Significance	$p < .4689$		$p < .4062$		$p < .5032$		$p < .4921$		$p < .1564$	

Courts[b]

	FCHA/CGSA (n = 27)		Clients (n = 11)		CRV (n = 7)		ARV (n = 10)		RR (n = 17) A/D?	N/LF
	yes	no	yes	not	yes	no	yes	no		
Not/somewhat helpful	70	74	64	74	71	73	70	73	53	79
Helpful	15	21	18	19	14	19	10	20	29	15
Very helpful	15	5	18	7	14	9	20	7	18	6
Significance	$p < .3835$		$p < .5253$		$p < .8641$		$p < .3768$		$p < .1078$	

Legal services[c]

	FCHA/CGSA (n = 30)		Clients (n = 14)		CRV (n = 8)		ARV (n = 12)		RR (n = 20) A/D?	N/LF
	yes	no	yes	not	yes	no	yes	no		
Not/somewhat helpful	50	71	50	65	60	64	50	65	43	70
Helpful	36	14	38	20	40	21	38	20	43	16
Very helpful	14	14	13	14	0	15	13	14	14	14
Significance	$p < .1442$		$p < .5623$		$p < .4752$		$p < .5623$		$p < .1063$	

TABLE 13—Concluded
Evaluations of mainstream interventions (random sample)

| | Medical services[d] | | | | | | | | | |
| | FCHA/CGSA (n = 30) | | Clients (n = 14) | | CRV (n = 8) | | ARV (n = 12) | | RR (n = 20) | |
	yes	no	yes	not	yes	no	yes	no	A/D?	N/LF
Not/somewhat helpful	23%	51%	29%	42%	13%	43%	17%	44%	40%	39%
Helpful	40%	29%	43%	32%	38%	33%	33%	34%	30%	35%
Very helpful	37%	20%	29%	26%	50%	24%	50%	22%	30%	36%
Significance	$p < .0520$		$p < .6168$		$p < .1725$		$p < .0901$		$p < .8911$	

Evaluations of mainstream interventions by gender

| | Police Help. | | | | | | Courts Help. | | | | | | Legal Help. | | | | | | Medical Help. | | | | | |
| | Not (%) | | Help. (%) | | Very (%) | | Not (%) | | Help. (%) | | Very (%) | | Not (%) | | Help. (%) | | Very (%) | | Not (%) | | Help. (%) | | Very (%) | |
	F	M	F	M	F	M	F	M	F	M	F	M	F	M	F	M	F	M	F	M	F	M	F	M
	60	46	14	8	26	46	65	86	23	9	12	5	54	80	27	15	19	5	32	43	31	40	27	27
Significance gender	$p < .2251$						$p < .1939$						$p < .1354$						$p < .6223$					

[a] Relationship-distressed women (A/D?) were significantly more likely to rate the police helpful or very helpful ($p < .0367$).
[b] Male abuse intervention clients and males who reported chronic and severe adult relationship violence were significantly more likely to rate the courts very helpful ($p < .0052$). Relationship-distressed (A/D?) respondents of both genders were considerably more likely to rate the courts helpful or very helpful (females: $p < .1228$; males: $p < .1341$).
[c] 'High risk' males (FCHA/CGSA) were significantly more likely to rate legal services helpful ($p < .0150$). Relationship-distressed females (A/D?) were considerably more likely to rate legal services helpful ($p < .1442$).
[d] 'High risk' females (FCHA and/or CGSA) were significantly more likely to rate medical interventions helpful or very helpful ($p < .0366$). Females who reported adult relationship violence were considerably more likely to rate medical services helpful or very helpful ($p < .1261$).

TABLE 14
Sexism as a major or important cause of abuse, controlling for gender (random sample)

	All respondents	All females	All males
Major/important	27%	25%	30%
		Significance gender p < .8554	

	All 'high risk' (FCHA and/or CGSA) Yes risks No risks	Female 'high risk' (FCHA and/or CGSA) Yes risks No risks	Male 'high risk' (FCHA and/or CGSA) Yes risks No risks
Major/important	31% 23%	35% 17%	22% 33%
Significance	*p < .5380*	*p < .2159*	*p < .8815*

	All clients Clients Not clients	Female clients Clients Not clients	Male clients Clients Not clients
Major/important	44% 22%	46% 19%	33% 29%
Significance	*p < .1544*	*p < .1000*	*p < 1.0000*

	All CRV III/IV Yes CRV No CRV	Female CRV III/IV Yes CRV No CRV	Male CRV III/IV Yes CRV No CRV
Major/important	63% 23%	67% 20%	50% 28%
Significance	*p < .0449*	*p < .0460*	*p < 1.000*

	All ARV III/IV Yes ARV No ARV	Female ARV III/IV Yes ARV No ARV	Male ARV III/IV Yes ARV No ARV
Major/important	57% 20%	55% 18%	67% 25%
Significance	*p < .0119*	*p < .0327*	*p .4125*

	All distressed A/D? N/LF	Female distressed A/D? N/LF	Male distressed A/D? N/LF
Major/important	29% 26%	27% 24%	33% 29%
Significance	*p < 1.0000*	*p < 1.0000*	*p < 1.0000*

Note: Sexism was the only alleged cause of abuse that 'high risk' respondents and respondents reporting serious adult relationship violence rated in a significantly or markedly different way than respondents not reporting risks or violence.

TABLE 15
Justifications for violence and abuse, controlling for gender (random sample)

	Justifications for male violence			Justifications for female violence		
	All	Females	Males	All	Females	Males
Provoked	10%	9%	11%	15%	14%	15%
Self-defence	49%	50%	48%	65%	61%	74%
Significance gender		*p < .9497*			*p < .3297*	

	All 'high risk'		Female 'high risk'		Male 'high risk'	
	Yes risks	No risks	Yes risks	No risks	Yes risks	No risks
Males: provoked	14%	6%	15%	3%	11%	11%
Males: self-defence	43%	54%	39%	60%	56%	44%
Females: provoked	20%	10%	19%	10%	22%	11%
Females: self-defence	57%	71%	54%	67%	67%	78%
Sign. male violence	*p < .3804*		*p < .1449*		*p < .8455*	
Sign. female violence	*p < .3614*		*p < .5274*		*p < .7408*	

	All clients		Female clients		Male clients	
	Clients	Not clients	Clients	Not clients	Clients	Not clients
Males: provoked	6%	10%	0%	12%	33%	8%
Males: self-defence	50%	49%	54%	49%	33%	50\%
Females: provoked	19%	13%	15%	14%	33%	13%
Females: self-defence	56%	67%	54%	63%	67%	75%
Sign. male violence	*p < .8715*		*p < .4343*		*p < .4276*	
Sign. female violence	*p < .7094*		*p < .8306*		*p < .5540*	

	All CRV III/IV		Female CRV III/IV		Male CRV III/IV	
	Yes CRV	No CRV	Yes CRV	No CRV	Yes CRV	No CRV
Males: provoked	13%	9%	0%	10%	50%	8%
Males: self-defence	63%	48%	67%	48%	50%	48%
Females: provoked	25%	13%	17%	14%	50%	12%
Females: self-defence	63%	65%	67%	60%	50%	76%
Sign. male violence	*p < .6270*		*p < .5853*		*p < .1480*	
Sign. female violence	*p < .6173*		*p < .8814*		*p < .3305*	

	All ARV III/IV		Female ARV III/IV		Male ARV III/IV	
	Yes ARV	No ARV	Yes ARV	No ARV	Yes ARV	No ARV
Males: provoked	7%	10%	0%	11%	33%	8%
Males: self-defence	50%	49%	46%	51%	67%	46%
Females: provoked	14%	15%	9%	16%	33%	13%
Females: self-defence	64%	65%	64%	60%	67%	75%
Sign. male violence	*p < .9395*		*p < .3899*		*p < .2106*	
Sign. female violence	*p < .9954*		*p < .8581*		*p < .5540*	

TABLE 15–*Concluded*
Justifications for violence and abuse, controlling for gender (random sample)

	All ratings		Female ratings		Male ratings	
	A/D?	N/LF	A/D?	N/LF	A/D?	N/LF
Males: provoked	19%	7%	20%	5%	17%	10%
Males: self-defence	57%	47%	53%	49%	67%	43%
Females: provoked	29%	10%	33%	7%	17%	14%
Females: self-defence	57%	68%	47%	66%	83%	71%
Sign. male violence	*p < .0845*		*p < .1428*		*p < .3943*	
Sign. female violence	*p < .0968*		*p < .0480*		*p < .6175*	

Notes

1: Theoretical and Political Contexts

1 Texts are, of course, empirical evidence. Talking and writing are a big part of what people 'actually experience and do.' This does not mean, as Blumer emphasizes, that reality shifts to the realm of imagery and conception. A core feature of 'reality' is that it talks back, that it refuses to bend to our conceptions. It is this 'obdurate' character of reality that both calls for and justifies empirical science. See Blumer, 1969: 22.

2 See Mead, 1934; Weber, 1949; 1958; Mills, 1959; Sartre, 1965; Berger and Luckman, 1966; Marx, 1968; Blumer, 1969; Buckley, 1967; Johnson, 1977; Giddens, 1976, 1979, 1983, 1992; Douglas, 1977; Therborn, 1980; Kemper, 1981; Reiss, 1981; Ferraro, 1983; Johnson and Ferraro, 1984; Lester, 1984; Denzin, 1984, 1987, 1989, 1994; Watzlawick, 1984a, 1984b; Bateson, 1985; Habermas, 1987; Weedon, 1987; Stets, 1988; Touraine, 1988; Best, 1989; Flax, 1990; Foucault, 1990; Hall, 1990; Richardson, 1990, 1994; Fine, 1993; Guba and Lincoln, 1994; Olesen, 1994; Ambert et al., 1995.

3 For examples of theoretical and empirical research on social problems since Blumer (1971), see Kitsuse and Spector, 1973; Spector and Kitsuse, 1974; Mauss, 1975; Schuyler, 1976; Pfohl, 1977; Schneider, 1978; Wiener, 1981; Tierney, 1982; Ferraro, 1983; Ferraro and Johnson, 1983; Loseke and Cahill, 1984; Gusfield, 1981, 1984, 1989; Aronson, 1984; Studer, 1984; Hazelrigg, 1985, 1986; Pfohl, 1985; Schneider and Spector, 1985; Woolgar and Pawluch, 1985; Schneider, 1985, 1993; Gillespie and Leffler, 1987; Kurz, 1987; Touraine, 1988; Best, 1989, 1990, 1993; Loseke, 1989, 1992; Walker, 1990; Dobash and Dobash, 1992; Ibarra and Kitsuse, 1993; Miller, 1993; Troyer, 1993. For work before Blumer, see Waller, 1936; Fuller and Myers, 1941; Becker, 1966, 1967.

4 The strict position created an impasse that has hindered the integration of empirical and conceptual work in social problems sociology for twenty years. Joel Best's (1989, 1993) contextual constructionism breaks this impasse through the pragmatic integration of allegedly incommensurable post-positivist and constructionist assumptions and practices, re-legitimizing the task C. Wright Mills identified as the central concern of sociology, the task of establishing empirical and theoretical links between personal troubles and public issues.

5 Guba and Lincoln (1994) identify positivist, post-positivist, constructionist, and critical approaches as contending paradigms. They maintain that except for positivism and post-positivism, these paradigms reflect incommensurable or contradictory positions on fundamental principles of ontology, epistemology, and methodology, and that a resolution depends on the emergence of a new meta-paradigm. Best simply brackets issues of 'epistemological consistency,' arguing that it is time to worry less about how we know what we know, and more about what we do know about social problems (Best, 1993).

6 Feminist or *violence against women* and non-feminist or *family violence* perspectives are discussed as ideal types. These ideal types do not typify what feminists and/or non-feminists generally have to say about violence and abuse; certainly many feminists construct abuse quite differently. Rather, the ideal types typify contending positions within a particular discourse. This discourse is evidenced in three widely read anthologies: *The Dark Side of Families* (1983), edited by Finkelhor et al.; *Feminist Perspectives on Wife Abuse* (1988), edited by Yllo and Bograd; and *Current Controversies on Family Violence* (1993), edited by Gelles and Loseke. For discussions of differences within and between feminisms, see Schechter, 1982; Breines and Gordon, 1983; Beaudry, 1985; Okun, 1986; Weedon, 1987; Harding, 1989, 1990; Hartsock, 1990; Flax, 1990; Thompson, 1992; Wolf, 1993; Ashe and Cahn, 1994; Sommers, 1994; Dobash and Dobash, 1995; Thompson and Walker, 1995.

7 Various accounts of the histories, discoveries, and re-discoveries of woman abuse, child abuse, and child sexual abuse are provided by Cleverdon, 1950; Pfohl, 1977; Dobash and Dobash, 1979, 1992; Schechter, 1982; Pleck, 1983; Breines and Gordon, 1983; Finkelhor, 1983; Light and Parr, 1983; Beaudry, 1985; Okun, 1986; Gordon, 1988; Blackman, 1989; Frankel-Howard, 1989; Best, 1990; Walker, 1990; McDonald and Peressini, 1991; Plummer, 1993.

8 I cannot overemphasize a point made repeatedly in feminist discourse: that there is no satisfactory way to define feminism other than as a contended

pluralism. For discussions of differences within and between feminisms, see Schechter, 1982; Breines and Gordon, 1983; Beaudry, 1985; Okun, 1986; Weedon, 1987; Harding, 1989, 1990; Hartsock, 1990; Flax, 1990; Thompson, 1992; Wolf, 1993; Ashe and Cahn, 1994; Sommers, 1994; Dobash and Dobash, 1995; Thompson and Walker, 1995.

9 Examples of these arguments can be found in Dobash and Dobash, 1979, 1992; Breines and Gordon, 1983; Wardell et al., 1983; Washburne, 1983; Beaudry, 1985; Stanko, 1985; Smith, 1987; Adams, 1988; Dankwort, 1988a, 1988b; Graham et al. 1988; Kelly, 1988, 1989; Pence and Shepard, 1988; Hamner and Maynard, 1989; Hoff, 1990; Holmes and Lundy, 1990; DeKeseredy and Hinch, 1991; Kaufman, 1992; McMahon and Pence, 1996.

10 Publications by feminists who employ or defend empiricist methods include Yllo, 1983, 1988, 1993; Finkelhor and Yllo, 1985; Bowker et al., 1988; Kelly, 1988, 1989; Schechter, 1988; Yllo and Straus, 1990; DeKeseredy and Hinch, 1991; Smith, 1994; Johnson and Sacco, 1995.

11 For discussion of the strengths and pitfalls of feminist epistemologies, the goals of feminist research, and the 'rewards and dangers' of research on domestic violence or woman abuse, see Dobash and Dobash, 1979, 1983, 1988, 1992; Stark and Flitcraft, 1983; Wardell et al., 1983; Gillespie and Leffler, 1987; Smith, 1987, 1997; Weedon, 1987, 1989; Hoff, 1988, 1990; Kelly, 1988, 1989; Alcoff, 1989; Hamner and Maynard, 1989; Harding, 1989, 1990; Hawkesworth, 1989; Longins, 1989; McCormack, 1989; Flax, 1990; Harstock, 1990; Hoffman, 1990; Richardson, 1990, 1994; Walker, 1990; Thompson, 1992; Miller, 1993; Clandinin and Connelly, 1994; Hirsh, 1994; Jacobson, 1994; Olesen, 1994; Thompson and Walker, 1995; Ronai et al., 1997.

12 Touraine (1988) argues that women achieve agency as they come to participate in *historicity*, the process through which society represents itself to itself, and women do this by and through participation in the women's movement.

13 In *context specific* research, the data at hand is interpreted in light of germane historical and structural phenomena; *institutional ethnography* entails a detailed mapping of the ways decisions and practices 'going on elsewhere' impinge upon the research setting; in *collaborative research*, study participants play a key role in the interpretation of the data; in *layered research* or autoethnography, the author is one of the subjects of the analysis. See Dobash and Dobash, 1979, 1983; Smith, 1987, 1997; Hoff, 1988, 1990; Ronai et al., 1997.

14 As Dorothy Smith (1997) makes explicit in 'Wife Abuse and Family Idealizations: The Violent Regulation of Family Regimes,' participants in *violence against women* discourse are generally 'uninterested' in the ways 'emotional

perversions' such as jealousy and possessiveness fuel violence (p. 120, note 1). Rather than attempt to establish causal links, Smith and others direct attention to the uses of male violence to enforce idealizations of male dominance and female subservience that are constituted 'quite outside the local practicality of family living' (p. 106).

15 For a discussion of epistemological differences between 'sociology of' and 'sociology for,' see Smith, 1987. For a recent discussion of the implications of 'crucial' differences between 'of' and 'for' approaches, see Olesen, 1994.

16 I derive the term 'therapeutic society' from Dobash and Dobash, 1992. For research, arguments, and reviews on this *family violence* position, see Steinmetz, 1977, 1978; Benjamin and Adler, 1980; Straus et al., 1980; Pizzey and Shapiro 1982; Berkowitz, 1983; Breines and Gordon, 1983; Fagen et al., 1983; Giles-Sims, 1983; Straus, 1983; Carlson, 1984; Denzin, 1984, 1987; Kalmuss, 1984; Neidig and Friedman, 1984; Roberts, 1984; Hotaling and Sugarman, 1986, 1990; Launius and Bernard, 1987; Morrison et al., 1987; Shupe, Stacey, and Hazelwood, 1987; Gelles and Straus, 1988; Gupta and Cox, 1988; MacEven and Garling, 1988; Huges et al., 1989; O'Leary et al., 1989; Stets and Pirog-Good, 1989; Stets and Straus, 1989, 1990; Cappell and Heiner, 1990; Carson et al., 1990; De Maris, 1990; Dibble and Straus, 1990; Fatout, 1990; Follingstad et al., 1990; Kantor and Straus, 1990; Lloyd, 1990; Straus and Gelles, 1990; Gelles and Conte, 1990; Straus and Smith, 1990; Suitor et al., 1990; Burkett, 1991; Egeland, 1993; Hamburger and Hastings, 1991; Herbert et al., 1991; Parker and Parker, 1991; Ray et al., 1991; Straus, 1991; Weatherford and Kaufman, 1991; Cascardi and O'Leary, 1992; McLaughlin et al., 1992; Pedersen and Thomas, 1992; Smith and Williams, 1992; Straus and Sweet, 1992; Wind and Silvern, 1992; Barnett and Fagan, 1993; Busby et al., 1993; Gelles, 1993b; Julian and McKenry, 1993; O'Leary, 1993; Straus, 1993a, 1993b; Walker, 1993; Jacobson et al., 1994; Pan et al., 1994; Rodgers, 1994; Stacey et al., 1994; Johnson, 1995; Johnson and Sacco, 1995; Lackey and Williams, 1995; Lenton, 1995; O'Keefe, 1995; Wilson et al., 1995; Barnett et al., 1996; Straus and Yodanis, 1996; Yelsma, 1996; Romkens, 1997; Ronai et al., 1997.

17 Denzin is a critical theorist (see Denzin 1989, 1994). His phenomenologies of domestic *family violence* (1984) and alcoholism (1987) are situated, perhaps uncomfortably, in *family violence* discourse. For other examples of qualitative *family violence* research, see Steinmetz, 1977; Gils-Sims, 1983; Shupe et al., 1987; Stets, 1988; Stacey et al., 1994; Eisikovits and Buchbinder, 1996.

18 Politically contentious findings regarding reciprocal and female-perpetrated violence are avoided when female-perpetrated acts are excluded

from consideration, as in the 1993 Statistics Canada *Violence against Women Survey*. See DeKeseredy and Hinch, 1991; Rodgers, 1994; Smith, 1994.

19 Denzin states that there are currently many variants and considerable over-lap between and among allegedly incommensurable positivist/post-positivist, constructionist, and critical paradigms. In contrast to Guba and Lincoln (1994), he states that any researcher, especially any qualitative researcher, 'can be more than one thing at the same time' (Denzin, 1994: 512).

20 As noted by Fine (1993), constructionist insights and assumptions have been incorporated into mainstream sociological practice. I would add that this incorporation is based on what Best (1993) terms a 'weak' reading.

21 *Family violence* studies consistently 'find' that women as well as men perpetrate violence. The real issue is what these findings mean. See Steinmetz, 1977, 1978; Straus et al., 1980; Berk et al., 1983; Coleman and Straus, 1983; Giles-Sims, 1983; Greenblat, 1983; Szinovacz, 1983; Kalmuss, 1984; Neidig and Friedman, 1984; Roberts, 1984; Browning and Duton, 1986; MacLeod, 1987, 1989; Shupe et al., 1987; Bowker et al., 1988; Gelles and Straus, 1988; Saunders, 1988; Stets, 1988; O'Leary et al., 1989; Sigler, 1989; Stets and Pirog-Good, 1989; Flynn, 1990; Follingstad et al., 1990; Hotaling and Sugarman, 1990; Stacey, 1990; Stets and Straus, 1990; Alexander et al., 1991; Barnes et al., 1991; Stets, 1991; Kurz, 1991, 1993; Loseke, 1991, 1992; Straus, 1991, 1993a, 1993b; McLaughlin et al., 1992; Straus and Sweet, 1992; Cambell, 1993; Fox, 1993; Gartner, 1993; Eaton, 1994; O'Leary et al., 1994; Stacey et al., 1994; Lenton, 1995; Szinovacz and Egley, 1995; Yelsma, 1996; Gray and Foshee, 1997; Römkens, 1997.

22 For further examples of inflammatory rhetoric and critiques of these practices, see Wardell et al., 1983; Yllo, 1988; Hoff, 1988, 1990; Schechter, 1988; Radford, 1989; Avis, 1992; Bograd, 1992; Erickson, 1992; Dobash and Dobash, 1992; Kaufman, 1992, Meth, 1992; Yllo, 1993; Murphy and O'Leary, 1994; Berliner, 1996, Eisikovits and Buchbinder, 1996; McMahon and Pence, 1996; O'Leary, 1996; Römkens, 1997.

23 McMahon and Pence (1996) assert that ongoing controversies over the gendered nature of abuse and how to address this are not exercises in denigration, nor are they about turf wars over who has the right to speak on the issue – they are about core 'conceptualizations' that abuse is rooted primarily in social political structures, as opposed to psychology. As in earlier debates, McMahon and Pence appear unable to recognize common ground; they refuse to recognize that O'Leary (1996), Straus (1993a, 1993b), and other proponents of couples counselling agree that violence is gendered regardless of whether women do or do not commit acts of violence, that all

intervenors have a responsibility to safeguard women's safety, and that the elimination of violence and coercion is the core, the primary, goal of counselling. On the other hand, O'Leary falls into polemics when he asserts 'certain ways to cope with the problem are often advanced to the exclusion and even denigration of other methods' because of 'political or theoretical differences.'

24 Publications by theorists and researchers who seek to bridge this divide include Okun, 1986; MacLeod, 1987; Schechter, 1988; McCormack, 1989; Hoff, 1990; Bograd, 1992; Campbell, 1993; Gelles and Loseke, 1993; Straus, 1993a; Ashe and Cahn, 1994; Eaton, 1994; Jacobson, 1994; Mahoney, 1994; Johnson, 1995; Eisikovits and Buchbinder, 1996, Dutton and Starzomski, 1997; Römkens, 1997.

25 There is no inherent or necessary contradiction between constructionist and feminist (or contextual constructionist and feminist) approaches. See Miller, 1993; and Denzin, 1994.

26 Richardson (1994) emphasizes that there are many avenues for sociological writers, and many audiences. Our research goal determines which audience we address, and it determines whether we draw on post-positivist, feminist, Marxist, historical, structural, post-structural, constructionist, interactionist, contextual constructionist, and/or other approaches. There is no singularly correct paradigm or theoretical orientation.

27 My goal is not to advance or refute either a *violence against women* or a *family violence* perspective on abuse. Both provide valuable insights, and both entail distortions. Nor do I focus on links between developments in the research community and historical processes of social activism and social change around abuse in the larger community of Canada or North America. Others, cited throughout this manuscript, have done an excellent job of this.

28 Schechter (1982) also noted that, on the grass-roots level, actors rarely adopt a pure position.

29 Denzin asserts that we can only apprehend interpreted worlds of interacting individuals, not so-called objective reality. However, he maintains that it is possible to 'capture' the world of lived experience by 'living one's way into the lives of the persons studied,' thereby seeing the world as one's interview subjects see it (Denzin, 1989: 43). I address problems associated with the concept 'authentic reality' in chapter 7.

30 As described by Blumer (1969: 38–46), a 'faithful interpretation' or analysis is one grounded in familiarity with what is actually going on in the sphere of life under study. It is grounded more in an exploratory attitude than in techniques. This attitude is marked by flexibility and by an alertness to the

need to constantly revise analytic concepts, images, and beliefs. For other discussions of 'truthful,' 'faithful,' and 'trustworthy' research, see Douglas, 1977, 1985; Lester, 1984; Denzin, 1989, 1994; Richardson, 1990; Lembert, 1994.

31 Many qualitative researchers seek to provide confirmation of the validity of their findings and interpretations by incorporating 'member responses' into a manuscript. This strategy adds to the data, but it does not resolve fundamental epistemological concerns around issues of validity and responsibility. For discussions on the values of qualitative research and the inescapability of the author's responsibility, see Sartre, 1965; Johnson, 1977; Denzin, 1989, 1994; Richardson, 1990, 1994; Clandinin and Connelly, 1994; Fine, 1994; Fontana and Frey, 1994; Lembert, 1994; Olesen, 1994; Ambert, 1995.

2: The Study, the Community, and 'The Problem'

1 Blumer (1971), Schneider (1985), and Best (1990) are among social problems analysts who note the importance of the media in mobilizing action around a social problem, and in shaping public responses to the problem.

2 The Township Resource Centre was funded through federal and provincial grants, and through grants provided by charitable organizations. It was one of many such facilities across Ontario that closed in the mid-1990s as a result of the withdrawal of provincial funding.

3 This does not mean that no one subscribed to feminism before the emergence of the Domestic Abuse Committee; rather, feminism emerged as an official voice with the formation of the Women's Action Group, renamed the Domestic Abuse Committee.

4 Some Domestic Abuse Committee participants described the committee as a more spontaneous grass-roots development, emerging from informal 'coffee talks.'

5 For discussions of problems associated with feminist or 'liberationist' and non-feminist or 'protectionist' shelters, see Ferraro, 1983; Beaudry, 1985; Davis, 1988; Hoff, 1990; Russell, 1990; McDonald and Peressini, 1991; Loseke, 1992; McKeel and Sporakowski, 1993. This literature is discussed in chapter 4.

6 The police were apparently correct that the spate of homicides was a 'statistical blip' since the fifth domestic homicide was the last through 1996.

7 Women were over-represented in the *random* sample, at a rate typical of surveys generally. In the overlapping and demographically less representative *couples* sample, the genders were balanced. Surveyed attitudes varied

more by whether respondents had experienced serious abuse over the life course than by gender or social demographics. On the relevance of gender to reporting patterns, see Stets and Straus, 1990; and Szinovacz and Egley, 1995.

8 Reported patterns reflect the responses of the 83 currently dating, married, and cohabiting *random* respondents. The reported attitudes and experiences of the full sample of 97 *survey* respondents were virtually identical. I rely on the responses of partnered respondents because non-partnered respondents did not complete the Conflict Tactics Scale.

9 In many studies, reported violence in past relationships is more severe or more serious than reported violence in current relationships. For a review of this issue, see Römkens, 1997.

10 In the Township survey and in surveys generally, the majority of respondents reject the notion that violence against partners is justifiable, except in the case of self-defence, especially when the perpetrator is male. Those who accept provocation as a justification are far more likely to engage in serious violence. See Straus et al., 1980; Greenblat, 1983; Hotaling and Sugarman, 1986; 1990; Ewing and Aubrey, 1987; Gelles and Straus, 1988; Sigler, 1989; Andrews and Brewin, 1990; Dibble and Straus, 1990; Barnett et al., 1996.

11 Methods and findings consistent with a *violence against women* perspective on abuse are discussed in chapter 1. See Dobash and Dobash, 1979, 1983,1988, 1992, 1995; Breines and Gordon, 1983; Wardell et al., 1983; Saunders, 1988; Hoff, 1991; Kurz, 1991, 1993; Loseke, 1991; Dobash et al., 1992; Thompson, 1992; Bowker, 1988, 1993; Straus, 1992; Fox, 1993; Gartner, 1993; Campbell, 1993; Smith, 1994; Thompson and Walker, 1994; Hamby et al., 1996; McMahon and Pence, 1996.

12 Methods and findings consistent with a *family violence* perspective on abuse are discussed in chapter 1. See Straus et al., 1980; Gelles and Straus, 1988; O'Leary et al., 1989; Stets and Pirog-Good, 1989; Stets and Straus, 1989, 1990; Kantor and Straus, 1990; Straus and Gelles, 1990; Yllo and Straus, 1990; DeKeseredy and Hinch, 1991; Pederson and Thomas, 1992; Smith and Williams, 1992; Straus, 1993a, 1993b; Yllo, 1993; Smith, 1994; Stacey et al., 1994; Johnson and Sacco, 1995; Lenton, 1995; Johnson, 1995; O'Keefe, 1995; O'Leary, 1996; Straus and Yodanis, 1996.

13 Throughout this book, statistical significance refers to Pearson correlations at values of $p < .0000$ through $p < .0500$ – conventionally regarded as outside the range of chance. Correlations are not – and this must be emphasized – proof of causal relationships.

14 Most *family violence* and *violence against women* researchers argue that substance abuse and domestic abuse are not causally related. See Dobash and

Dobash, 1979; Gils-Sims, 1983; Spieker, 1983; Pahl, 1985a; Okun, 1986; Frankel-Howard, 1989; Bain et al., 1991; Gelles, 1993a. Some interpret alcohol abuse as a contributing factor or empirical correlate. See Coleman and Straus, 1983; Gottheil et al., 1983; Heath, 1983; Denzin, 1987; Gordon, 1988; Gelles and Straus, 1989; Hotaling and Sugarman, 1990; Kantor and Straus, 1990; Suitor et al., 1990; Barnes et al., 1991; Hamburger and Hastings, 1991; Weatherford and Kaufman, 1991; Barnett and Fagan, 1993; Gelles, 1993; Julian and McKerry, 1993; Pan et al., 1994; Rodgers, 1994; O'Keefe, 1995. Flanzer (1993) argues that the link is causal.

15 These patterns are far less evident in the smaller, less representative, and more 'risk resilient' dual-partner *couples* sub-sample. See table 9.

16 Respondents reporting serious violence in a current or previous adult relationship were highly likely to identify sexism as important, especially if female. However, these respondents regarded substance abuse and family-of-origin issues as equally important. See table 14, including note.

17 Next to female-perpetration, the intergenerational hypothesis is the most controversial of all *family violence* constructs. For arguments and research refuting the intergenerational hypothesis, see Breines and Gordon, 1983; MacEven and Garling, 1988; Hotaling and Sugarman, 1990; Loseke, 1991; Kurz, 1991; Dobash and Dobash, 1992; Dobash et al., 1992; Kaufman and Zigler, 1993. Approaches to pro-feminist group counselling for male abusers and female victims are described in Hamner and Maynard, 1987; Adams, 1988; Dankwort, 1988a, 1988b; Pence and Shepard, 1988; Holmes and Lundy, 1990; Hoff, 1990; Avis, 1992; Bograd, 1992; Dobash and Dobash, 1992; Kaufman, 1992; Meth, 1992; Dobash et al., 1996; McMahon and Pence, 1996.

18 For arguments and research supporting the intergenerational hypothesis, see Straus et al., 1980; Pizzey and Shapiro, 1982; Fagen et al., 1983; Straus, 1983; Carlson, 1984; Denzin, 1984; Kalmuss, 1984; Hotaling and Sugarman, 1986, 1990; Okun, 1986; Shupe et al., 1987; Huges et al., 1989; Gelles and Straus, 1989; Cappell and Heiner, 1990; Carson et al., 1990; DeMaris, 1990; Fatout, 1990; Flynn, 1990; Gelles and Conte, 1990; Bain et al., 1991; Barnes et al., 1991; Hamburger and Hastings, 1991; Smith and Williams, 1992; Busby et al., 1993; Egeland, 1993; Rodgers, 1994; O'Keefe, 1995. Approaches to more traditionally oriented counselling for abusers, victims, and couples are described in Geller and Wasserstrom, 1984; Neidig and Friedman, 1984; Roberts, 1984; Sonkin et al., 1985; Nosco and Wallace, 1988; Gelles and Conte, 1990; Wallace and Nosco, 1991; Straus, 1993a, 1993b; Stacey et al., 1994; O'Farrell and Murphy, 1995; O'Leary, 1996.

19 I discuss psycho-educational and cognitive behavioural counselling inter-

ventions in chapter 5. These approaches appear to be equally effective or equally ineffective, depending on how one interprets the data. See Gondolf, 1997.

20 For arguments against research on differences, see Wardell et al., 1983; Stanko, 1985, 1988; Kelly, 1988, 1989; Dobash and Dobash, 1992.

21 On economic status as a risk marker and its relationship to other risks, see reviews by Hotaling and Sugarman, 1986, 1990; and DeKeseredy and Hinch, 1991. See also Straus et al., 1980; Gelles and Straus, 1988; Rodgers, 1994.

22 In chapter 5, I discuss *family violence* characterizations of differences between domestically violent and non-violent males and females, and links between domestic violence and child sexual abuse. See Herman, 1981; Renvoize, 1978, 1982; Sonkin et al., 1985; Launius and Benard, 1987; MacLeod, 1987; Gupta and Cox, 1988; Carson et al., 1990; Gelles and Conte, 1990; Hamburger and Hastings, 1991; Parker and Parker, 1991; Ray et al., 1991; Canavan et al., 1992; Cascardi and O'Leary, 1992; Wind and Silvern, 1992; Apt and Hurlbert, 1993; Busby et al., 1993; O'Leary, 1993; Loftus, 1994; Jacobson et al., 1994.

23 Female respondents reporting client experience or childhood risks and/or their own or their partner's substance abuse were significantly more likely to prefer or accept feminists as intervention board and staff; those reporting chronic or severe adult relationship violence or current relationship distress were noticeably more likely to do so. See table 10.a.

24 Attitudes about the relevance of female culpability, substance abuse, family-of-origin abuse, and economic stress varied little by reported abuse experience. Some *violence against women* researchers interpret survey respondents' attitudes as mere documentation of the hegemonic status of 'therapeutic' and therefore *family violence* thinking in contemporary society. See Dobash and Dobash, 1992; Smith, 1997. For scholarly discussions of 'facts' and 'myths' about domestic violence, see Okun, 1986; Ewing and Aubrey, 1987. For a constructionist treatment of these issues, see Watzlawick, 1984a, 1984b.

25 Across genders, respondents in 'high risk' categories were noticeably less likely to prefer community leaders. In contrast, the minority who preferred feminists were overwhelmingly 'high risk' females. See tables 10.a–10.d.

3: Mobilization of Action: Struggles for Control

1 According to media reports and personal interviews, the twelve-year-old girl was found partially disrobed and chained to a school-yard fence during

the lunch break. Charges were laid and then dropped since the girl later claimed she had agreed to participate in 'the game.' The older sister of a classmate told me the kids all knew that the boys had 'stuck things up her,' and that the girl was simply too afraid to prosecute.

2 This uncooperative officer was transferred out of the Township (interview: police inspector Tom, 1991).

3 The Women's Directorate is a provincial agency responsible for channelling public funds to projects that address issues of concern to women.

4 I subsequently learned that Township Family Services counsellor Fiona also conducted woman abuse groups for male abusers and female victims through the Regional Woman Abuse Program, and that Alice provided individual counselling for women and men through Township Family Services.

5 Many feminist researchers attribute residents' resistance to *violence against women* constructions of abuse to the pervasive influence of 'the dominant ideology.' For discussions and examples of this hegemony argument, see Therborn, 1980; Beaudry, 1985; Dobash and Dobash, 1992; Richardson, 1994; Smith, 1997.

6 In the Community Response Workshop, Kathryn did not present herself as a Domestic Violence Committee member. Kathryn was, in fact, an alternate on this committee. Her primary alliance was with the Domestic Abuse Committee.

7 I established formal contact with the Domestic Abuse Committee shortly after the Abuse Awareness Workshop. Up until this time, my research was focused on the activities of the Domestic Violence Committee.

8 This is a prime example of the rhetorical use of statistics (Best, 1990). The national rate Charles cited includes emotional and physical abuse. In my survey pretest, administered to housing co-op residents, at least one co-op household in ten struggled with chronic or severe physical violence; many more reported episodic minor violence (approximately a third of co-op households participated in the pretest).

9 This is another example of the rhetorical use of statistics (Best, 1990). In expressing data on intergenerational risks in percentage terms (1000% and 600%), Straus et al. (1980) unintentionally invite lay readers to misread the risk of violence in adult relationships as 1000 times higher for males who witness spousal violence in comparison to males who do not, and 600 times higher for females who witness spousal violence in comparison to females who do not; rather than as 10 times and 6 times higher.

10 For refutations of analyses of abuse as gender-neutral, see Dobash and Dobash, 1979, 1983, 1988, 1992, 1995; Breines and Gordon, 1983; Wardell et

al., 1983; Saunders, 1988; DeKeseredy and Hinch, 1991; Hoff, 1990; Kurz, 1991, 1993; Loseke, 1991; Dobash et al., 1992; Bowker et al., 1993; Campbell, 1993; Smith, 1994.

11 As noted in previous chapters, many *family violence* sociologists, Straus included, acknowledge that abuse is gendered, at least in its consequences.

12 With a lawsuit pending, I elected not to interview core members of 'the opposition' (as the consent letter makes clear, research material can be subpoenaed). My analysis of their position is consequently based on public statements, public discussions, radio interviews, and reports of Domestic Violence Committee and Township Resource Centre – affiliated respondents who either opposed or supported the 'opposition's' position.

13 For discussions of feminism and social change, see Mauss, 1975; Wiener, 1981; Schechter, 1982; Tierney, 1982; Pleck, 1983; Breines and Gordon, 1983; Light and Parr, 1983; Schneider, 1985a; Okun, 1986; Davis, 1988; Gordon, 1988; Touraine, 1988; Blackman, 1989; Walker, 1990; Dobash and Dobash, 1992; Wolf, 1993.

14 White ribbons are worn in memory of the 1989 Montreal massacre.

15 A Township jury acquitted the accused on the grounds that he had no way of knowing his advances were unwelcome. His accuser testified that she was too frightened to verbally or physically resist (follow-up interview: Kathryn, 1993).

4: Implementation of a Plan of Action: Struggles with Control

1 The shelter director did not formally participate in the study but was present at a Domestic Abuse Committee meeting in 1991, where she was introduced as a consultant who served on a shelter board in another community. I did not encounter her again until the shelter opening in June 1992. She did not participate in formal interviews.

2 Lisa and Julia both enrolled in this abuse advocacy course with the express hope of obtaining a staff position at the new shelter.

3 Edna subsequently informed me that neither agency received the funding; instead, a spokesperson from the Ministry of Community and Social Services lectured both boards on the importance of inter-agency cooperation.

4 See Bowker et al., 1988, for a scholarly formulation of the argument that female abuse of children is a response to male victimization.

5 For discussion of the role of feminism in establishing shelters, various shelter models, and the problems associated with implementing supportive and empowering shelter practices, see Pizzey and Shapiro, 1982; Schechter,

1982; Ferraro, 1983; Beaudry, 1985; Pahl, 1985; Berk et al., 1986; Okun, 1986; MacLeod, 1987, 1989; Davis, 1988; Hoff, 1990; Russell, 1990; McDonald and Peressini, 1991; Dobash and Dobash, 1992; Loseke, 1992; McKeel and Sporakowski, 1993; Gagne, 1996.

6 See especially Schechter, 1982; Beaudry, 1985; MacLeod, 1987, 1989; Davis, 1988; Russell, 1990; McDonald and Peressini, 1991; Loseke, 1992.

7 In some U.S. jurisdictions, publicly funded women's shelters are only available to women on social assistance (Davis, 1988). On the disenchantment of social service clients, see Eisikovits and Buchbinder, 1996.

8 See especially Berk et al., 1986; Bowker and Maurer, 1986; Kurz, 1987; Eisikovits and Buchbinder, 1996.

9 Despite widespread rumours of problems in shelters, in general, and the Township shelter, in particular, the new shelter was commonly full beyond capacity (follow-up interviews through, 1992). This is not surprising considering the disproportionately high support for shelters among survey respondents reporting chronic and severe violence, whether female or male, but especially if female. See tables 4 and 11.

5: Counselling and Therapeutic Intervenors

1 I contrast the perspectives of RWAP and RSAP counsellors with those of a private therapist encountered through the, 1992 survey on violence and abuse. Her daughter, who was one of the 83 partnered *random* survey respondents, arranged the interview.

2 For discussions of differences between pro-feminist and mainstream or non-feminist counselling programs, see Hamner and Maynard, 1987; Adams, 1988; Dankwort, 1988a, 1988b; Pence and Shepard, 1988; Holmes and Lundy, 1990; Hoff, 1990; Avis, 1992; Bograd, 1992; Dobash and Dobash, 1992; Kaufman, 1992; Meth, 1992; Berliner, 1996; McMahon and Pence, 1996; O'Leary, 1996.

3 For descriptions of the aims and practices of more mainstream counselling for spouse or woman abuse, see Neidig and Friedman, 1984; Roberts, 1984; Rosewater, 1984; Sonkin et al., 1985; Nosco and Wallace, 1988; Gelles and Conte, 1990; Wallace and Nosko, 1991; Straus, 1993a, 1993b; Stacey et al., 1994; O'Farrell and Murphy, 1995.

4 Cognitive-behavioural and psycho-educational approaches have comparable outcomes as measured by recidivism. See Gondolf, 1997.

5 McKendy (1992) reports that clients of a pro-feminist batterer program display little resistance to the idea that they are abusive and that they need to stop being abusive. However, they resist and resent assertions that male

partners hold all the power in relationships, that men are solely responsible for the interactive realities they participate in, and that emotions are irrelevant to action. McKendy attributes high attrition rates to a systematic silencing of the men's emotional realities.

6 Alcoholics Anonymous and Narcotics Anonymous were the only locally available substance abuse programs during the research period.

7 See, for instance, Herman, 1981; Renvoize, 1982; Bass, 1988; Gupta and Cox, 1988; Carson et al., 1990; Gelles and Conte, 1990; Gordon, 1990; Burkett, 1991; Parker and Parker, 1991; Canavan et al., 1992; Busby et al., 1993; Hanson et al., 1994; Gilgun, 1995; Ronai, 1997.

8 For *family violence* characterizations of male abusers and discussions of differences between community-identified and agency-identified 'batterers,' see Denzin, 1984, 1987; Gondolf, 1985a; Sonkin et al., 1985; Launius and Benard, 1987; Nosko and Wallace, 1988; Dodge and Bates, 1990; Fatout, 1990; Hamburger and Hastings, 1991; Wallace and Nosko, 1991; O'Leary, 1993; Jacobson et al., 1994.

9 For *family violence* characterizations of abused women and the relationship between woman abuse and child sexual abuse, see Herman, 1981; Launius and Benard, 1987; MacLeod, 1987; Morrison et al., 1987; Gupta, 1988; Carson et al., 1990; Hotaling and Sugarman, 1990; Burkett, 1991; Parker and Parker, 1991; Ray et al., 1991; Canavan et al., 1992; Cascardi, 1992; Wind and Silvern, 1992; Apt and Hurlbert, 1993; Busby et al., 1993; Feldman-Summers and Pope, 1994; Loftus et al., 1994.

10 For *family violence* characterizations of the dynamics of abusive relationships, see Pizzey and Shapiro, 1982; Gils-Sims, 1983; Denzin, 1987; Morrison et al., 1987; Shupe et al., 1987; Nosko and Wallace, 1988; Stets, 1988; Lloyd, 1990; Jacobson et al., 1994; Stacey et al., 1994.

11 No researcher suggests that all or even most 'high risk' individuals perpetrate or sustain violence or abuse in adult relationships. As *random* and *couples* data displayed in tables 8 to 9 demonstrate, many individuals and couples display remarkable resilience with respect to childhood traumas. See Werner and Smith, 1992.

12 Strong resident support for professionally run therapeutic interventions is predictable in light of the alleged hegemonic status of therapeutic thinking in contemporary society (Dobash and Dobash, 1992; Smith, 1997).

13 See Best (1990) on congruities in conceptualizations of abuse between abuse 'experts' and survey respondents reporting abusive experiences, both of whom tend to view key issues differently than do survey respondents generally, in studies cited by Best, and in this study.

14 On factors associated with client 'disenchantment' or resistance to abuse

intervention, see Bowker and Maurer's (1986) evaluation of abuse victim characteristics and program effectiveness; McKendy's (1992) discussion of batterer program recidivism and 'ideological practices' that contradict or silence men's emotional realities; and Eisikovits and Buchbinder's (1996) analysis of abuse intervenors' and female clients' mutual 'disenchantment' as a consequence of discordant expectations of counselling outcomes.

15 As noted in chapter 3, Fiona moved to another community prior to the opening of the Township shelter in June of 1992.

6: Enforcement, Legal, and Medical Intervenors

1 As recounted by Township residents encountered in many contexts, the ways in which police meet these responsibilities vary greatly. Some officers reportedly supported and assisted abused women. Others were reportedly judgmental and non-supportive.

2 Information cards listed the Regional Women's Shelter, Township Family Services, the Regional Woman Abuse Program, the Regional Sex Abuse Program, the Children's Aid Society, and the Township Legal Clinic.

3 In a number of publications, Domestic Violence Committee and Domestic Abuse Committee activists asserted the Township had 10 domestic violence calls per one thousand population compared to 3.2 per thousand for the Region. The Regional Women's Shelter's information manual was one of several sources claiming wife battering to be the major cause of homicide in Canada, a 'fact' many Domestic Abuse Committee activists cited as common knowledge. Finally, the Regional Women's Shelter's information manual claimed that 'domestic abuse calls are second only to motor vehicle accidents as the most common request for police service.'

4 The nature of the remaining 48 incidents was not specified in field notes.

5 Traditional relationships refer to those in which the wife has no job or career outside the home.

6 Some *violence against women* and *family violence* proponents argue in favour of a strong, and in some instances a punitive, police and court response. Others express concerns about the extension of social control. See Kelly, 1988, 1989; MacLeod, 1989; Radford, 1989; Sherman, 1992; Berk, 1993; Buzawa and Buzawa, 1993; Gelles, 1993a; Kurz, 1993; Schmidt and Sherman, 1993; Stark, 1993; Straus, 1993b; Snider, 1994. In Canada and the United States, courts commonly mandate abusers to 'male batterer' programs. See chapter 5.

7 Both probation and parole officers participated in less formal discussions through 1992.

8 Clients on probation have not yet served time in jail; those on parole have. The officers reported that the vast majority of their clients are on probation, mostly for property offences.

9 Flyers were reportedly distributed to over eleven thousand households.

10 The physician estimated that serious patterns of physical wife abuse occurred in close to 10 per cent of the families serviced by her clinic. For a discussion of the medical profession's response to domestic violence in Ontario at this time, see Bain et al., 1991.

7: Victims, Perpetrators, and Survivors

1 The cases summarized in this chapter were drawn from approximately 50 first-hand accounts of adult relationship violence obtained in formal research contexts. These include 17 survey accounts (17/98, including one respondent who was not able to relate to the questionnaire but who provided qualitative data), 13 pretest accounts (13/24 volunteers recruited through the Township housing co-operative and the resource centre), and 20 in-depth interviews. Numerous other first-hand accounts were provided in less formal research contexts.

2 A number of researchers emphasize the importance of sharing stories with respondents (see, for instance, Denzin, 1989, 1994; Ronai, 1997). I routinely shared information about my personal life, history, and biases during the natural course of conversation on abuse. I found, however, that my respondents were generally uninterested in my experiences and attitudes. On the other hand, they were very interested in telling me about theirs, and shared with me the belief that there is something important to learn both from what they had experienced (or were experiencing) and from what they thought about this experience.

3 'Survival' refers to the existential state in which an individual sees herself or himself as having left abuse behind. It is the final phase of Ferraro and Johnson's (1983) 'victimization process,' or career. For a feminist analysis of this phenomenon, see Hoff, 1990.

4 On the embeddedness of abuse in both interpersonal and social-political processes, see Steinmetz, 1977; Giddens, 1979, 1992; Benjamin and Adler, 1980; Giles-Sims, 1983; Ferraro and Johnson, 1983; Lester, 1984; Denzin, 1984, 1987, 1989; Shupe et al., 1987; Stets, 1988; McKendy, 1992; Stacey et al., 1994; Eisikovits and Buchbinder, 1996; Römkens, 1997.

5 In social interactionist discourse, social dis-ease refers to something more than 'personal pathologies' (Dobash and Dobash, 1992) or 'emotional perversions' (Smith, 1997) associated with jealousy, possessiveness, substance

abuse and the like. It also refers to emotionally laden experiences of constraint and powerlessness rooted in actors' 'authentic' or intuitive knowledge of their situation in a classist, racist, sexist social structure. See Denzin, 1984; and McKendy, 1992.

6 A number of researchers argue that spouse abuse and substance abuse are similar, both in dynamics and in etiology. See Spieker, 1983; Barnett and Fagan, 1993; Flanzer, 1993; and O'Farrell and Murphy, 1995.

7 Denzin acknowledges that males/husbands can be victims, that females/ wives can be perpetrators, and that spousal violence is often reciprocal. At the same time, he states that domestic family violence is predominantly male-perpetrated.

8 Denzin acknowledges that women can also be alcoholics. He maintains that more alcoholics are male but refers to the alcoholic through use of both the female and the male pronoun. I use the male pronoun in my abbreviated presentation of Denzin's argument.

9 Denzin's phenomenologies of abuse should be read in the context of his general theorizing on social processes. See Denzin, 1989, 1994.

10 Denzin's concept 'authentic reality' is consistent with a realist ontology. As he makes clear (Denzin, 1994), this ontological position is typical of a number of prevailing critical approaches, many of which combine a realist ontology, a subjectivist epistemology, and a transformative ethnographic methodology. Ontological positions are, of course, not provable.

11 This is a core premise of social interactionist theory. See Mead, 1934. Its significance to recognizing 'victimization' is brilliantly articulated in Ferraro and Johnson, 1983.

12 For discussions of women's reasons for staying, see Ferraro and Johnson, 1983; Johnson and Ferraro, 1984; Loseke and Cahill, 1984, 1992; Roberts, 1984; Neidig and Friedman, 1985; MacLeod, 1987; Herbert et al., 1991; Hoff, 1990; Bowker, 1993; Mahoney, 1994; Eisikovits and Buchbinder, 1996.

13 For discussions on the problematic relationship between data and interpretation, see Blumer, 1969; Douglas, 1985; Richardson, 1990, 1994; Denzin, 1994; Fontana and Frey, 1994; Lembert, 1994; Olesen, 1994.

14 As Denzin (1989, 1994) and myriad others have pointed out, telling a story is inescapably an act of interpretation. There is never only one 'true' interpretation. For other discussions of this issue, see Sartre, 1965; Johnson, 1977; Richardson, 1990, 1994; Clandinin and Connelly, 1994; Fine, 1994; Fontana and Frey, 1994; Lembert, 1994; Olesen, 1994; Ambert, 1995.

15 Some feminist researchers question the ethics of in-depth interviewing. Their concerns relate to the manipulative process of establishing rapport,

the influence of the interviewer on the study, the inherent power imbalance in interviewer/interviewee relationships, and the inevitability of transforming research subjects into objects (see Fontana and Frey, 1994). Some feminist researchers incorporate interviewees' responses to the text that emerge from interviews. This strategy addresses some but not all of the above concerns. In defence of traditional in-depth interviewing, it can be said that it provides research subjects with the opportunity to share their own understandings and knowledge of experience; it provides them with a voice. Regardless of whether interviewees do or do not 'collaborate' in producing published texts, as researchers, authors, and readers, it is our responsibility to acknowledge the mediating processes of selecting, editing, ordering, and interpreting that situate these tellings in texts.

16 Tracy's and Yvonne's accounts should be read in the context of child sexual abuse and its consequences, discussed in chapter 5.

17 Tracy used the hide-a-bed couch as her bed.

18 Without mentioning names, I asked a Township Family Services counsellor to advise me as to whether I should report this child's situation to the Children's Aid Society. She told me that the situation was already being monitored, and that, at any rate, a report of verbal threats would not elicit a CAS response.

19 Tracy indicates that as a child she was manipulated into sex and sex play by her father, maternal grandfather, and maternal uncle, but in contrast to her sister-in-law Yvonne, she does not report that these incestuous experiences were accompanied by violence or the threat of violence.

20 Tracy did not see herself as violent or abusive, despite recounting incidents in which she initiated violence or teased partners to the point where she thought abuse was inevitable. Tracy also did not see herself as a substance abuser. She reported that she frequently went to bars and that she planned one day to run a bar, but that she only drank very moderately.

21 Another woman encountered at this party participated in a subsequent interview, a 'hard-living' woman in her later thirties who reported that she freely and frequently engaged in violence against dating partners.

22 I took detailed field notes on my conversation with Kim immediately after the party.

23 Though 'experts' across the feminist/non-feminist divide reject the notion that substance abuse 'causes' domestic violence or woman abuse, this is especially true in *violence against women* discourse. Sam's account strongly supports this 'expert' position.

24 I paraphrase Denzin, who paraphrases Marx. See Marx, 1968.

8: A Researcher's Construction of 'The Problem': Conclusion

1 For summaries of the survey data, see tables 4, 5, and 14. 'Sexism' was the only proposed 'cause' of abuse that survey respondents reporting adult relationship violence rated differently than other respondents. Among women, the difference was statistically significant.

2 For an analysis of data on risk management in the larger and more representative 'risk vulnerable' *random* sample, and in the smaller and less representative 'risk resilient' dual-partner *couples* sub-sample, see table 9.

3 Women reporting current relationship violence were actually more likely to rate male violence as justifiable than females not reporting violence. See Table 15.

4 Two-thirds of all survey respondents, and an even higher percentage of women, identified power and control as a major or important 'motive' behind abusive practices. See table 4.

5 In the mid-1990s, the Township Resource Centre lost provincial funding, and closed. This unforeseen development rendered the 'access to services' argument less relevant.

6 See Yvonne's account in chapter 7 of difficulties associated with stopping abusive practices.

7 Caringella-MacDonald and Humphries (1991) describe positive outcomes associated with a 'feminist peacemaking' community approach to the problem of sexual assault.

8 As Watzlawick (1984b) argues, and as research on problems in women's shelters reviewed in chapter 4 demonstrates, these reifications are not simply or wholly a function of the content of ideologies; rather, they are the consequences of human tendencies to forget that ideologies are merely perspectives, merely lenses. As self-critical feminist theorist Hirsh points out, theories (and implicitly ideologies) are unavoidably based on images that mask or foreclose others. More importantly, all images have the potential to turn perverse (Hirsh, 1994:3).

9 A series of articles in the *National Post* in November 1998 that 'expose' and criticize feminist-run women's shelters and related woman abuse services as radically dysfunctional are but one example of an ongoing feminist backlash fuelled by the activities of a recently emergent and highly vocal men's rights movement (see LaFramboise, 1998).

10 This is not to say that all lenses, or claims, are equally viable. Some are insupportable, empirically and morally. Some are 'bogus,' others are pernicious – those promoting or justifying torture or genocide, for instance. This

in not true of either *violence against women* or *family violence* perspectives. As argued throughout this book, both are grounded in empirically supportable 'facts' about our historically situated and intersubjectively mediated social world, and both aim at the alleviation of human misery.

11 General systems and communication theorists have long argued that zero-sum control is associated with destructive outcomes. See Buckley, 1967; Reiss, 1981; Watzlawick, 1984a, 1984b; Bateson, 1985.

12 Along with other essentially mainstream sociologists, I regard 'facts' as refutable constructions or representations of actions, events, and relationships evidenced in the empirical social world. Facts may or may not be 'true,' that is, supportable, but they are never the full 'truth.' See Blumer, 1969; Giddens, 1976, 1983; Best, 1993; Loseke and Gelles, 1993; Searle, 1993.

13 Social problems theorists have tended to argue that it is theoretically unfruitful, politically inappropriate, or epistemologically impossible to assess the content of truth-claims, and therefore to address bad faith and related issues. Best's 'But Seriously Folks' (1993) re-legitimizes attempts to do so, epistemological inconsistencies notwithstanding. See the review of social problems discourse in chapter 2.

Appendices

1 These ethical guidelines are outlined in the pamphlet entitled *Code of Ethics* printed by the American Sociological Association and distributed to members in the spring of 1991.

2 Concerns about the safety of participants prevented the researcher from making requests to approach partners for participation in the couples follow-up when the first partner reported current or past patterns of violent abuse.

Bibliography

Adams, D. (1988). Treatment models of men who batter: A profeminist analysis. In *Feminist perspectives on wife abuse*, ed. K. Yllo and M. Bogard, pp. 176–99. Newbury Park: Sage Publications Inc.

Alcoff, L. (1989). Justifying feminist social science. In *Feminism and science*, ed. N. Tuana, pp. 85–103. Bloomington: Indiana University Press.

Alexander, P.C., S. Moore, and E.R. Alexander III. (1991). What is transmitted in the intergenerational transmission of violence? *Journal of Marriage and the Family*, 53(3): 657–68.

Ambert, A., P.A. Adler, P. Adler, and D.F. Detzner. (1995). Understanding and evaluating qualitative research. *Journal of Marriage and the Family* 57(4): 879–93.

Andrews, B., and C.R. Brewin. (1990). Attributions of blame for marital violence: A study of antecedents and consequences. *Journal of Marriage and the Family* 52(3): 757–68.

Apt, C., and D.F. Hurlbert. (1993). The sexuality of women in physically abusive marriages: A comparative study. *Journal of Marriage and the Family* 8(1): 57–67.

Aronson, N. (1984). Science as claims-making activity: Implications for social problems research. In *Studies in the Sociology of Social Problems*, ed. J.W. Schneider and J.I. Kitsuse, pp. 1–30. Norwood: Ablex Publishing Corporation.

Ashe, M., and N. Cahn. (1994). Child abuse: A problem for feminist theory. In *The public nature of private violence: The discovery of domestic abuse*, ed. M.A. Fineman and R. Mykitiuk, pp. 166–94. New York: Routledge.

Avis, J.M. (1992). Where are all the family therapists? Abuse and violence within families and family therapy's response. *Journal of Marital and Family Therapy* 18(3): 225–32.

Bain, J., O. Bearinger, D. Currie, K. Finkel, L. Hargot, B. Lent, D. Miller, B. Pressman, T. Rolfe, and B. Wybrow. (1991). *Reports on wife assault: A medical perspective, approaches to treatment of the male batterer and his family.* Committee on Wife Assault, Ontario Medical Association.

Barnes, G.E., L. Greenwood, and R. Sommer. (1991). Courtship violence in a Canadian sample of male college students. *Family Process* 40: 37–44.

Barnett, O.W., and R.W. Fagan. (1993). Alcohol use in male spouse abusers and their female partners. *Journal of Family Violence* 8(1): 1–25.

Barnett, O.W., T.F. Martinez, and M. Keyson. (1996). The relationship between violence, social support, and self-blame in battered women. *Journal of Interpersonal Violence* 11(2): 221–33.

Bass, E. (1988). *Courage to heal: A guide for women survivors of child sexual abuse.* New York: Harper and Row.

Bateson, G. (1985). *Steps to an ecology of mind.* 13th ed. New York: Balantine Books.

Beaudry, M. (1985). *Battered women.* 1st ed. Montreal: Black Rose Books.

Becker, H.S. (1966). Introduction. In *Social problems: A modern approach,* ed. H.S. Becker, pp. 1–31. New York: John Wiley and Sons.

– (1967). Whose side are we on? *Social Problems* 14: 239–47.

Benjamin, M., and S. Adler. (1980). Wife abuse implications for socio-legal policy and practice. *Canadian Journal of Family Law* 2(4): 339–67.

Berger, P.L., and T. Luckmann. (1966). *The social construction of reality.* New York: Doubleday.

Berk, R.A. (1993). What the scientific evidence shows: On the average, we can do no better than arrest. In *Current controversies on family violence,* ed. R.J. Gelles and D.R. Loseke, pp. 323–36. Newbury Park: Sage Publications Inc.

Berk, R.A., S. Fernstermaker Berk, D.R. Loseke, and D. Rauma. (1983). Mutual combat and other family violence myths. In *The dark side of families: Current family violence research,* ed. D. Finklehor, R.J. Gelles, G.T. Hotaling, and M.A. Straus, pp. 197–212. Beverly Hills: Sage Publications Inc.

Berk, R.A., P. Newton, and S.F. Berk. (1986). What a difference a day makes: An empirical study of the impact of shelters for battered women. *Journal of Marriage and the Family* 48: 481–90.

Berkowitz, L. (1983). The goals of aggression. In *The dark side of families: Current family violence research,* ed. D. Finklehor, R.J. Gelles, G.T. Hotaling, and M.A. Straus, pp. 166–81. Beverly Hills: Sage Publications Inc.

Berliner, L. (1996). Intervening in domestic violence: Should victims and offenders or couples be the focus? *Journal of Interpersonal Violence* 11(3): 449–50.

Best, J. (1989). Extending the constructionist perspective: A conclusion – and an introduction. In *Images of issues: Typifying contemporary social problems*, ed. J. Best, pp. 243–53. New York: Aldine De Gruyter.

– (1990). *Threatened children: rhetoric and concern about child-victims*. Chicago: University of Chicago Press.

– (1993). But seriously folks: The limitations of the strict constructionist interpretation of social problems. In *Reconsidering social constructionism: Debates in social problems theory*, ed. J.A. Holstein and G. Miller, pp. 129–47. New York: Aldine De Gruyter.

Blackman, J. (1989). *Intimate violence: A study of injustice*. New York: Columbia University Press.

Blumer, H. (1969). *Symbolic interactionism, perspective and method*. Englewood Cliffs, NJ: Prentice-Hall.

– (1971). Social problems as collective behavior. *Social Problems* 18(3): 298–306.

Bograd, M. (1992). Values in conflict: Challenges to family therapists' thinking. *Journal of Marital and Family Therapy* 18(3): 245–56.

Bowker, L.H. (1993). A battered woman's problems are social, not psychological. In *Current controversies on family violence*, ed. R.J. Gelles and R. Loseke, pp. 154–65. Newbury Park: Sage Publications Inc.

Bowker, L.H., M. Arbitell, and J.R. McFerron. (1988). On the relationship between wife beating and child abuse. In *Feminist perspectives on wife abuse*, eds. K. Yllo and M. Bogard, pp. 158–74. Newbury Park: Sage Publications Inc.

Bowker, L.H., and L. Maurer. (1986). The effectiveness of counselling services utilized by battered women. *Women and Therapy* 5(4): 65–82.

Breines, W., and L. Gordon. (1983). The new scholarship on family violence. *Journal of Women in Culture and Society* 8(3): 490–531.

Browning, J., and D. Duton. (1986). Assessment of wife assault with the Conflict Tactics Scale: Using couple data to quantify the differential reporting effect. *Journal of Marriage and the Family* 48: 375–9.

Buckley, W. (1967). *Sociology and modern systems theory*. 1st ed. New York: Prentice-Hall.

Burkett, L.P. (1991). Parenting behaviors of women who were sexaully abused as children in their families of origin. *Family Process* 30: 421–34.

Busby, D.M., G.L. Steggell, E. Glenn, and D.W. Adamson. (1993). Treatment issues for survivors of physical and sexual abuse. *Journal of Marital and Family Therapy* 19(4): 377–92.

Buzawa, E.S., and C.G. Buzawa. (1993). The scientific evidence is not conclusive: Arrest is no panacea. In *Current controversies on family violence*, eds. R.J. Gelles and D.R. Loseke, pp. 337–56. Newbury Park: Sage Publications Inc.

Campbell, A. (1993). *Men, women, and aggression.* New York: Basic Books.

Canadian Centre for Justice Statistics. (1994). *Family violence in Canada.* 89-5410XPE. 1st ed. Ottawa. Statistics Canada.

Canavan, M.M., W.J. Meyer, and D. Higgs. (1992). The female experience of sibling incest. *Journal of Marital and Family Therapy* 18(2): 129–42.

Cappell, C., and R.B. Heiner. (1990). The intergenerational transmission of family aggression. *Journal of Marriage and the Family* 5(2): 135–52.

Caringella-MacDonald, S., and D. Humphries. (1991). Sexual assault, women and the community: Organizing to prevent sexual violence. In *Criminology as peacemaking*, ed. H. Pepinsky and R. Quinney, pp. 98–113. Bloomington: Indiana University Press.

Carlson, B.E. (1984). Children's observations of interparental violence. In *Battered women and their families: Intervention strategies and treatment programs*, ed. A.R. Roberts, pp. 147–67. New York: Springer Publishing Company.

Carson, D.K., K.M. Gertz, M.A. Donaldson, and S.A. Wonderlich. (1990). Family of origin characteristics and current family relationships of female adult incest victims. *Journal of Family Violence* 5(2): 153–71.

Cascardi, M., and D.K. O'Leary. (1992). Depressive symptomatology, self-esteem and self-blame in battered women. *Journal of Family Violence* 7(4): 249–59.

Clandinin, D.J., and F.M. Connelly. (1994). Personal experience methods. In *Handbook of qualitative research*, eds. N.K. Denzin and Y.S. Lincoln, pp. 413–27. Thousand Oaks: Sage Publications.

Cleverdon, C.L. (1950). *The woman suffrage movement in Canada.* Toronto: University of Toronto Press.

Coleman, D.H., and M.A. Straus. (1983). Alcohol abuse and family violence. In *Alcohol, drug abuse and aggression*, eds. E. Gottheil, K.A. Druley, T.E. Skoloda, and H.M. Waxman, pp. 104–24. Springfield: Charles C. Thomas.

– (1990). Marital power, confict, and violence in a nationally representative sample of american couples. In *Physical violence in American families: Risk factors and adaptations to violence; 8,145 families*, eds. M.A. Straus and R.J. Gelles, pp. 287–304. New Brunswick, NJ: Transaction Publishers.

Dankwort, J. (1988a). The challenge of accountability in treating wife abusers: A critique from Quebec. *Canadian Journal of Community Mental Health* 7(2): 103–17.

– (1988b). Programs for men who batter: A snapshot. *Vis A Vis* 6(2): 1–3.

Davis, N.J. (1988). Shelters for battered women: social policy response to interpersonal violence. *Social Science Journal* 25(4): 401–19.

DeKeseredy, W.S., and R. Hinch. (1991). *Woman abuse: Sociological perspectives.* Toronto: Thompson Educational Publishing, Inc.

DeMaris, A. (1989). Attrition in batterers' counseling: The role of social and demographic factors. *Social Science Review* 63: 142–54.

– (1990). The dynamics of generational transfer in courtship violence: A biracial exploration. *Journal of Marriage and the Family* 53(1): 219–31.

Denzin, N.K. (1984). Toward a phenomenology of domestic, family violence. *American Journal of Sociology* 90(3): 483–513.

– (1987). *The alcoholic self.* 1st ed. Newbury Park: Sage Publications.

– (1989). *Interpretive interactionism.* Newbury Park: Sage Publications.

– (1994). The art and politics of interpretation. In *Handbook of Qualitative Research*, ed. N.K. Denzin and Y.S. Lincoln, pp. 500–15. Thousand Oaks: Sage Publications.

Dibble, U., and M.A. Straus. (1990). Some social structure determinants of inconsistency between attitudes and behavior: The case of family violence. In *Physical violence in American families: Risk factors and adaptations to violence: 8,145 families*, ed. M.A. Straus and R.J. Gelles, pp. 167–81. New Brunswick, NJ: Transaction Publishers.

Dobash, R.E., and R.P. Dobash. (1979). *Violence against wives: A case against the patriarchy.* 1st ed. New York: The Free Press.

– (1988). Research as social action: The struggle for battered women. In *Feminist perspectives on wife abuse*, eds. K. Yllo and M. Bogard, pp. 51–74. Newbury Park: Sage Publications Inc.

– (1992). *Women, violence, and social change.* 1st ed. London: Routledge.

Dobash, R.P., and R.E. Dobash. (1983). The context-specific approach. In *The dark side of families: Current family violence research*, ed. D. Finklelhor, R.J. Gelles, G.T. Hotaling, and M.A. Straus, pp. 261–76. Beverly Hills: Sage Publications Inc.

– (1995). Reflections on findings from the Violence against Women Survey. *Canadian Journal of Criminology* 37(3): 457–84.

Dobash, R.P., R.E. Dobash, K. Cavanagh, and R. Lewis. (1996). *Re-education programmes for violent men – an evaluation.* Research findings, 46. Edinburgh: Home Office Research and Statistics Directorate.

Dobash, R.P., R.E. Dobash, M. Wilson, and M. Daly. (1992). The myth of sexual symmetry in marital violence. *Social Problems* 39(1): 71–91.

Dodge, K.A., J.E. Bates, and G.S. Pettit. (1990). Mechanisms in the cycle of violence. *Science* 250: 1678–1683.

Douglas, J.D. (1977). Existential sociology. In *Existential sociology*, ed. J.D. Douglas and J.M. Johnson, pp. 3–73. Cambridge: Cambridge University Press.

– (1985). *Creative interviewing.* Beverly Hills: Sage Publications.

Dutton, D.G., and A.J. Starzomski. (1997). Personality predictors of the

Minnesota Power and Control Wheel. *Journal of Interpersonal Violence* 12(1): 70–82.

Eaton, M. (1994). Abuse by any other name: Feminism, difference, and intralesbian violence. In *The Public Nature of Private Violence: The Discovery of Domestic Abuse*, ed. M.A. Fineman and R. Mykitiuk, pp. 195–223. New York: Routledge.

Egeland, B. (1993). A history of abuse is a major risk factor for abusing the next generation. In *Current controversies on family violence*, ed. R.J. Gelles and D.R. Loseke, pp. 197–208. Newbury Park: Sage Publications Inc.

Eisikovits, Z., and Buchbinder, E. (1996). Pathways to disenchantment: battered women's views of their social workers. *Journal of Interpersonal Violence* 11(3): 425–40.

Erickson, B.M. (1992). Feminist fundamentalism: Reactions to Avis, Kaufman, and Bograd. *Journal of Marital and Family Therapy* 18(3): 263–7.

Ewing, C.P., and Aubrey, M. (1987). Battered women and public opinion: Some realities about the myths. *Journal of Family Violence* 2(3): 259–64.

Fagan, J.A., Stewart, D.K., and Hansen, K.V. (1983). Violent men or violent husbands? Background factors and situational correlates. In *The dark side of family violence: current family violence research*, ed. D. Finkelhor, R.J. Gelles, G.T. Hotaling, and M.A. Straus, pp. 49–67. Beverly Hills: Sage Publications Inc.

Fatout, M.F. (1990). Consequences of abuse on the relationships of children. *Families in Society*, 71(2): 76–81.

Feldman-Summers, S., and K.S. Pope. (1994). The experience of 'forgetting' childhood abuse: A national survey of psychologists. *Journal of consulting and Clinical Psychology* 62(3): 636–9.

Ferraro, K.J., (1983). Negotiating trouble in a battered women's shelter. *Urban Life* 12(3): 287–306.

Ferraro, K.J., and J.M. Johnson. (1983). How women experience battering: the process of victimizaiton. *Social Problems* 30(3): 325–39.

Fine, G.A. (1993). The sad demise, mysterious disappearance, and glorious triumph of symbolic interactionism. *Annual Journal of Sociology* 19(61): 61–87.

Fine, M. (1994). Working the hyphens: Reinventing self and other in qualitative research. In *Handbook of Qualitative Research*, ed. N.K. Denzin and Y. Lincoln, pp. 70–82. Thousand Oaks: Sage Publications.

Finkelhor, D. (1983). Common Features of Family Abuse. In *The Dark Side of Families: Current Family Violence Research*, ed. D. Finklehor, R.J. Gelles, G.T. Hotaling, and M.A. Straus, pp. 17–28. Beverly Hills: Sage Publications Inc.

Finkelhor, D., and K. Yllo (1985). *License to rape: Sexual abuse of wives*. 1st ed. New York: The Free Press.

Flanzer, J.P. (1993). Alcohol and other drugs are key causal agents of violence. In *Current controversies on family violence*, ed. R.J. Gelles and D.R. Loseke, pp. 171–81. Newbury Park: Sage Publications Inc.

Flax, J. (1990). Thinking fragments: Psychoanalysis, feminism, and post-modernism in the contemporary west. 1st ed. Berkeley: University of California Press.

Flynn, C.P. (1990). Relationship violence by women: Issues and implications. *Family Relations* 39(2): 194–7.

Follingstad, D.R., L.L. Rutledge, B.J. Berg, E.S. Hause, and D.S. Polek. (1990). The role of emotional abuse in physically abusive relationships. *Journal of Marriage and the Family* 5(2): 108–17.

Fontana, A., and J.H. Frey. (1994). Interviewing: The art of science. In *Handbook of qualitative research*, ed. N.K. Denzin and Y.S. Lincoln, pp. 361–76. Thousand Oaks: Sage Publications.

Foucault, M. (1980). *The history of sexuality*. New York: Vintage Books.

Fox, B.J. (1993). On violent men and female victims: A comment on DeKeseredy and Kelly. *Canadian Journal of Sociology*, 18, 321–4.

Frankel-Howard, D. (1989). *Family violence: A review of theoretical and clinical literature*. Ottawa: Health and Welfare Canada.

Fuller, R.C., and R.R. Myers. (1941). The natural history of a social problem. *American Sociological Review* 6, 320–8.

Gagne, P. (1996). Identity, strategy, and feminist politics: clemency for battered women who kill. *Social Problems* 43(1): 77–93.

Gartner, R. (1993). Studying woman abuse: A comment on DeKeseredy and Kelly. *Canadian Journal of Sociology* 18: 313–20.

Geller, J., and J. Wasserstrom. (1984). Conjoint therapy for the treatment of domestic violence. In *Battered women and their families*, ed. A.R. Roberts, pp. 31–64. New York: Springer Publishing Company.

Gelles, R.J. (1993a). Constraints against family violence: How well do they work? *American Behavioral Scientist* 36(5): 575–86.

– (1993b). Though a sociological lens: Social structure and family violence. In *Current controversies on family violence*, ed. R.J. Gelles and D.R. Loseke, pp. 31–46. Newbury Park: Sage Publications Inc.

– (1993c). Alcohol and other drugs are associated with violence – they are not its cause. In *Current controversies on family violence*, ed. R.J. Gelles and D.R. Loseke, pp. 182–96. Newbury Park: Sage Publications Inc.

Gelles, R.J., and J.R. Conte. (1990). Domestic violence and sexual abuse of children: A review of research in the eighties. *Journal of Marriage and the Family* 52: 1045–58.

Gelles, R.J., and D.R. Loseke. (1993). Conclusion: Social problems, social policy, and controversies on family violence. In *Current controversies on family violence*, ed. R.J. Gelles and D.R. Loseke, pp. 357–66. Newbury Park: Sage Publications Inc.

Gelles, R.J., and M.A. Straus. (1988). *Intimate violence: the definitive study of the causes and consequences of abuse in the American Family.* 1st ed. New York: Simon and Schuster.

Giddens, A. (1976). *New rules of sociological methods: A positive critique of interpretive sociologies.* London: Hutchinson and Company.

– (1979). *Central problems in social theory.* Berkeley: University of California Press.

– (1983). *Profiles and critiques in social theory.* 1st ed. Berkeley: University of California Press.

– (1992). *The transformation of intimacy.* Cambridge: Polity Press.

Giles-Sims, J. (1983). *Wife battering: A systems theory approach.* New York: The Gilford Press.

Gilgun, J.F. (1995). We shared something special: The moral discourse of incest perpetrators. *Journal of Marriage and the Family* 57(2): 265–81.

Gillespie, D.L., and A. Leffler. (1987). The politics of research methodology in claims-making activities: Social science and sexual harassment. *Social Problems* 34(5): 490–501.

Goffman, E. (1961). *Asylums.* New York: Anchor Books.

Gondolf, E.W. (1985a). Anger and oppression in men who batter: Empiricist and feminist perspectives and their implications for research. *Victimology* 10: 311–24.

– (1985b). *Men who batter: An integrated appraoch for stopping wife abuse.* Miami: Learning Publications Inc.

– (1997). Batterer programs: What we know and need to know. *Journal of Interpersonal Violence* 12(1): 83–98.

Gordon, L. (1988). *Heroes of their own lives: The politics and history of family violence,* Boston 1880–1960. New York: Viking.

Gordon, M. (1990). Males and females as victims of childhood sexual abuse: An explanation of the gender effect. *Journal of Family Violence* 5(4): 321–32.

Gottheil, E., K.A. Druley, T.E. Skoloda, and H.M. Waxman. (1983). Aggression and addiction: Summary and overview. In *Alcohol, drug abuse and aggression,* ed. E. Gottheil, K.A. Druley, T.E. Skoloda, and H.M. Waxman, pp. 333–56. Springfield: Charles C. Thomas.

Graham, D.L., E. Rawlings, and N. Rimini. (1988). Survivors of terror: Battered women, hostages, and the stockholm syndrome. In *Feminist perspectives on wife abuse,* ed. K. Yllo and M. Bograd, pp. 217–33. Newbury Park: Sage Publications.

Gray, H.M., and V. Foshee. (1997). Adolescent dating violence: Differences between one-sided and mutually violent profiles. *Journal of Interpersonal Violence* 12(1): 126–41.

Greenblat, C.S. (1983). A hit is a hit is a hit ... Or is it? Approval and tolerance of the use of physical force by spouses. In *The dark side of families: Current family violence research*, ed. D. Finkelhor, R.J. Gelles, G.T. Hotaling, and M.A. Straus, pp. 235–60. Beverly Hills: Sage Publications.

Guba, E.G., and Y.S. Lincoln. (1994). Competing paradigms in qualitative research. In *Handbook of qualitative research*, ed. N.K. Denzin and Y.S. Lincoln, pp. 105–17. Thousand Oaks: Sage Publications.

Gupta, G.R., and S.M. Cox. (1988). A Typology of incest and possible intervention strategies. *Journal of Marriage and the Family* 3(4): 299–312.

Gusfield, J.R. (1981). *The culture of public problems: Drinking-driving and the symbolic order.* Chicago: University of Chicago Press.

– (1984). On the side: Practical action and social construtionism in social problems theory. In *Studies in the sociology of social problems*, ed. J.W. Schneider and J.I. Kitsuse, pp. 31–49. Norwood: Ablex Publishing Corporation.

– (1989). Constructing the ownership of social problems: Fun and profits in the welfare state. *Social Problems* 36(5): 431–41.

Habermas, J. (1987). *The philosophical discourse of modernity.* 1st ed. Cambridge: MIT Press.

Hall, J.R. (1990). Epistemology and sociohistorical inquiry. *Annual Review of Sociology* 16: 329–51.

Hamburger, K.L., and J.E. Hastings. (1991). Personality correlates of men who batter and nonviolent men: Some continuities and discontinuities. *Journal of Family Violence* 6(2): 131–47.

Hamby, S.L., V.C. Poindexter, and B. Gray-Little. (1996). Four measures of partner violence: Construct similarity and classification differences. *Journal of Marriage and the Family* 58(1): 127–39.

Hanmer, J., and M. Maynard. (1989). Introduction: Violence and gender stratification. In *Women, violence and social control*, ed. J. Hanmer and M. Maynard, pp. 1–12. Houndmills: Macmillan.

Hanson, R.F., J.A. Lipovsky, and B.E. Saunders. (1994). Characteristics of fathers in incest families. *Journal of Interpersonal Violence* 9(2): 155–69.

Harding, S. (1989). Is there a feminist method? In *Feminism and science.* ed. N. Tuana, pp. 17–32. Bloomington: Indiana University Press.

– (1990). Feminism, science, and the anti-enlightenment critiques. In *Feminism/postmodernism*, ed. L.J. Nicholson, pp. 83–106. New York: Routledge.

Hartsock, N. (1990). Foucault on power: A theory for women? In *Feminism/postmodernism*, ed. L.J. Nicholson, pp. 157–75. New York: Routledge.

Hawkesworth, M.E. (1989). Knowers, knowing, known: Feminist theory and claims of truth. *Signs* 14(3): 533–57.

Hazelrigg, L.E. (1985). Were it not for words. *Social Problems* 32(3): 234–7.

– (1986). Is there a choice between 'Constructionism' and 'Objectivism'? *Social Problems* 33(6): 1–13.

Heath, D.B. (1983). Alcohol and aggression: A 'Missing Link' in world wide perspective. In *Alcohol, drug abuse and aggression*, ed. E. Gottheil, K.A. Druley, T.E. Skoloda, and H.M. Waxman, pp. 89–103. Springfield: Charles C. Thomas.

Herbert, T.B., R.C. Silver, and J.H. Ellard. (1991). Coping with an abusive relationship: I. How and why do women stay? *Journal of Marriage and the Family* 53(2): 311–25.

Herman, J.L. (1981). *Father-daughter incest.* Cambridge: Harvard University Press.

Hirsh, S.F. (1994). Section one, images of violence: Introduction. In *The public nature of private violence: The discovery of domestic abuse*, ed. M.A. Fineman and R. Mykitiuk, pp. 3–10. New York: Routledge.

Hoff, L.A. (1988). Collaborative feminist theory and the myth of objectivity. In *Feminist perspectives on wife abuse*, ed. K. Yllo and M. Bogard, pp. 269–81. Newbury Park: Sage Publications Inc.

– (1990). *Battered women as survivors.* London: Routledge.

Hoffman, L. (1990). Constructing realities: An art of lenses. *Family Process*, 29(1): 1–12.

Holmes, M., and C. Lundy. (1990). Group work for abusive men: A profeminist response. *Canadian Mental Health* 38(4): 12–17.

Hotaling, G.T., and D.B. Sugarman. (1986). An analysis of risk markers in husband to wife violence: The current state of knowledge. *Violence and Victims*, 101–24

– (1990). A risk marker analysis of assaulted wives. *Journal of Family Violence* 5(1): 1–13.

Huges, H.M., D. Parkinson, and M. Vargo. (1989). Witnessing spouse abuse and experiencing physical abuse: A 'double whammy'? *Journal of Marriage and the Family* 4(2): 197–209.

Ibarra, P.R., and J.I. Ktisuse. (1993). Vernacular constituents of moral discourse: An interactionist proposal for the study of social problems. In *Reconsidering social constructionism: Debates in social problems theory*, ed. J.A. Holstein and G. Miller, pp. 25–58. New York: Aldine De Gruyter.

Jacobson, N.S. (1994). Rewards and dangers in researching domestic violence. *Family Process* 33(1): 81–6.

Jacobson, N.S., J.M. Gottman, J. Waltz, R. Rushe, J. Babcock, and A. Holtzworth-Munroe. (1994). Affect, verbal content, and psychophysiology in the arguments of couples with a violent husband. *Journal of Consulting and Clinical Psychology* 62(5): 982–8.

Johnson, H., and V. Sacco. (1995). Researching violence against women: Statistics Canada's National Survey. *Canadian Journal of Criminology* 37(3): 281–304.

Johnson, J.M. (1977). Behind the rational appearances: Fusion of thinking and feeling in sociological research. In *Existential sociology*, ed. J.D. Douglas and J.M. Johnson, pp. 201–28. Cambridge: Cambridge University Press.

Johnson, J.M., and K.J. Ferraro. (1984). The victimized self: The case of battered women. In *The existential self in society*, ed. J.A. Kotarba and A. Fontana, pp. 119–30. Chicago: University of Chicago Press.

Johnson, M.P. (1995). Patriarchal terrorism and common couple violence: Two forms of violence against women. *Journal of Marriage and the Family* 57(2): 283–94.

Julian, T.W., and P.C. McKerry. (1993). Mediators of male violence towards female intimates. *Journal of Family Violence* 8(1): 39–56.

Kalmuss, D. (1984). The intergenerational transmission of marital aggression. *Journal of Marriage and the Family* 46: 11–19.

Kantor, D., and W. Lehr. (1975). *Inside the family.* San Francisco: Jossey-Bass.

Kantor, G.K., and M.A. Straus. (1990). The 'drunken bum' theory of wife beating. In *Physical violence in American families: Risk factors and adaptations to violence; 8,145 families*, ed. M.A. Straus and R.J. Gelles, pp. 203–26. New Brunswick, NJ: Transaction Publishers.

Kaufman, G. Jr., (1992). The mysterious disappearances of battered women in family therapists' offices: Male privilege colluding with male violence. *Journal of Marital and Family Therapy* 18(3): 233–43.

Kaufman, J., and E. Zigler. (1993). The intergenerational tranmission of abuse is overstated. In *Current controversies on family violence*, ed. R.J. Gelles and D.R. Loseke, pp. 209–21. Newbury Park: Sage Publications Inc.

Kelly, L. (1988). How women define their experiences of violence. In *Feminist perspectives on wife abuse*, ed. K. Yllo and M. Bograd, pp. 114–32. Newbury Park: Sage Publications.

– (1989). The continuum of sexual violence. In *Women, violence and social control*, ed. J. Hanmer and M. Maynard, pp. 46–60. Houndmills: Macmillan.

Kemper, T.D. (1981). Social constructionist and positivist approaches to the sociology of emotions. *American Journal of Sociology* 87(2): 336–62.

Kitsuse, J., and M. Spector. (1973). Toward a sociology of social problems: Social conditions, value judgements, and social problems. *Social Problems* 20(3): 407–19.

Kleidman, R. (1994). Volunteer activism and professionalism in social movement organizations. *Social Change* 41(2): 257–76.

Kurz, D. (1987). Emergency department responses to battered women: Resistance to medicalization. *Social Problems* 34(1): 69–81.

– (1991). Corporal punishment and adult use of violence: A critique of discipline and deviance. *Social Problems* 38(2): 155–61.

– (1993). Physical assaults by husbands: A major social problem. In *Current controversies on family violence*, ed. R.J. Gelles and D.R. Loseke, pp. 88–103. Newbury Park: Sage Publishers Inc.

Lackey, C., and K.R. Williams. (1995). Social bonding and the cessation of partner violence across generations. *Journal of Marriage and the Family* 57(2): 295–305.

LaFramboise, D. (1998). Battered shelters. *National Post* 1(17): B1.

Launius, M.H., and J.L. Bernard. (1987). Interpersonal problem-solving skills in battered, counseling and control women. *Journal of Family Violence* 2(2): 151–62.

Lembert, L.B. (1994). A narrative analysis of abuse. *Journal of Contemporary Ethonography* 22(4): 411–41.

Lenton, R.L. (1995). Power versus feminist theories on wife abuse. *Canadian Journal of Criminology* 37(3): 305–30.

Lester, M. (1984). Self: Sociological portraits. In *The existential self in society*, ed. J. Kotarba and A. Fontana, pp. 18–68. Chicago: University of Chicago Press.

Light, B., and J. Parr. (1983). *Canadian women on the move 1867–1920*. Toronto: New Hogtown Press.

Lloyd, S.A. (1990). Conflict types and strategies in violent marriages. *Journal of Family Violence* 5(4): 269–84.

Loftus, E.F., M. Garry, and J. Feldman. (1994). Forgetting sexual trauma: What does it mean when 38% forget? *Journal of Counsulting and Clinical Psychology* 62(6): 1177–81.

Longins, H.E. (1989). Can there be a feminist science? In *Feminism and science*, ed. N. Tuana, pp. 45–57. Bloomington: Indiana University Press.

Loseke, D.R. (1989). Images of issues: Typifying contemporary social problems. In *Images of issues*, ed. J. Best, pp. 191–206. New York: Aldine De Gruyter.

– (1991). Reply to Murry A. Straus: Readings on discipline and deviance. *Social Problems* 38(2): 162–66.

– (1992). *The battered woman and shelters*. Albany: State University of New York Press.

Loseke, D.R., and S.E. Cahill. (1984). The social construction of deviance: Experts on battered women. *Social Problems* 31(3): 296–310.

Loseke, D.R., and R.J. Gelles. (1993). Introduction: Examining and evaluating controversies on family violence. In *Current controversies on family violence,* ed. R. Gelles and D. Loseke, pp. ix–xvii. Newbury Park: Sage Publications Inc.

MacEven, K.E., and J. Garling. (1988). Multiple stressor, violence in the family of origin, and marital aggression: A longitudinal investigation. *Journal of Marriage and the Family* 3(1): 73–87.

MacLeod, L. (1980). *Wife battering in Canada: The vicious circle.* 1st ed. Ottawa: Canadian Advisory Board on the Status of Women.

– (1987). *Battered but not beaten: Preventing wife battering in Canada.* Ottawa: Canadian Advisory Council on the Status of Women.

– (1987). *Wife battering and the web of hope: Progress, dilemmas and visions of prevention.* Ottawa: Health and Welfare Canada.

Mahoney, M. (1994). Victimization or oppression? Women's lives, violence, and agency. In *The public nature of private violence: The discovery of domestic abuse,* ed. M.A. Fineman and R. Mykitiuk, pp. 53–92. New York: Routledge.

Mann, R.M. (1991). Victimization and agency. Paper presented at the Annual Meeting of the Canadian Sociology and Anthropology Association, Kingston, Ontario.

Marx, K. (1968). The eighteenth prumiare of Louis Bonaparte. In *Karl Marx and Frederick Engels: Selected Works,* pp. 97–180. New York: International Publishers.

Mauss, A.L. (1975). *Social problems as social movements.* 1st ed. Philadelphia: J.B. Pippincott Co.

McCormack, T. (1989). Feminism and the new crisis in methodology. In *The effects of feminist approaches on research methodologies,* ed. W. Tomm, pp. 13–30. Waterloo: Wilfred Laurier University Press.

McDonald, L., and T.L. Peressini. (1991). Social policy and sheltering in the 1990s. Paper presented at the Annual Meeting of the Canadian Sociology and Anthropology Association, Kingston, Ontario.

McKeel, A.J., and M.J. Sporakowski. (1993). How shelter counselors' views about responsibility for wife abuse relate to services they provide to battered women. *Journal of Marriage and the Family* 8(2): 101–11.

McKendy, J.P. (1992). Ideological practices and the management of emotions: The case of 'wife abusers.' *Critical Sociology* 19(2): 61–80.

McLaughlin, I.G., K.E. Leonard, and M. Senchak. (1992). Prevalence and distribution of premarital aggression among couples applying for a marriage license. *Journal of Marriage and the Family* 7(4): 309–19.

McMahon, M., and E. Pence. (1996). Replying to Dan O'Leary. *Journal of Interpersonal Violence* 11(3): 452–55.

Mead, G.H. (1934). *Mind, self, and society.* Chicago: University of Chicago Press.

Meth, R.L. (1992). Marriage and family therapists working with family violence: Strained bedfellows or compatible partners? A commentary on Avis,
Kaufman, and Bograd. *Journal of Marital and Family Therapy* 18(3): 257–61.

Meyer, D., and N. Whittier. (1994). Social movement spillover. *Social Problems*
41(2): 277–98.

Miller, G. (1993). New challenges to social constructionism: Alternative per-
spectives on social problems theory. In *Reconsidering social constructionism:
Debates in social problems theory,* ed. J.A. Holstein and G. Miller, pp. 253–78.
New York: Aldine De Gruyter.

Mills, C.W. (1959). *The sociological imagination.* 1st ed. London: Oxford University Press.

Morrison, R.L., V.B. Hasselt, and A.S. Bellack. (1987). Assessment of assertion
and problem solving skills in wife abusers and their spouses. *Journal of
Family Violence* 2(3): 227–38.

Murphy, C.M., and K.D. O'Leary. (1994). Research paradigms, values, and
spouse abuse. *Journal of Interpersonal Violence* 9(2): 207–23.

Neidig, P.H., and D.H. Friedman. (1984). *Spouse abuse: A treatment program for
couples.* Champaign: Research Press Company.

Nosko, A., and B. Wallace. (1988). Group work with abusive men: A multi-
dimensional model. *Social Work with Groups* 11(3): 33–52.

O'Farrell, T.J., and C.M. Murphy. (1995). Marital violence before and after alcoholism treatment. *Journal of Consulting and Clinical Psychology* 63(2): 256–62.

O'Keefe, M. (1995). Predictors of child abuse in maritally violent families. *Journal of Interpersonal Violence* 10(1): 3–35.

O'Leary, K.D. (1993). Through a psychological lens: Personality traits, personality disorders, and levels of violence. In *Current controversies on family violence,* ed. R. Gelles and D. Loseke, pp. 7–30. Newbury Park: Sage Publishers,
Inc.

– (1996). Physical aggression in intimate relationships can be treated within a
marital context under certain circumstances. *Journal of Interpersonal Violence*
11(3): 450–2.

O'Leary, K.D., J. Barling, I. Arias, and A. Rosenbaum. (1989). Prevalence and
stability of physical aggression between spouses: A longitudinal analysis.
Journal of Consulting and Clinical Psychology 57(2): 263–8.

O'Leary, K.D., J. Malone, and A. Tyree. (1994). Physical aggression in early
marriage: Prerelationship and relationship effects. *Journal of Consulting and
Clinical Psychology* 62(3): 594–602.

Okun, L. (1986). *Woman abuse: Facts replacing myths.* Albany: State University of
New York Press.

Olesen, V. (1994). Feminisms and models of qualitative research. In *Handbook of qualitative research*, ed. N.K. Denzin and Y.S. Lincoln, pp. 158–74. Thousand Oaks: Sage Publications.

Pahl, J. (1985a). Marital violence and marital problems. In *Private violence and public policy*, ed. J. Pahl, pp. 29–43. London: Routledge and Kegan Paul.

– (1985b). Marriage and marriage breakdown. In *Private violence and public policy*, ed. J. Pahl, pp. 44–56. London: Routledge and Kegan Paul.

Pan, H.S., P.H. Neidig, and K.D. O'Leary. (1994). Predicting mild and severe husband-to-wife physical aggression. *Journal of Consulting and Clinical Psychology* 62(5): 975–81.

Parker, S., and H. Parker. (1991). Female victims of child sexual abuse: Adult adjustment. *Journal of Family Violence* 6(2): 183–97.

Pederson, P., and C.D. Thomas. (1992). Prevalence and correlates of dating violence in a Canadian university sample. *Canadian Journal of Behavioral Science* 24(4): 490–501.

Pence, E., and M. Shepard. (1988). Integrating feminist theory and practice: The challenge of the battered woman's movement. In *Feminist perspectives on wife abuse*, ed. K. Yllo and M. Bogard, pp. 282–98. Newbury Park: Sage Publications Inc.

Pfohl, S. (1977). The 'Discovery' of child abuse. *Social Problems* 24(3): 310–23.

– (1985). Toward a sociological deconstruction of social problems. *Social Problems* 32(3): 228–32.

Pizzey, E., and J. Shapiro. (1982). *Prone to violence*. Feltham: Hamlyn Paperbacks.

Pleck, E. (1983). Feminist responses to crimes against women. *Signs* 8(3): 451–70.

Plummer, C.A. (1993). Prevention is appropriate, prevention is successful. In *Current controversies on family violence*, ed. R.J. Gelles and D.R. Loseke, pp. 288–305. Newbury Park: Sage Publications.

Radford, J. (1989). Policing male violence – policing women. In *Women, violence and social control*, ed. J. Hanmer and M. Maynard, pp. 30–45. Houndmills: Macmillan.

Ray, K.C., J.L. Jackson, and R.M. Townsley. (1991). Family environments of victims of intrafamilial and extrafamilial child sexual abuse. *Journal of Family Violence* 6(4): 365–74.

Reiss, D. (1981). *The family's construction of reality*. Cambridge: Harvard University Press.

Renvoize, J. (1978). *Web of violence*. London: Routledge and Kegan Paul.

– (1982). *Incest: A family pattern*. London: Routledge and Kegan Paul.

Richardson, L. (1990). Narrative and sociology. *Journal of Contemporary Ethnography* 19(1): 116–35.

– (1994). Writing: A method of inquiry. In *Handbook of qualitative research*, ed. N.K. Denzin and Y.S. Lincoln, pp. 516–29. Thousand Oaks: Sage Publications.

Riggs, D.S., and M.B. Caulfield. (1997). Expected consequences of male violence against their female dating partners. *Journal of Interpersonal Violence* 12(2): 229–40.

Roberts, A.R. (1984). Intervention with the abusive partner. In *Battered women and their families: Intervention strategies and treatment programs*, ed. A.R. Roberts, pp. 84–115. New York: Springer Publishing Company.

Rodgers, K. (1994). Wife assault: The findings of a national survey. *Juristat*, 14(9): 1–22.

Römkens, R. (1997). Prevalence of wife abuse in the Netherlands: Combining quantitative and qualitative methods in survey research. *Journal of Interpersonal Violence* 12(1): 99–125.

Ronai, C.R. (1997). Discurisve constraint in the narrated identities of childhood sex abuse survivors. In *Everyday sexism in the third millennium*, ed. C.R. Ronai, B.A. Zsembic, and J.R. Feagin, pp. 123–36. New York: Routledge.

Ronai, C.R., B.A. Zsembic, and J.R. Feagin. (1997). Introduction: Living with everyday sexism in the third millennium. In *Everyday sexism in the third millennium*, ed. C.R. Ronai, B.A. Zsembic, and J.R. Feagin, pp. 1–11. New York: Routledge.

Rosewater, L.B. (1984). Feminist theory: Implications for practioners. In *Women and mental health policy*, ed. L.E. Walker, pp. 267–79. Beverly Hills: Sage Publications.

Russell, M. (1990). Second stage shelters: A consumers report. *Canada's Mental Health* 38(2/3): 24–6.

Sartre, J.P. (1965). *Being and nothingness*. 2nd ed. New York: The Citadel Press.

Saunders, D.G. (1988). Wife abuse, husband abuse, or mutual combat? A feminist perspective on the empirical findings. In *Feminist perspectives on wife abuse*, ed. K. Yllo and M. Bogard, pp. 90–113. Newbury Park: Sage Publications Inc.

Schechter, S. (1982). *Women and male violence*. Boston: South End Press.

– (1988). Building bridges between activists, professionals, and researchers. In *Feminist perspectives on wife abuse*, ed. K. Yllo and M. Bogard, pp. 299–312. Newbury Park: Sage Publications Inc.

Schmidt, J.D., and L.W. Sherman. (1993). Does arrest deter domestic violence? *American Behavioral Scientist* 36(5): 601–9.

Schneider, J.W. (1978). Deviant drinking as a disease: Alcoholism as a social accomplishment. *Social Problems* 24(4): 361–82.

– (1985a). Social problems theory: The constructionist view. *Annual Review of Sociology* 11: 209–27.

- (1985b). Defining the definitional perspective on social problems. *Social Problems* 32(3): 232–4.
- (1993). 'Members only': Reading the constructionist text. In *Reconsidering social constructionism: Debates in social problems theory*, ed. J.A. Holstein and G. Miller, pp. 103–116. New York: Aldine De Gruyter.
Schneider, J.W., and M. Spector. (1985). Social problems theory: The constructionist view. *Annual Review of Sociology* 11, 209–27.
Schuyler, M. (1976). Battered wives: An emerging social problem. *Social Work*, 21(6): 488–91.
Searle, J.R. (1993). Rationality and realism, what is at stake? *Daedalus* 122(4): 55–83.
Sherman, L.W. (1992). *Policing domestic violence*. New York: The Free Press.
Shupe, A., W.A. Stacey, and L.R. Hazlewood. (1987). *Violent men, violent couples: The dynamics of domestic violence*. Lexington: Lexington Books.
Sigler, R.T. (1989). *Domestic violence in context: An assessment of community attitudes*. Toronto: Lexington Books.
Smith, D. (1987). *The everyday world as problematic: A feminist sociology*. Toronto: University of Toronto Press.
- (1997). Wife abuse and family idealizations: The violent regulation of family regimes. In *Everyday sexism in the third millennium*, ed. C.R. Ronai, B.A. Zsembic, and J.R. Feagin, pp. 105–122. New York: Routledge.
Smith, J.P., and J.G. Williams. (1992). From abusive household to dating violence. *Journal of Marriage and the Family* 7(2): 153–65.
Smith, M.D. (1994). Enhancing the quality of survey data on violence against women: A feminist approach. *Gender and Society*, 8(1): 109–25.
Snider, L. (1994). Feminism, punishment, and the potential of empowerment. *Canadian Journal of Law and Society* 9(1): 75–104.
Sommers, C.H. (1994). *Who stole feminism? How women have betrayed women*. 1st ed. New York: Simon and Schuster.
Sonkin, D.J., D. Martin, and L.E. Walker. (1985). *The male batterer, A treatment approach*. Springer Publishing Co.
Spector, M., and J. Kitsuse. (1974). Social problems: A re-formulation. *Social Problems* 21(2): 145–59.
Spieker, G. (1983). What is the linkage between alcohol abuse and violence? In *Alcohol, drug abuse and aggression*, ed. E. Gottheil, K.A. Druley, T.E. Skoloda, and H.M. Waxman, pp. 125–36. Springfield: Charles C. Thomas.
Stacey, J. (1990). *Brave new families: Stories of domestic upheaval in late twentieth century America*. New York: Basic Books.
Stacey, W.A., L.R. Hazlewood, and A. Shupe. (1994). *The violent couple*. Westport: Praeger.

Stanko, E.A. (1985). *Intimate intrusions: Woman's experience of male violence*. London: Routledge and Kegan Paul.

Stark, E. (1993). Mandatory arrest of batterers: A reply to its critics. *American Behavioral Scientist* 36(5): 651–80.

Stark, E., and A. Flitcraft. (1983). Social knowledge, social policy, and the abuse of women: The case against patriarchial benevolence. In *The dark side of families: Current family violence research*, ed. D. Finkelhor, R.J. Gelles, G.T. Hotaling, and M.A. Straus, pp. 330–48. Beverly Hills: Sage Publications Inc.

Statistics Canada. (1993). Violence against women survey: Survey highlights 1993. 11-001E (ISSN 0827-0465). *The Daily* [Ottawa].

Steinmetz, S.K. (1977). *The cycle of violence: Assertive, aggressive, and abusive family interaction*. New York: Praeger.

– (1978). The battered husband syndrome. *Victimology* 2, 499–509.

Stets, J.E. (1988). *Domestic violence and control*. New York: Springer-Verlag.

– (1992). Interactive processes in dating aggression: A national study. *Journal of Marriage and the Family* 54(1): 165–77.

Stets, J.E., and M.A. Pirog-Good. (1989). Patterns of physical and sexual abuse for men and women in dating relationships: A descriptive analysis. *Journal of Family Violence* 4(1): 63–76.

Stets, J.E., and M.A. Straus. (1989). The marriage license as a hitting license. A comparison of assaults in dating, cohabitating, and married couples. *Journal of Family Violence* 4(2): 161–80.

– (1990). Gender differences in reporting martial violence and its medical and psychological consequences. In *Physical violence in American families: Risk factors and adaptations to violence; 8,145 families*, ed. M.A. Straus and R.J. Gelles, pp. 151–80. New Brunswick, NJ: Transaction Publishers.

Straus, M.A. (1983). Ordinary violence, child abuse, and wife-beating: What do they have in common? In *The dark side of families: Current family violence research*, ed. D. Finkelhor, R. Gelles, G.T. Hotaling, and M.A. Straus, pp. 213–34. Beverly Hills: Sage Publications.

– (1991). New theory and old canards about family violence research. *Social Problems* 38(2): 180–97.

– (1993a). Physical assults by wives: A major social problem. In *Current controversies on family violence*, ed. R.J. Gelles and D.R. Loseke, pp. 67–87. Newbury Park: Sage Publications Inc.

– (1993b). Identifying offenders in criminal justice research on domestic assault. *American Behavioral Scientist* 36(5): 587–600.

Straus, M.A., and Gelles, R.J. (1990). Wife's marital dependency and wife abuse. In *Physical violence in American families: Risk factors and adaptations to violence: 8,145 families*, ed. M.A. Straus and R.J. Gelles, pp. 369–82. New Brunswick, NJ: Transaction Publishers.

Straus, M.A., R. Gelles, and S. Steinmetz. (1980). *Behind closed doors*. New York: Anchor Books.

Straus, M.A., and C. Smith. (1990). Family patterns and primary prevention of family violence. In *Physical violence in American families*, ed. M.A. Straus and R.J. Gelles, pp. 507–26. New Brunswick, NJ: Transaction Publishers.

Straus, M.A., and S. Sweet. (1992). Verbal aggression in couples: Incidence rates and relationships to personal characteristics. *Journal of Marriage and the Family* 54(2): 346–57.

Straus, M.A., and C.L. Yodanis. (1996). Corporal punishment in adolescence and physical assaults on spouses later in life: What accounts for the link? *Journal of Marriage and the Family* 58(4): 825–41.

Studer, M. (1984). Wife beating as a social problem: The process of definition. *International Journal of Women's Studies* 7(5): 412–22.

Suitor, J.J., K. Pillemer, and M.A. Straus. (1990). Marital violence in life course perspective. In *Physical violence in American familis*, ed. M.A. Straus and R.J. Gelles, pp. 305–17. New Brunswick: Transaction Publishers.

Szinovacz, M.E. (1983). Using the couple as a methodological tool: The case of marital violence. *Journal of Marriage and the Family* 45(3): 633–44.

Szinovacz, M.E., and L.C. Egley. (1995). Comparing one-partner and couple data on sensitive marital behaviors: The case of marital violence. *Journal of Marriage and the Family* 57(4): 847–65.

Therborn, G. (1980). *The ideology of power and the power of ideology*. 2nd ed. London: Verso Editions.

Thompson, L. (1992). Feminist methodology for family studies. *Journal of Marriage and the Family* 54(1): 3–18.

Thompson, L., and A.J. Walker. (1995). The place of feminism in family studies. *Journal of Marriage and the Family* 57(4): 995–1010.

Tierney, K.J. (1982). The battered women movement and the creation of the wife beating problem. *Social Problems* 29(3): 207–20.

Touraine, A. (1988). *Return of the actor*. Minneapolis: University of Minnesota Press.

Troyer, R.J. (1993). Revised social constructionism: Traditional social science more than a postmodernist analysis. In *Reconsidering social constructionism: Debates in social problems theory*, ed. J.A. Holstein and G. Miller, pp. 117–28. New York: Aldine De Gruyter.

Walker, G.A. (1990). *Family violence and the women's movement*. 1st ed. Toronto: University of Toronto Press.

Walker, L.E. (1984). *The battered woman syndrome*. 1st ed. New York: Springer Publishing Company.
– (1993). The battered woman syndrome is a psychological consequence of abuse. In *Current controversies on family violence*, ed. R.J. Gelles and D.R. Loseke, pp. 133–53. Newbury Park: Sage Publications Inc.
Wallace, B., and A. Nosko. (1991). Working with shame in the group treatment of male batterers. Unpublished manuscript.
Waller, W. (1936). Social problems and the mores. *American Sociological Review* 1: 922–34.
Walsh, F. (1982). *Normal family processes*. New York: The Guilford Press.
Wardell, L., D.L. Gillespie, and A. Leffler. (1983). Science and violence against wives. In *The dark side of families: Current family violence research*, ed. D. Finklehor, R.J. Gelles, G.T. Hotaling, and M.A. Straus, pp. 69–84. Beverly Hills: Sage Publications Inc.
Washburne, C.K. (1983). A feminist analysis of child abuse and neglect. In *The dark side of families: Current family violence research*, ed. D. Finkelhor, R.J. Gelles, G.T. Hotaling, and M.A. Straus, pp. 289–92. Beverly Hills: Sage Publications Inc.
Watzlawick, P. (1984a). Components of ideological 'realities.' In *The invented reality: How do we know what we believe we know? (contributions to constructivism)*, ed. P. Watzlawick, pp. 206–47. New York: W.W. Norton.
– (1984b). Epilogue. In *The invented reality: How do we know what we believe we know? (Contributions to constructivism)*, ed. P. Watzlawick, pp. 325–32. New York: W.W. Norton.
Weatherford, V.L.C., and E.R. Kaufman. (1991). Adult children of alcoholics: An exploration of axis II disorder replicated in dysfunctional family patterns. *Journal of Family Violence* 6(4): 319–35.
Weber, M. (1949). *The methodology of the social sciences*. 1st ed. New York: The Free Press.
– (1958). *From Max Weber: Essays in sociology*. 6th ed. New York: Oxford University Press.
Weedon, C. (1987). *Feminist practice and poststructuralist theory*. 1st ed. New York: Basil Blackwell.
Werner, E.E., and R.S. Smith. (1992). *Overcoming the odds*. Ithaca: Cornell University Press.
Wiener, C. (1981). *The politics of alcoholism*. 1st ed. New Brunswick, NJ: Transaction Books.
Wilson, M., H. Johnson, and M. Daly. (1995). Lethal and non-lethal violence against wives. *Canadian Journal of Criminology* 37(3): 331–62.

Wind, T.W., and L. Silvern. (1992). Type and extent of child abuse as predictors of adult functioning. *Journal of Family Violence* 7(4): 261–81.

Wolf, N. (1993). *Fire with fire*. 1st ed. Toronto: Random House.

Woolgar, S., and D. Pawluch. (1985). Ontological gerrymandering: The anatomy of social problems explanations. *Social Problems* 32(3): 214–27.

Yelsma, P. (1996). Affective orientations of perpetrators, victims, and functional spouses. *Journal of Interpersonal Violence* 11(2): 141–61.

Yllo, K.A. (1983). Using a feminist approach in quantitative research: A case study. In *The dark side of families: Current family violence research*, ed. D. Finkelhor, R.J. Gelles, G.T. Hotaling, and M.A. Straus, pp. 277–88. Beverly Hills: Sage Publications.

– (1988). Political and methodological debates in wife abuse research. In *Feminist perspectives on wife abuse*, ed. K. Yllo and M. Bogard, pp. 28–50. Newbury Park: Sage Publications Inc.

– (1993). Through a feminist lens: Gender, power, and violence. In *Current controversies on family violence*, ed. R.J. Gelles and D.R. Loseke, pp. 47–62. Newbury Park: Sage Publications Inc.

Yllo, K.A., and M.A. Straus. (1990). Patriarchy and violence against wives: The impact of structural and normative factors. In *Physical violence in American families*, ed. M.A. Straus and R.J. Gelles, pp. 383–99. New Brunswick: Transaction Publishers.

Author Index

Subject Index

abuse, as social problem: emergence in Canada and world, 4–8; emergence in Township, 22–6; and feminist/non-feminist polarizations, x, 5, 8–11, 13–15, 30–6, 197–200, 281–2n10

abuse activism. *See* Domestic Abuse Committee; Township Women's Shelter

abuse awareness workshops, 40–54

abuse discourses: and ideal types, 8, 264n6; as ideological lenses, competing myths, contending hegemonies, 8–11, 13–15, 89, 113, 134, 204–5, 264n6, 281n8; and inflammatory rhetoric, 13–15, 203, 267nn22–3; and key controversies, 8–16, 31–8, 52, 133–4, 265n9, 266n17, 266–7n18, 267–8n21, 268n23, 270–1n14, 271nn17–18, 273–4n10, 274n11; 276nn8–10. See also *family violence; violence against women*

abuse survival, survivors. *See* survival; survivors

abused women: abuse discourses and survey data on, 8–15, 31–8, 133–8, 232–62 (tables 3–15), 276n9,

279n7; and agency, competency, responsibility, 79, 82–3, 87, 116, 124–5, 141–4; and alcohol and drug problems, 42–3, 69–70, 73, 81, 102, 128, 142–3, 165–71, 176–8; and anger, assertiveness, boundaries, dependency, empathy, jealousy, power and control, and self-esteem problems, 92–5, 99–101, 122–3, 125, 140–3, 145–54, 163, 171–2, 280n20; and child abuse perpetration, 69–70, 80–1, 274n4; childhood trauma and child sex-abuse histories of, 45–7, 52, 82, 96–7, 102–4, 119, 126–7, 142–3, 145–54, 156–64, 165–71, 172, 179, 186, 272n22; counselling and therapy 'needs' of, 82–3, 122, 125, 152–3, 163–4, 172, 178; excitement 'needs' of, 94–5, 140–1, 143–4; violence perpetration and provocation by, 42, 48–50, 69–71, 80–1, 93–4, 120–1, 129, 142–3, 146, 149–50, 165–72, 175–6, 188–90

abusive men: abuse discourses and survey data on, 8–15, 31–7, 89–91,

14; and residents' attitudes (lay theories), 30–7, 108–9, 130, 136–7, 142, 164, 169–70, 179–80, 184, 195, 234–62 (tables 4–15), 257n.a, 272n24, 273n5, 276nn12–13, 280n23; *violence against women* and *family violence* as contending for, 89, 113

history, historicity: and abuse issue (current context), 4–5, 8, 195, 206; and epistemologies, 12; and feminist movement, 8, 265n12, 274n13

hope: and modernism, 16; and the Township shelter process, 206–7, 223–6

humanism: and TWS/DAC participants, 120, 129, 224–5

ideal types: *violence against women* and *family violence* as, 16, 264n6

ideological wrangles: and shelter problems, 68, 132

ideologies (lenses, conceptualizations, representations): abuse discourses as, 8–11, 13–15, 89, 113, 134, 204–5, 264n6, 281n8; community development and feminism as, 22–6; and control or ownership struggles, x, 4, 16, 136, 207, 267n23, 281–2n10; and distortions, reifications, and 'bad faith,' xi, 87, 204–6, 281n8; and empirical methods, ix, 4, 10, 12–15, 17, 268n9; and lay theories, 108–9, 142, 164, 169–7, 179–80, 184, 195, 257n.a, 272n24, 273n5, 276nn12–13, 280n23; and modernism, post-modernism, 11–13; and reality construction, 3–4, 6, 9, 12, 132, 136; *violence against*

women and *family violence* as, 8–11, 13–15, 89, 113, 134, 205, 264n6

incest. *See* child sex abuse

inflammatory rhetoric, 13–15, 203, 267n22

inter-agency cooperation. *See* coordinated abuse system

intergenerational abuse: abuse discourses and survey data on, 10–11, 33–5, 234–46 (tables 4–9), 271nn17–18; and extended families, 143, 145–9, 191–2, 199–200; gender and social class effects in, 82, 96–7, 107–8, 117, 124–7; and mutating trajectories, 34, 36, 102–4, 106; TWS/DAC participants' ambivalent and contending perspectives on (key controversy), 34, 46, 51–4, 81–2, 89, 96–7, 98, 102–4, 116–20, 125–7, 129; victims, perpetrators, and survivors of, 139–91

intervention clients: dissatisfactions and preferences, 33, 42–3, 67–8, 72–4, 76, 86–7, 152–3, 163–4, 169–70, 241–3 (tables 7–8), 247–62 (tables 10–15), 272n23, 275–6n5, 276–7n14

jealousy and infidelity: abuse discourses and survey data on, 134–5, 235 (table 4), 265–6n14, 278–9n5; TWS/DAC participants' contending perspectives on, 95, 104, 120, 125; and victims, perpetrators, and survivors, 139–40, 146–7, 150–3, 155, 159, 162–3, 168, 170, 174–5, 177–8, 183, 186–9, 191. *See also* promiscuity

Jekyll and Hyde types. *See* abusive men

key controversies. *See* alcohol and
drug abuse; childhood trauma;
female-perpetrated violence;
intergenerational abuse; sexism;
social class; Township, as exceptional
knowledge, knowledgeability. *See*
agency; epistemologies; social
interactionism

lawsuits. *See* Domestic Abuse Committee, the opposition
lay theories: survey and interview
data, 30–7, 108–9, 130, 136–7,
142, 164, 169–70, 179–80, 184, 195,
234–62 (tables 4–15), 257n.a,
272n24, 273n5, 276nn12–13,
280n23
lived experience of abuse. See *domestic abuse*, dynamics of, as lived
experience
love: and abuse, 41–3, 94–5, 100–2,
137, 140, 146–7, 150–2, 155, 173,
179, 192–4

mainstream interventions: and survey data, 31–7, 108–9, 130, 236
(table 4), 255–9 (tables 11–13); and
TWS/DAC process, 23, 60, 113–32.
See also Domestic Abuse Committee, activists and affiliated professionals
male-perpetrated violence. *See* abusive men
media, the, 19–20, 25, 28–9, 40, 58,
60–1, 124, 269n1, 272–3n1
men: as 'bullies,' 57; as (not) 'the
enemy,' 65, 75, 79, 129; as 'the male
hierarchy,' 62, 87, 200; as (not)
'monsters,' 24, 50; as necessary or

valued DAC participants and shelter board members, 20, 24, 53–4,
63, 65; as 'the old boys,' 56, 58–9,
65, 131
mission statement: of TRC, 22; of
TWS, 68

narcissism, 4, 91, 135, 155, 165
newcomers and established residents, 29–30, 118, 124, 126, 128–9
normality of abuse, 104, 137–8,
144–5, 156–7, 159, 192–3. *See also*
pathology of abuse

object aggression (throwing and
smashing things): in *family violence*
discourses, 10–11; and survey
data, 232–46 (tables 3–9); and victims, perpetrators, and survivors,
177, 179, 181–2, 187
objective and putative realities. *See*
epistemologies; social interactionism; social problems processes
official plan. *See* coordinated abuse
system; social problems processes
Olympian plane, 12, 15
ownership. *See* social problems processes

pathology of abuse: and abuse discourses, 11, 34–6, 134–6, 138, 200;
TWS/DAC participants' references to, 50, 102, 130; and victims,
perpetrators, and survivors, 139,
144, 151–2, 155–8, 165, 170, 179,
183, 192–3. *See also* normality of
abuse
patriarchy. *See* feminisms; *violence
against women*
police: dislike of 'domestics,' 115–16;

56, 60–71, 74–6, 109–11, 113, 118, 122–4, 131–2, 200–2, 274n2; control issues and bad faith in, 63–5, 70–7, 201–3; and executive retreat, 109–10; funders and funding of, 21, 26–8, 40, 47, 54–5, 57–8, 76; and media, 19, 25, 27–30, 40, 60–1, 63–4, 76; and mobilization, 19–20, 25, 40–54, 57; and official plan, 22–4, 54–5, 60, 67–8; polarizations and outcomes in, 23, 29, 34, 39, 54–76, 86–7, 107–10, 118, 121–2, 124, 132, 200–3, 204–5, 223–6; residents' support for, 32, 37, 61, 64, 85–6, 236 (table 4), 247–55 (tables 10–11), 275n9

Township Women's Shelter, the director, 60–2, 67–8, 70–6, 109–11, 202, 274n1

Township Women's Shelter, the opposition. *See* Domestic Abuse Committee, the opposition

truths, truth claims, ix–xi, 6–7, 12–13, 16–17, 27, 32, 51–2, 74, 114–15, 277n3, 282n12

unintended outcomes. *See* social problems processes; Township Women's Shelter, polarizations and outcomes in

us against them, x–xi, 24, 63, 86–7, 110–11, 132, 203–5

Utopian position, 12

victim blaming, 36, 129, 155–6

victimization process. *See* cycle of violence

victims, perpetrators, and survivors, personal interviews: Anne, 139–44; Hank, 185–91; Keith, 172–8; Kim, 165–71; Sam, 179–85; Tracy, 145–54; Yvonne, 156–64; researcher's analysis of, 133–9, 144–5, 154–6, 164–5, 171–2, 178–9, 185, 191–5, 278n1, 279–80n15, 280nn18, 22

violence against women: 5, 8–16, 31–7, 52, 62, 89–90, 97, 113, 133–4, 138, 198–201, 203, 205–7, 223, 264n6, 266nn16–17, 267n21, 270n11, 273–4n10, 277n6

weapons: abuse discourses and survey data on, 11, 32, 234–47 (tables 4–9); and domestic homicides, 27–8; and victims, perpetrators, and survivors, 149–50, 155, 158, 166, 174, 179–85, 189–90

women's shelters: abuse discourses and survey data on, 10, 13, 32, 36, 84–5, 236 (table 4), 247–61 (tables 10–15), 269n5; and client dissatisfaction, 42, 67–8, 76, 87, 274–5nn5–7; and feminist backlash, xi, 281n9; power and control problems in, 42, 79, 85, 87

women's 'toleration' of abuse, 10, 28, 36, 70, 80, 83–4, 102–3, 117–18, 125–6, 128–9, 137, 139–41, 143–4, 146, 155, 165, 279n12